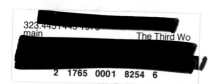

The Third World
and Press Freedom

edited by

Philip C. Horton

FOREWORD BY

John Chancellor

THE THIRD WORLD
AND PRESS FREEDOM

PRAEGER PUBLISHERS
Praeger Special Studies

New York • London • Sydney • Toronto

Library of Congress Cataloging in Publication Data
Main entry under title:

The Third World and press freedom.

    1. Underdeveloped areas—Journalism. 2. Liberty
of the press. 3. News agencies. I. Horton, Philip C.
PN4736.T48   323.44'5   78-17072
ISBN 0-03-045551-0

PRAEGER SPECIAL STUDIES
383 Madison Avenue, New York, N.Y., 10017,
U.S.A.

Published in the United States of America in 1978
by Praeger Publishers,
A Division of Holt, Rinehart and Winston, CBS Inc.

89 038 987654321

Printed in the United States of America

Foreword

JOHN CHANCELLOR

This is a book about freedom and responsibility. It is also about the meaning of those concepts, and it shows us how different people, from different worlds, can define freedom and responsibility in very different ways. It is a book about something called "news", a word with a host of definitions. And it is a book about culture, politics and geography.

These essays were prepared for a Conference on "the Third World and Press Freedom" held in 1977 in New York City under the auspices of the Edward R. Murrow Center of the Fletcher School of Law and Diplomacy, Tufts University. Among those attending the Conference were representatives of some of the great international news agencies, as well as scholars, diplomats, and journalists from the United States, Europe, Latin America, Africa, the Arab World, and Asia.

The group spent two days in sometimes heated and sometimes good-natured discussion of several significant questions: the responsibility of the news services of the developed countries to readers, listeners and viewers of news in the developing world; the ability of journalists in the developing world to organize themselves in groups which cross national boundaries; and the elusive, vexatious problem of news itself—what it is, and what some participants thought it ought to be.

The New York Conference was, in one sense, another response to a challenge from the Third World, a challenge to the international journalistic institutions of the developed countries. It is said in the Third World, and repeated endlessly on such intergovernmental forums as UNESCO, that a) the international wire services and the major newspapers with syndicated foreign coverage do not give the whole world a fair picture of Third World events, especially with respect to social and economic development, and that b) the Third World itself is denied useful information about itself because of the international media's bias against events in the developing world.

The challenge seems simple enough: provide more accurate, comprehensive, and meaningful worldwide coverage of news from the Third World, and provide more accurate and useful information about the Third World to the developing countries themselves. But, as the New York Conference demonstrated, it is more complicated than that. For one thing, there is a considerable gap between the definition of good journalism in the developed world and in the developing world.

On one side, to cite recent examples, we have seen the *New York Times* locked in a Constitutional battle with the Federal government over the Pentagon Papers, the *Washington Post* fighting the White House in the Watergate affair, and *The Sunday Times* of London fighting in the British courts about the Thalidomide case. These examples show a press fighting to defend its right to report things that governments do not want reported.

On the other side, one African participant offered this view: "Many young countries have fragile political structures that cannot withstand endless scrutiny by the news media of the shortcomings of those in power or the failures of economic and social development programmes." The gap, clearly, is wide, indeed.

Yet most journalists from developed countries familiar with the problems discussed here would admit that there are significant shortcomings in the international reportage of the Third World, most particularly in the deadline journalism of the news agencies, weekly magazines, radio, and television. There are sins of commission: the "look-at-the-antics-of-the-funny-natives" stories written by visiting journalists; the easy labelling of some leaders in ideological terms, when the true situation calls for more sophisticated interpretation; and the oversimplication of news reports from countries with ancient and complex tribal or religious histories. There are sins of omission: the failure of editors to use stories written on the not-so-sexy topics of agricultural, industrial or social development, and the reluctance of news managers to establish permanent bureaus in countries which do not produce enough "news"—under the developed-country definition of news.

James Reston of the *New York Times* once defined news as a chronicle of conflict and change. It would seem to be a valid criticism of international coverage of events in the Third World to say that the developed countries pay attention to the conflicts, but not enough attention to the changes in those countries. Walter Lippmann wrote, "Journalism must give man a picture of the world upon which they can act?" Yet, is it the responsibility of the developed countries to provide citizens of the Third World with pictures of the world upon which they can act?

Is it the responsibility of editors in New York, London and Paris to provide stories to their readers on Swaziland's new system for irrigating orange groves, Tanzania's rural health services, or inland fisheries in Nepal? No one questions the utility of such information among countries in the developing world. Can such information be provided, and exchanged, by news pools within the Third World itself? Such information surely falls into the category of news for developing countries, just as the Nepalese inland fisheries fall outside the category of news for readers in the rest of the world.

The idea of Third World news pools has merit, but the danger is that such arrangements will result in government-to-government communication, and not in a free flow of information. There are about 25 national news agencies in Africa and all but 3 are government controlled. An independent journalist would like to see those figures reversed, but that is not likely to happen.

What is likely to happen is the situation of a correspondent for a nongovernmental Asian news agency, serving Third World clients, as described by one of the Conference participants: the correspondent, he writes, "... knows how far he can go in handling a delicate story without compromising his professional position and without treading on too many tender toes. Maybe, at times, he sacrifices a good story that he would have written if conditions were different. But quite often by sacrificing one story, he manages to write three others."

In some parts of the world, that is acceptable journalism. There are European and American journalists who operate in that fashion. Yet, if the press is to do its job, and not become an agency of government, there must be treading on tender toes. The basic task is to create a system under which the journalist is not only allowed to operate freely, but is protected from harm if he does so. This has been difficult even in old countries with traditions of constitutional guarantees. It is doubly difficult for a new country.

The United States, for example, has shown itself to be strong and secure enough to accept a free and generally unfettered press; but what of a weak country emerging from colonial times into a shaky young statehood? But if that shaky young statehood is to develop into a strong and secure state, capable of protecting the rights of its citizens, a free and unfettered press becomes a necessity.

The dynamics of national growth rarely, if ever, allow a controlled press, serving the needs of the government and controlled by the government, to shed its governmental skin and become truly free. The press needs to be free at the beginning.

Nevertheless, despite the differences of viewpoint which often surfaced between the Third World participants at the New York conference and their colleagues from the developed world, it can be said that gatherings of this kind are producing changes in attitude which can only be beneficial in the future. Editors at international news organizations are learning to pay a different kind of attention to news from the Third World. Correspondents visiting the Third World are learning that their reporting demands more understanding and sophistication.

As an American reading these papers, I am struck by another, underlying theme of this conference and others like it. Our Third World colleagues are urging us to use our freedom to assume more responsibility, while we are telling them of their responsibility to be free.

Preface

PHILIP C. HORTON

In the spring of 1977, the Murrow Center of the Fletcher School of Law and Diplomacy organized a two-day conference at the Time-Life Building in New York City on "The Third World and Press Freedom." Its purpose was twofold: to examine the social, political, and legal issues raised by Third World complaints and criticism of the Western wire services and news media; and to explore possible solutions acceptable to both the developing and the developed nations to problems concerning the admittedly massive imbalance of the international flow of news. The topics of the papers commissioned for the conference, presented here for the first time in book form, were selected to serve both these ends.

Most of the participants and observers at the New York meetings would agree, I believe, that much of its unique significance and the follow-on activities it generated flowed from two particular features of the conference design. Unlike most intergovernmental conferences of recent years where these particular issues were debated by politicians and international civil servants, the New York Conference was specifically designed for professional news managers, men who, whatever their ideological bent or political affiliation, would be completely familiar with the real-life problems and complexities of news operations. Thus, most of the participants at New York, apart from academics, were newsmen and most of the papers were authored by them. Government officials for the most part were invited as observers.

Our purpose was not to eliminate or sidestep the ideological issues —indeed there was a fair amount of political rhetoric and bickering in the opening session—but rather to open up areas of shared professional experience and concern, and in this way to encourage cooperative efforts to identify and correct some of the shortcomings of international news coverage. In short, professionalism and cooperation were the keynotes of the New York Conference.

The success of this approach was witnessed in the final plenary session by a clear consensus that a follow-on conference should be convened in the following year, preferably in one of the Third World countries. Such a conference was held in Cairo in April 1978 and attracted 39 senior newsmen from 20 of the developing countries, together with a large delegation of American and European news executives. It was probably the first of its kind to be jointly designed and funded by American and Third World institutions. Our cosponsors in this undertaking were the Middle East News Agency and Cairo University.

Unfortunately the Soviet bloc and its followers take a jaundiced view of such cooperative efforts. They promote instead the argument that the western news media are the instruments of "capitalist domination," agents of "cultural imperialism" and "neocolonialism" which the developing world would do well to eschew in favor of the Soviet example.

Publication of the papers of the New York Conference, it is hoped, will provide a countervailing view and foster a wider recognition that most of the Third World countries are, in fact, by no means wedded to the Soviet model of strict government control of the news media. As we learned at the New York Conference, many of their leading editors, even in countries where the press is largely or partly controlled by the government, are prepared to work for greater press freedom in their own countries in the belief that over the longer term it will be in the national self-interest. The vast diversity of the developing world and its rapid rate of change will continue, we believe, to offer many opportunities for further cooperation while confounding the sweeping generalizations and simplistic arguments of propagandists and ideologues of whatever persuasion.

In recent decades, we in this country have learned that American-style democracy cannot successfully be exported or imposed on other countries. The same holds true for the Western concept of a totally free and independent press. Like all freedoms, press freedom is relative and subject to political, social, economic, and even ethical constraints. As an ideal, it must be defended, fought for, and promoted by all possible means, but always with the recognition that, like the perfectibility of man, it can never be wholly or absolutely achieved.

Such recognition argues for greater patience and flexibility in dealing with the problems of a pluralistic world, including those of the news media which can, and almost certainly will, play an important role, for better or worse, in determining the course of North-South relations in the coming years.

Acknowledgments

For making possible both the conference and the commissioned papers, we are deeply indebted to a number of private foundations: the Mary L. Markle Foundation, the MacCormick Charitable Trust, the Philip L. Graham Fund, the New York Times Foundation, the Poynter Fund; to Time Inc. for donating its conference facilities and hospitality; and to UNESCO for contributing to the travel costs of our colleagues from the developing countries.

Special thanks are owed to Ernest Kohlmetz of Guilford, Connecticut, for his skilful assistance in editing the papers, and to members of the faculty and student body of the Fletcher School for their steady encouragement. Above all, I am grateful to the members of the Planning Committee for the New York Conference, who provided invaluable advice and guidance throughout the planning phase and the proceedings of the conference itself:

Edward W. Barrett
George Beebe
Philip Foisie
Edmund A. Gullion
William G. Harley
Richard C. Hottelet

John Hughes
Clayton Kirkpatrick
Frank Tremaine
Leonard R. Sussman
Stanley M. Swinton
Barry Zorthian

List of Acronyms

ACAN	Agencia Centroamericana de Noticias
AFP	Agence France-Presse
ANSA	Agencia Nazionale Stampa Associata
AP	Associated Press
ARNA	Arab Revolution News Agency
CANA	Caribbean News Agency
CTK	Ceskoslovenska Piskova Kancelar
DEPTHnews	Development, Economics, and Population Themes News
DPA	Deutsche-Presse Agentur
IPS	Interpress Service
MENA	Middle East News Agency
TASS	Telegrafnoye Agentstvo Sovietskovo Soyuza
TWNA	Third World News Agency
UPI	United Press International
USIA	United States Information Agency
WAFA	Wakalep Anba El-Falastinieh

Contents

1. NEWS FLOW IN THE THIRD WORLD:
An Overview

ROGER TATARIAN

The developing discussions between the industrialized nations and the Third World are not concerned solely with a more equitable distribution of the world's economic wealth. Also at issue is something less tangible but no less vital—news and information.

The Asian, African, and Latin American nations known variously as the Third World or the nonaligned or developing nations are demanding a "New Order of Information," together with the "New International Economic Order" called for by the Sixth Special Session of the United Nations General Assembly in 1974.

These nations are questioning and even rejecting traditional concepts of freedom in the international flow of news and information, saying these concepts serve only those who control the lines of communication. These countries are demanding a "more balanced" flow of news between the developed and developing worlds and are asserting a still-evolving "right to communicate" for nations lacking in the means of communications.

In tones of mounting intensity, Third World governments and commentators are portraying all Western forms of communications—the news media, television, and cinema—as agents of "cultural aggression" or of "cultural imperialism." But the principal fire is aimed at the four Western-based international news agencies that today are the major suppliers of news and pictures to the world press and radio. These agencies—the Associated Press (AP) and United Press International (UPI) of the United States, Agence France-Presse (AFP) of France, and Reuters of Britain—are assailed as remnants of a colonial past. They are charged with being more interested in denigrating the young developing states than in reporting their positive accomplishments.

1

This growing scrutiny of the news agencies has coincided with the establishment of national or government-operated information agencies in many Third World countries. Eighty-five Third World governments, meeting in Colombo, SRI Lanka, in August 1976, ratified the formation of what is known as the Nonaligned News Agencies Pool for the interchange of news among their various news agencies and information services.

The proliferation of national agencies, most of them government run, and the creation of the Nonaligned Pool have combined to cause some fears in the West that these official entities may be used to drive out the Western agencies and further restrict the free flow of information in the world. The Third World reply to this, is that the pool seeks only to supplement the work of the global agencies with a dimension of news now felt to be lacking (see the chapters by Biola Olasope and Narinder K. Aggarwala).

But the rhetoric that has accompanied the birth of the pool has at times seemed so hostile that misgivings linger. Western media have given much attention to the statement by Abbas Sykes, Tanzania's ambassador to the United Nations Educational, Scientific and Cultural Organization (UNESCO), that "we don't want Western journalists in our countries. They should take their news from us."

Aggarwala, an Indian journalist serving with the United Nations Development Programme (UNDP), comments in his chapter that few developing countries share Sykes' sentiment. Yet the establishment of this official news pool presents a high potential for repression by governments that are, for the most part, authoritarian.

UNESCO itself has come under criticism in the West for fostering government involvement in the international flow of news, and the agency has become the forum of increasingly sharp confrontations with Cold War overtones. This situation in UNESCO has stemmed from a campaign within the agency by the Soviet Union to proclaim news to be a legitimate instrument of state policy.

The U.S. government and U.S. media have strongly opposed the Soviet declaration on the "use" of information that was proposed to the 1974 UNESCO general conference and revised for the next biennial meeting, but the declaration has natural attractions for strong central governments and a close vote on it had been expected at UNESCO'S Nineteenth Biennial General Conference in Nairobi, Kenya, in the fall of 1976. A combination of able diplomacy and economic pressure by the United States averted a showdown at Nairobi, although the issue is on the agenda for the UNESCO biennial in 1978.

The sum total of all these pressures on free-press traditions has served to arouse the Western press and particularly the press of the

United States as it rarely has been aroused. Major U.S. journalistic figures went to UNESCO meetings in San Jose, Costa Rica, and in Nairobi in 1976 to oppose measures that they felt would threaten the free flow of information in the world. And many representatives of the press are working with academic institutions and foundations to formulate some constructive response to the complaints in the Third World about the status quo in international news collection and distribution.

Once the Soviet declaration had been shunted aside at Nairobi, the conference went on to approve a proposal for a concerted effort to establish some new order for global news distribution. What progress these efforts in and out of UNESCO make may help determine how the controversial Soviet declaration on the "uses" of information by government will fare when it comes up again before a UNESCO membership dominated by Third World governments.

The Soviet declaration is a powerful lure for any regime bent on consolidating and perpetuating itself. The Soviet Union has had longer than any modern state to appreciate the advantages of official control of news as a lever of power. This is not to suggest that the desire for power is either the exclusive or dominant motive in the creation of national news agencies in the Third World, but that it *is* a factor cannot convincingly be denied. There are, however, other reasons why existing patterns of news flow are not felt to be satisfactory. Some of the complaints have a basis in fact. Some are more reasonable than others. Still others are based on cultural, psychological, and even emotional grounds and can, if erroneous, probably be erased only with the passage of time.

The search for a constructive response from the West must take into account the reasonable proposition that no corrective plan or suggestion will have universal appeal. The Third World is no monolith. No doubt some states will prefer to keep their news media captives of government. There, the best that can be hoped for is that the frontiers be kept open to outside reporters. The question of access is vital not only for the news agencies but also for individual newspapers, radio, and television. Thus all facets of the profession need to participate in this undertaking.

Before examining specific complaints from the Third World against present international news patterns, it is necessary to make some distinctions in terminology and to review major postwar developments concerning international communications, particularly the role of UNESCO.

In discussing international news agencies, Third World and UNESCO spokesmen do not usually place the Soviet Telegrafnoye

Agentstvo Sovietskovo Soyuza (TASS) in the same category as AP, UPI, AFP, and Reuters. TASS does have a widespread geographical presence, as does the Hsinhua agency of the People's Republic of China (PRC), and an intercontinental scope of operations is a prime requisite of a global news service. Yet there is another test that neither TASS or Hsinhua can pass, and that is the capability to report things critical of their home governments. Both TASS and Hsinhua are totally financed and directed by their respective governments and simply do not transmit anything that runs contrary to official policy. They are thus more official information agencies and less news agencies in the sense that news is generally understood.

This is admittedly a distinction not likely to win universal acceptance. But it may be significant that even in the Third World, references to the "major" news agencies are most frequently intended to mean AP, UPI, AFP, and Reuters. The special nature of TASS and Hsinhua apparently does not go unobserved. Whatever their other shortcomings, the four Western agencies are free of the kind of domination the Soviet and the PRC agencies are subject to and thus can be qualified as the dominant news agencies of the world, with West Germany's Deutsche-Presse Agentur (DPA) and Japan's Kyodo perhaps the closest behind.

The term "propaganda" is a tendentious one and is therefore being avoided in the ensuing discussion. But it must be borne in mind that propaganda is the main function of official news agencies and information services. Propaganda is one of the two currents in the global stream of information. The other is news. The purpose of news is simply to inform. Propaganda also can be informative, but that is incidental to its main function which is to influence, to persuade, or to promote. Governments are interested in influencing, persuading, and promoting. News agencies are not.

UNESCO AND FREE FLOW: RETREAT OR ADVANCE?

UNESCO's role in the present controversy over world news flow is itself the subject of controversy. Indeed, it would be miraculous if UNESCO could avoid controversy, having, as it does, a constituency holding two irreconcilable attitudes toward freedom of expression.

It is not only the traditional postwar clash between communist and Western ideology that contributes to this. It is also the fact that most Third World nations are authoritarian and practice, to some extent, the totalitarian concept of regulated news that is generally embraced in the communist world.

A numerical majority of UNESCO's members have no deep ideological attachment to freedom of expression and have given growing support to plans, programs, and projects to inject governments more and more into the arena of news and information. The resultant alarm in the West has produced charges that UNESCO's bureaucracy is leading rather than following its members in this trend (see Gunnar R. Naesselund's chapter in defense of UNESCO).

It would be grossly unfair to portray UNESCO as uniformly controversial, even on information matters. It has, for example, supported lowered telegraphic rates for press messages, worked for the development of greater technical facilities, mounted massive campaigns to combat illiteracy, and is, among other things, a vital source of statistics measuring the problems existing in the world of communication. Among its present activities is an effort to promote an international code to ensure the physical safety of journalists professionally engaged in the international arena.

What is causing some concern in the West, however, is that UNESCO's original preoccupation with expanding the international channels for the flow of communication has given way to a preoccupation with the *content* of this information and to fostering the idea that government control is a positive social imperative.

UNESCO takes the official position that it does not lead but follows. Thus UNESCO Director General Amadou-Mahtar M'Bow of Senegal declared to the opening of the Intergovernmental Conference on Communications Policies in Latin America and the Caribbean in San Jose, Costa Rica, on July 12, 1976:

> UNESCO, for its part, has no communication policy to propose to its Member States. UNESCO states problems, raises questions, promotes the exchange of experiences and reflections on the current situation and trends, and on ways and means of formulating policies. It is for each country, in the light of the world's cumulative experience, to define its policy on the basis of its own options, its economic and social situation and its needs in the field of communication.

This protestation of neutrality is not found convincing by many. UNESCO's experts also propose solutions, and their manner of presentation can and does amount to subtle advocacy. A meeting of UNESCO experts in Bogota in 1974, for example, proposed four options for national policies on broadcasting, all of which envisaged government control of content.

Some of UNESCO's critics accuse it of fostering "creeping totalitarianism," as did a *Wall Street Journal* commentary on October 27, 1977.

Be that as it may, the UNESCO bureaucracy does have a palpable tilt. To argue that the tilt is solely a response to UNESCO membership fails to indicate the influence of UNESCO's experts in causing it, and in any case does not alter the fact that a tilt is present. It manifests itself throughout UNESCO literature.

No great measure of neutrality is reflected in M'Bow's references to the Western news agencies in his Costa Rican address.

> Even today many observers find that the selection of news as most often practiced by certain large international news agencies systematically stresses the phenomena of tension or violence in the countries of the Third World. On the other hand, in many cases, they feel that those agencies keep silent on events of a positive nature which occur with increasing frequency in those same countries. The evil is aggravated at the level of the individual mass communication medium where a further and still more restrictive selection is made, as a result of which the user is only provided with a caricature of the day's news, sketched in a few hasty lines. It thus comes about that the peoples of Latin American and the Caribbean region ... see their races reflected from afar in mirrors that deform them.

Nor does Makaminan Makagiansar, UNESCO assistant director general for culture and communication, writing in the April 1977 issue of the UNESCO *Courier,* reflect neutrality:

> UNESCO is engaged in reflection on the establishment of the "new world order" which has been on the agenda of the United Nations since 1974. To a great extent, this new order will depend on improved access to information, on more effective communication, on a more equitable distribution of the mass media with their immense potential for promoting mutual understanding between men and nations, and ultimately on ensuring that information becomes once again a liberating force rather than an instrument of subjection.

Even without UNESCO, Third World dissatisfaction with the work of the world agencies would doubtlessly have been inevitable if for no other reason than that they are headquartered in the "imperialist" world. It is no exaggeration to suggest that it is as much their nationality as what they do or do not do that makes the Western agencies the subject of so much suspicion and attack today. But neither is it an exaggeration to suggest that UNESCO has accelerated and crystallized the dissatisfaction with the Big Four.

United Nations agencies began to interest themselves in the international flow of information immediately after World War II. The UN

Conference on Freedom of Information in Geneva in 1948 was attended by representatives of 54 governments and observers from eight international organizations. Great attention was paid to remedying deficiencies in mass communications facilities in the world and even then there was a recommendation for the development of national news agencies.

Another key date was 1959, when the Economic and Social Council (ECOSOC) requested UNESCO to make a worldwide survey of press, radio, film, and television development. This UNESCO did with a series of three regional meetings with media and government representatives. The meeting for Southeast Asia was held in Bangkok in January 1960; for Latin America in Santiago, Chile, in February 1961; and for Africa in Addis Ababa in the spring of 1962.

At that early stage, as can be seen in the following passage from an early report by a director general of UNESCO, it was not the nature and tone of the flow of information, but the physical facilities for it, that was the focus of attention. The report said its preparation had been guided by two premises:

> The first is that a prerequisite to freedom of information is the existence of adequate mass communication facilities. Nearly 70% of the total population of the world, living in more than 100 countries, at present lack these facilities to a degree that denies them full enjoyment of this basic human right. The second premise is that development of the information media forms part of economic development as a whole and therefore may be assisted by resources drawn from technical assistance programs. Such assistance in the mass communication field is of growing importance at a time when underdeveloped countries are seeking to attain in a matter of years a level of advancement which it has taken the developed countries centuries to achieve.

Vittorino Veronese of Italy opened the Bangkok conference in 1960 with a speech that emphasized that a lack of physical facilities was the great obstacle to the development of press, radio, film, and television in Southeast Asia:

> In this matter of facilities UNESCO has adopted the criterion that a country is insufficiently provided with information media if it has less than ten copies of a daily newspaper, less than five radio receivers and less than two cinema seats for every 100 people. The simple application of this criterion shows that almost all of the countries of Southeast Asia lack the means which would enable them to benefit from the knowledge which would be made available to them.
> This serious state of affairs hinders social advancement. It is, surely, a commonplace today to emphasize that economic and social

progress goes hand in hand with development of the information media. But we have not, perhaps, given sufficient attention to its implication for the development of insufficiently developed countries. In any event, at a time when these countries are combating illiteracy and striving to carry out programs of economic development, they find themselves deprived of the potent and indispensable aid of the means of communication.

Here, as far back as 1960, some grumbling manifested itself at the work of the world news agencies but it had not yet taken on the intensity that characterizes so much of the Third World rhetoric today. The report on the Bangkok discussions on news agencies and telecommunications said at one point:

It was also noted that the flow of news between the various countries in the region, as well as the exchange of news between Asia and the rest of the world, is largely in the hands of the world news agencies. *Although the latter have made praiseworthy efforts to meet new requirements for more news about Asia in general, it remains true that they are based in the West, where their most important clients are also located, and that both their selection and their treatment of news must necessarily be influenced by these clients' interests* [emphasis added]. Consequently, the Southeast Asian countries are not sufficiently provided with news about one another or with news from an Asian point of view, about the rest of the world. These tasks are not being adequately done, at present, either by the world agencies or by the national agencies in the region.

The foregoing is noteworthy on two counts. First, it indicates that the mere fact the Big Four are based in the industrialized West explains much of the suspicion of them. And second, it sounds a theme dear to Third World commentators—that the Western agencies are seriously responsive only to the needs of their subscribers in the West.

A 1961 UNESCO report on news agency development in Latin America found that only Cuba among the Latin American nations had an agency "which distributes news regularly to other countries in the region." The reference presumably is to Castro's agency Prensa Latina, a politicized entity that could hardly be called a new service in the Western meaning of the world.

This report said that Latin America was much more highly developed than Southeast Asia or Africa when it came to newspapers and broadcasting stations, and that this fact would normally contribute to news agency development. And yet, the report said, "it appears paradoxical, on economic grounds, that there should be fewer national news agencies in Latin America than in either of these two other regions."

The report cited a trend toward economic and social integration in Latin America as another factor that would be favorable toward the development of news agencies. But it added:

> Three negative factors offset these positive ones. Most important, perhaps, is the fact that the extensive services of the world news agencies are distributed in Spanish and Portuguese. This would diminish, for Latin American agencies, the "translation function" which is important among news agencies in Southeast Asia. There is, in addition, a severe lack of trained Latin American senior news agency staff, particularly in management and administration. The third obstacle arises from the high or disparate rates charged for transmitting news within the area and to other regions.

There is in the foregoing a querulous observation that the big Western agencies, by providing adequate service and doing so in the language of the receiving countries, are rather unsportingly reducing the need for a national agency.

As recently as 1962, UNESCO literature was making a distinction between news and official government information that is much more difficult to find today. A UNESCO report on the 1962 African regional conference previously mentioned said *inter alia:*

> In making plans for the development of news agencies, the meeting pointed out, it was first of all necessary to define the function of a news agency. For one thing, a distinction should be made between the straightforward work of collecting and distributing news and the quite separate activities of publishing, advertising and publicity. A distinction should also be made between a national news agency and a government information department, even though the news agency might be government-sponsored. . . .
>
> The meeting agreed that, in the long term, the cooperative type of news agency, owned and operated by its member newspapers, would probably best fulfill the functions of an impartial news gathering and distributing enterprise, since the various political persuasions and tastes of its members would tend to guarantee objectivity. However, it was recognized that full ownership and control of news agencies by the press would very likely not be possible at present in countries where newspapers were still few in number and limited in financial resources, or where a multiplicity of strongly differing political parties made cooperation particularly difficult even on the professional level.

This effort to draw a distinction between a bona fide news service and an organ of government appears not to preoccupy UNESCO today.

Two UNESCO conferences that appear to have been particularly significant in the shift in emphasis and policy within UNESCO were the meetings of experts in Bogota, Colombia, in July 1974 and in Quito, Ecuador, in June 1975. Both dealt with communications policies and news exchanges in Latin America and were preparatory to the Latin American Intergovernmental Conference held in July 1976 at San Jose, Costa Rica.

The concept of nationalizing news and information functions took a great step forward at these two meetings. The report of the UNESCO experts at Bogota proposed to define a national communication policy as "a set of prescriptions and norms laid down to guide the behavior of communications institutions in a country."

"It was considered necessary," the report said, "to stress the role of the government or the state in order to link the national development policy with that of communications."

Private ownership of media came under question at Bogota in a manner that left little doubt about the ideological orientation of many of the experts. They agreed that a national development policy was the standard by which a national communications policy should be defined. And since private enterprises, in the language of the report, "have definite individual and commercial aims," it was questionable whether or how private enterprises could be integrated with development policy.

"The need for political, economic and cultural independence," the experts said, "is forcing the member states of the region to assume overall control over their national mass communication policy, a control which has hitherto been exercised partly in practice by private cultural enterprise."

The Bogota experts were particularly sharp in attacking the "pernicious" qualities of commercial broadcasting, both in radio and television, and their dedication to state control was reflected in the four different formulas they proposed for operating broadcast media. All provided for firm government operation or regulation—not technical regulation, as in the United States, but regulation of content.

The Bogota experts also stressed the concept of access and participation by "the people" in the communication process, a concept that clearly required the intervention of government as representative of the people.

The Quito conference of experts in 1975 went forward in much the same spirit, with major attention devoted to news agencies. One group of experts said that government-run news agencies were "reliable tools for development" and should be encouraged. They recommended the creation of a news agency for the Latin American and Caribbean area by forming a federation of national agencies.

However radical or extreme some of these proposals may have sounded to the world of the libertarian press, they did not represent the most radical views among the experts gathered at Quito. One proposal, which was defeated by a majority, urged that national news agencies be given a monopoly in distributing inside a country any outside news that referred to the internal affairs of that country.

The fact that this proposal was on the agenda at all indicated how far UNESCO had moved from the 1962 admonition to itself about the importance of maintaining a distinction between "the straightforward work of collecting and distributing news" and other activities, and also between a national news agency and a government information department.

An unprecedented storm over UNESCO and news policy erupted in the months preceding the Costa Rica conference. Background papers for the conference circulated by UNESCO experts included the following possible ingredients for national policies on mass communications:

• Government-run news agencies could be given exclusive rights to disseminate information from outside the country (the same idea that had come up at Quito).

• Legal measures might be considered to permit the arrest of correspondents of international press organizations that published or distributed material regarded as critical by the country where the correspondent was posted.

• Independent print and broadcast media could be nationalized. (The left-wing military government of Peru had provided precedent for this in 1974 by nationalizing all six of the country's independent dailies.)

These provisions stirred understandable alarm in the Western press, alarm not dispelled when UNESCO disavowed the proposals as representative of UNESCO policy: the proposals simply represented the views of the experts who prepared them. The Inter-American Press Association (IAPA), which represents some of the most prestigious newspapers in the western hemisphere, sent a strong delegation to Costa Rica. Freedom House in New York, one of the earliest critics of UNESCO's press policies, called a special news conference to call attention of free journalists everywhere to the issues involved.

In Costa Rica, during the conference, the IAPA delegation met with UNESCO officials in attendance and then issued a statement saying that UNESCO's "tendency" to recommend policy that "could undermine freedom of the press remains unchanged.] . . The highest authorities of UNESCO have repeatedly stated that it is not their intention to limit or undermine freedom of expression ... It is clear, however, that freedom of expression means one thing to UNESCO and another to the Inter-American Press Association."

Inside the conference hall, Director General M'Bow felt it necessary to make reference to the storm raised by IAPA, and he did not overlook the fact that some of Latin America's biggest newspapers—most of them members of IAPA—were owned and controlled by wealthy old-line families. What, he asked, "can be the true meaning of the term 'freedom of expression' today" in countries and conditions such as these?

M'Bow then went on to explain UNESCO's changing objectives. International communications, he said, remain concentrated in a "few limited points of the globe" that also control the developing satellite technology with all of its potential for even greater saturation of the world.

"Considerations of this kind," M'Bow said, "are what have led UNESCO to speak no longer of 'freedom of information' alone, but also of 'access to and participation in communication,' no longer only of 'freedom of information' but also of 'balanced flow of information.' In short, it is a question of going beyond the stage of mere information in an effort to reach that of communication, because if there is to be communication, information can no longer be a one-way affair."

Referring back to the growing technological hold on communication channels, he said, "This situation is deplored by the many people who feel that it cannot long continue without seriously imperilling international understanding and consequently the maintenance of peace and harmony between nations."

In the foregoing statements by the IAPA, as representatives of classic Western press traditions, and by M'Bow and Third World spokesmen, there can be seen sharply divergent interpretations of free expression, a divergence that goes to the heart of the present problem. To members of the IAPA and other Western journalists, "Free Flow of Information" means today what it meant in 1948 when it was proclaimed by the United Nations to be a right of all men—that news should travel freely and without hindrance around the world.

To many in the Third World, "free flow" is a self-serving concept devised in 1948 by the West, and particularly by the two U.S. news agencies, to ensure their domination of world news channels. In its place, Third World commentators are now calling for "balanced flow" or "equilibrated" flow of news and are beginning to articulate what is being called a "right to communicate" and a right to "equality of access" to communications systems.

The reason for this change in terminology is touched upon by E. Lloyd Sommerlad, chief of UNESCO's Division of Communication and Research Policies, in a paper presented for a communications conference sponsored by the Asia Mass Communication and Information Center and held in Sri Lanka in April 1975. He wrote:

> The concept of the "free flow of information" has increasingly come under critical scrutiny in recent years. At the 1974 General Conference of UNESCO, the program for the Division of Free Flow of Information and International Exchanges gave rise to a debate which showed that Third World countries particularly considered that "the concept of free flow was outdated and belonged to the nineteenth century." Free flow should be seen within the framework of freedom and the equality of access both to media and to information. Some delegates observed the "free flow" had little meaning for those lacking the necessary infra-structures and the means to communication.

This relegation of "free flow" to a past era is popular with Third World commentators. When the Nonaligned News Agencies Pool was being formed in New Delhi in July 1976 before the Colombo summit meeting, which ratified the pool, Indira Gandhi's minister of information, V. C. Shukla, said that the idea of free flow of information "fits insidiously into the package of other kinds of 'freedom' still championed by the adherents of the 19th century liberalism."

As for the "right to communicate," Sommerlad said it was not just a new name for free flow of information:

> It has much wider dimensions. It takes two to communicate and the essential new ingredient in the "right" is the idea of dialogue, interaction, exchange, response, sharing, in a two-way flow with mutual respect. While the central idea in free flow is the dissemination of information, the essence of communication is interchange.

Sommerlad acknowledged the extreme difficulty in agreeing upon what could constitute a "balanced" news flow. The standard, he said, could hardly be simply a quantitative one. The imbalance was firstly a reflection of world political power, he said, and secondly, "a matter of different values just as much as it is a quantitative measure." And associated with this are the implications of dependency, which so restricts choice and limits initiative."

"The balance that is sought," Sommerlad said, "is essentially a harmony—an equilibrium which is not upset by an overwhelming intrusion of information or entertainment which is not relevant to needs or in conformity with cultural values."

To many in the West, the implications of these distinctions represent little but a retreat from the principles of Geneva.

THE SOVIET DIMENSION

Ironically, it took a Soviet initiative to direct the full attention of the Western press to the policy drifts within UNESCO with regard to news and information. The initiative was Moscow's effort to win UNESCO approval of a controversial Soviet resolution on the "uses" of the mass media by governments.

This move had its origins in a resolution adopted by the Sixteenth Biennial General Conference of UNESCO in 1970, authorizing the director general to assist member states in the formation of mass communications policies. At the 1972 general conference, the Soviet and Byelorussian delegations introduced a resolution for the preparation of a declaration on "the fundamental principles governing the use of the mass media."

At the 1974 general conference, the United States and others opposed the form of the Soviet-proposed resolution and the director-general was asked to prepare a revised draft for UNESCO's 1976 biennial conference in Nairobi. Intergovernmental experts were summoned to a conference at UNESCO headquarters in Paris in mid-December 1975 to prepare the draft for the Nairobi conference in late 1976. The Soviet delegation in Paris brought in the revised draft, which would shortly arouse thundering editorial broadsides from the free world and, in the process, assail UNESCO and call serious attention to the coincidental dissatisfaction in the Third World with the work of the Western news agencies.

The Soviet proposal was formally entitled "A Draft Declaration on Fundamental Principles Governing the Use of the Mass Media in Strengthening Peace and International Understanding and in Combating War Propaganda, Racism and Apartheid." In the words of William G. Harley of the U.S. Commission for UNESCO, the title alone "was reason enough to postpone it."

"But there were more serious reasons for postponement," Harley said in a background paper for the commission:

> It was clearly a Soviet plot to extend the USSR philosophy of state control of the media into the international sphere and thereby give it UNESCO sanction. Stripped of its lofty rhetoric, the Declaration was nothing more than a set of directives on what the media of the world should say and do to foster these objectives. The United States took

a jaundiced view of the whole business but did not have the votes to knock the resolution out and so agreed, without enthusiasm, to try and work out such areas of agreement as might be possible, while repeating its feeling that a much more productive course for UNESCO to follow would be to help develop the opportunities for all peoples to receive information and to articulate their views through the mass media.

It had been agreed at the outset that the 85 nations assembled in Paris would avoid votes and work on concensus. But this agreement broke down after Yugoslavia introduced the resolution to equate Zionism with racism. When Algeria forced this to a showdown vote, the United States and 12 other nations walked out. With the most potent opposition gone, the Paris meeting sailed ahead and approved the draft resolution for submission to UNESCO's Nineteenth Biennial General Conference in Nairobi in October-November 1976.

The drama of the Paris meeting, more than any other one thing, served to alert the free press to the Soviet initiative, its great support in the Third World, and its threat to a free flow of information. This broad concern was sharpened, as has been seen, by events surrounding the UNESCO conference at San Jose, Costa Rica, in July 1976. A few weeks later, in July, came the ministerial conference of nonaligned nations in New Delhi, where the Third World states voted to establish a pooling arrangement among their national news agencies. This action, together with the accompanying attacks on the Western news agencies and concern over the pending Soviet resolution, now made it certain that the approaching Nairobi conference would get a degree of press scrutiny rarely afforded UNESCO meetings.

IAPA held its annual meeting in Williamsburg, Virginia, shortly before the Nairobi conference. UNESCO was closely identified with the Soviet declaration in many of the statements by the assembled publishers and editors of major western-hemisphere newspapers.

"The status of the press in the Americas is not encouraging," said a statement by IAPA's Committee on Freedom of the Press and Information (IAPA *News,* October/November 1976). "The enemies of free journalism, who at one time were only dictators, grow and multiply. The communications media live under severe pressures, and, with UNESCO in the vanguard of the enemy, it is time to prepare for a long uphill struggle."

George Beebe of the *Miami Herald,* then chairman of IAPA's executive committee, said the main threat of many UNESCO proposals "is to spread the influence of the Russian school of press control into the Third World. This is not a red scare. This is a red reality."

Beebe said IAPA's main fear "is not over the formation of national news agencies, which could be completely legitimate, but over suggestions that these agencies have control of the news flow in and out of countries."

Jerry W. Friedheim, executive vice-president and general manager of the American Newspaper Publishers Association (ANPA), said the approaching Nairobi meeting was "possibly the world's greatest challenge to a free press." He too spoke of a UNESCO thrust, saying, "We must rescue UNESCO from its flirtation with the policies that would serve the aims of tyrants rather than the aims of freedom and liberty" (IAPA *News,* October/November 1976).

The Williamsburg meeting among other things also appealed to the governments of Colombia, Costa Rica, Mexico, and Venezuela to reconsider the support they had given at the UNESCO conference in Costa Rica to various proposals calling for government involvement in information policy.

After Williamsburg, Beebe flew to Nairobi in his capacity as chairman of the World Press Freedom Committee, an organization representing not only IAPA but also the International Press Institute (IPI), the Inter American Association of Broadcasters, and a dozen other national and international organizations.

The U.S. government had also been active in the months before Nairobi in a less public manner. U.S. diplomats had been calling on Third World countries to mobilize support against the Soviet resolution, and the U.S. delegation at Nairobi proved an effective and eloquent one. Clayton Kirkpatrick, editor and vice-president of the *Chicago Tribune,* was a member of the delegation, and he spoke out strongly against the resolution and particularly against arguments that too much was being made of a proposal that would in any event not have the force of law. He said:

> Acceptance of the draft would put the moral sanction of UNESCO on the side of a controlled and subservient mass media. It is cynicism unworthy of the ideals of this Organization to adopt this resolution under the pretext that it is not significant. If the draft has no real significance, honesty and respect for the opinions of mankind require that it be abandoned.

In the end, the Soviet declaration was sidetracked until the next general conference of UNESCO in 1978. The conference instead approved a Tunisian proposal committing UNESCO to some practical steps to improving information systems in the Third World.

The Tunisian proposal in effect gave the Nonaligned News Agencies Pool special status within UNESCO by "inviting" the UNESCO director general to pay "special attention" to its activities. The resolution praised UNESCO's efforts in "assisting in liberating the developing countries from the state of dependence, which still characterizes their communication and information systems." It also called for studies and measures "to ensure a more balanced and diversified exchange of news than that which currently exists between developing countries."

The sidetracking of the Soviet resolution at Nairobi was made possible by able diplomacy and the support of moderate Third World countries. But there can be no doubt that an implicit U.S. threat to withdraw from UNESCO helped convince Director General M'Bow that it would be fiscally more prudent—the United States being UNESCO's largest single contributor—to avoid a bruising confrontation at Nairobi and a possible debacle at UNESCO's first general conference on African soil.

The United States was already deeply and deliberately in arrears in its UNESCO assessments when the Nairobi conference began. The economic aspect of the negotiations is spelled out by Leonard R. Sussman, the executive director of Freedom House, in his "Mass News Media and the Third World Challenge" (The Washington Papers, vol. 46, Beverly Hills and London, Sage Publications). Sussman wrote:

> The United States had paid $3.2 million in arrearages shortly before coming to Nairobi in order to vote there. By mid-1977, the United States, which is committed to provide 25% of UNESCO's annual budget, would owe UNESCO some $90 million in arrearages, current dues and other assessments. The only vocal U.S. opinion on the issue favored withdrawing funds until UNESCO reached satisfactory positions on critical confrontational issues. Mr. M'Bow paid a hasty visit to Secretary of State Kissinger just before the biennial opened; in turn, M'Bow was visited privately by members of the UNESCO Commission. In the hectic hours before the sessions opened, M'Bow sent a trusted aide to the United States to make certain the threats of withholding further funds, and even of withdrawing from UNESCO formally, were not empty gestures. M'Bow was assured they were not. He apparently accepted these estimates and devised the negotiating group as a face-saving format for those backing the Soviet resolution.

Under this format, the negotiating group at Nairobi was asked to study the Soviet draft in order to improve chances for a compromise, but it was understood all along that it would not be heard from again at Nairobi. But since it was assured a place on the agenda for UNESCO's general conference in 1978, the battle was far from over.

The Soviet declaration gives the customary tip of the hat to freedom of information as a principle, but subsequent language makes clear that its main intent is to put UNESCO's mark of legitimacy on the Soviet concept of news as an instrument of state policy.

The opening articles speak in generalities about the need for promoting the spread of information for the reduction of international tensions, and so on, and for the development of media to "correct the existing disequilibrium and for the training of personnel."

Article II does contain a mutual pledge of "non-interference" in each other's affairs, a further license—if one were needed—for any state to protest any reporting that it regarded as domestic interference.

The Soviet bid for Arab and Afro Asian support is contained not only in the title of the draft but also in Article VIII, which says: "The voices of those struggling against apartheid and other forms of racial discrimination, colonialism, neo-colonialism and foreign occupation by aggression, and unable to be heard within their own territory, should be given expression through the mass media of other countries with due respect for the sovereignty of the host countries."

While a previous article, number V, states in a general way that the media should avoid any justification of religious hatred, the right of protest enunciated in Article VIII is so drawn as to make it inapplicable to Jews in the Soviet Union.

Articles X, XI, and XII are clearly the most significant.

Article X: States, institutions or groups which consider that the circulation of erroneous news reports has seriously impaired their action with a view to the strengthening of peace and international understanding, and their efforts to combat war propaganda, racism and apartheid, should be able to rectify such news reports through the mass media.

Article XI: It is the duty of professional organizations in the field of mass communication to define and promote standards of professional ethics on a national and international level to support their members in the responsible exercise of their profession.

Article XII: States are responsible for the activities in the international sphere of all mass media under their jurisdiction.

Article XII has evoked the sharpest controversy because it is subject to two interpretations, either of which is wholly unacceptable to the West. The first would be that since the AP, UPI, and *New York Times* correspondents in Moscow for example, are, clearly under Soviet jurisdiction, the Soviet government could hold itself responsible for their reportage of Soviet affairs—or, in more practical terms, that these correspondents would be answerable to the Soviet government for their reportage.

The other interpretation would be that since AP, UPI, and the *New York Times* are organically U.S. corporations, the U.S. government is responsible for everything they say and write about the Soviet Union.

The full import of Articles X and XII is lost if they are read in isolation. Article X gives governments a right of access to news media whenever they feel they have been the victim of erroneous news reports. And Article XII, under one interpretation, would place upon another government the obligation of providing such access if the news medium in question were under its jurisdiction. Foreign ministries would thus become press ombudsmen for each other.

"While the State Department may patiently turn back formal complaints from foreign ambassadors with polite explanations how a free press operates, the onus thereafter will be on the United States for having defied an international agreement," says Sussman in "Mass Media and the Third World Challenge."

THE NONALIGNED NEWS AGENCIES POOL: A FIRST ASSESSMENT

The Nonaligned News Agencies Pool, ratified in August 1976 by the 85 nations attending the Fifth Nonaligned Summit Conference in Colombo, is the Third World's most ambitious effort to make its voice heard in the international arena.

The pool concept began to gain impetus at the Fourth Nonaligned Summit in Algiers in 1973, which recommended some form of cooperative action by the various Third World national news agencies. From the beginning, the initiative was seized by the Yugoslav agency, Tanjug. On January 18, 1975, it announced that it would act as the vehicle for the interchange of information between itself and 10 other nonaligned countries (see the chapter by Pero Ivacic on Tanjug's role).

The constitution for the pool was drawn up at a ministerial conference in New Delhi in July 1976, and the project was formally launched at the Colombo summit in the following month. In a report to the New Delhi conference, Tanjug reported that the pool that it had launched some 18 months previously had already attracted the participation of about 40 national agencies.

Yugoslavia had in the intervening time consolidated the role of Tanjug as the key relay center for the pool. It launched a $13 million modernization program for Tanjug, including the construction of four 38,000-watt radio transmitters to expedite short wave radioteletype transmission of Tanjug news and offerings from pool members in three languages—French, Spanish, and English.

Also, Yugoslavia had in 1975 begun offering seminars at Yugoslav universities to Third World journalists on such things as the role of information in "decolonization," in "strengthening economic and social independence," and in "promoting cultural interaction in the Third World."

The New Delhi and Colombo conferences were held during the period of Prime Minister Gandhi's authoritarian rule in India. As the host to the ministerial conference, she strongly articulated her dissatisfaction with the work of the big world news agencies and signaled India's intention of rivaling Yugoslavia as a leader of the nonaligned pool movement.

Her government had forced India's four news agencies to merge into a single new agency, named Samachar, and Samachar was in great evidence at the Colombo conference, providing coverage not only for India but for nonaligned countries without their own coverage.

Samachar had also announced other plans that clearly were intended to strengthen India's bid for a leadership role in the field of Third World information. This included a statement that Samachar would station from 40 to 50 correspondents around the world not only to report to Indian readers but "to make Samachar's expertise in news coverage available to the developing world." A half dozen or so additional correspondents were in fact abroad for Samachar when Gandi's emergency rule was terminated at the polls in March 1977. The new Indian government was quick to restore traditional press freedoms. Samachar was allowed to continue only until mid-November when the government formally denounced it as an "aberration" of the emergency. Samachar was dissolved, permitting the four merged agencies to resume independent operation. While the Indian government remains committed to the Nonaligned Pool, it has made it publicly clear that it in no way regards the pool as a replacement for the traditional sources of news but rather as a supplement to them. In effect, Yugoslavia's premier role in the operating of the pool remains assured for the time being.

Briefly, this is how the pool works. Participants (news agencies or government informatrion services where no news agencies exist) send selected items for the pool to Tanjug in Belgrade at their own expense. There is supposed to be a daily limit of 500 words on each contributor, but this is not rigidly enforced. Since Tanjug, outside of the pool arrangement, receives the full file of many of these agencies, it can also select items from those files for inclusion in the pool section of its daily transmissions. Tanjug translates and transmits all pool offerings in Spanish, French, and English, "scrupulously respecting the substance of the news received," in the words of Pero Ivacic, general director of Tanjug. "The publication rate of items from the Pool newscast is still modest," Ivacic reported in the April 1977 issue of the UNESCO *Courier,* "but it is improving daily. The quality, substance and presentation of the material provided is also constantly improving, while an increasing number of news agencies of non-aligned countries are actively participating in the Pool."

While no statistical data are yet available on the use of pool material, an analysis of the content is provided in a study by Edward T. Pinch of the U.S. State Department's Senior Seminar in Foreign Policy. The study was based on Tanjug's file for every eighth day of transmission during the first quarter of 1977. This yielded a total of 327 items. These were studied to determine national participation, the general subject matter of the stories, their possible interest to Western media, and their bias for or against the United States.

While Tanjug reported that 41 news agencies and organizations were participating in the pool at the time of the study, contributions from only 26 showed up in the samples. Of these, 10 contributors provided one percent or less of the items in the pool. The study showed that 60 percent of the contents of the pool was provided by just seven countries. The breakdown by percentages was as follows:

17	Yugoslavia
12	Egypt
7	Iraq
6 (each)	Cuba, Qatar, Sri Lanka, Libya
5	Cyprus
4 (each)	India, Morrocco
3 (each)	Vietnam, Ghana, UN Office of Public Information
2 (each)	Indonesia, Tunisia, Sudan
1 (or less)	North Korea, Malaysia, Palestine Liberation Organization, Saudi Arabia, Mexico, Venezuela, Algeria, Bangladesh, Syria, Interpress

(Interpress Service [IPS] is a Rome-based organization that relays the Tanjug file and pool file to Latin America where it is further redistributed by the Cuban agency, Prensa Latina. Tanjug describes IPS as a "private, non-governmental news agency" dedicated to Third World news. The fact that IPS is a link between one Communist state and another should be noted in speculating about its own political orientation.)

In his study, Pinch noted that only one of the top seven contributors to the pool (Sri Lanka) had an established tradition of press freedom. "Other nations with a traditionally democratic press such as Cyprus, India, Mexico, and Venezuela, contributed lesser amounts," Pinch said. "If this pattern of participation continues in the future, input from the Third World's democracies will continue at about 17%, which is roughly proportional to their membership in the Nonaligned Movement."

This study also sought to determine how much of the Nonaligned Pool's offerings might be found usable in Western journalistic terms. Items were rated "high" if they were felt to be of potential interest to newspapers, news magazines, radio, or television in the West. A "medium" rating was given to items of more limited potential; items in this category, for example, might be found usable in specialized journals or provide the basis for further investigation. Items rated "low" were those felt, for a variety of reasons, not to be of any interest to Western media. On this basis, 22% were rated "high," 26% as "medium," and 52% as "low."

"The 22% figure for the 'high' column is probably greater than critics of Third World journalism would anticipate," Pinch said. He observed, however, that this did not necessarily mean that this 22 percent was news that was not obtained by the Western media from other sources. In fact, much of it was attributable to sources already available to all media.

The study found that news items sent to the pool by Jordan and Qatar did best in the "high" category because "these stories have solid news content and are low in ideological polemics."

The "real surprise" of this part of the study, Pinch observed, was the showing of Cuba's Prensa Latina, which won a "high" rating for nine out of 21 stories. The Prensa Latina file, he said, is not free of the rhetoric that reduces Western placement potential but its jargon "is comparatively crisp, is less pervasive, and usually does not obscure the news content."

With regard to overt bias in reference to the United States, the study said it found "surprisingly little. . . . Even more surprising," it added, "is that of the 9% of stories found to have a bias, 4% were in favor of the U.S."

Bias, it should be noted, was defined as attitudes aimed directly toward the United States itself, rather than for or against positions taken by the United States in the international arena. If the yardstick were for and against U.S. positions, the balance clearly would be strongly against the United States. In any case, as Pinch himself cautions repeatedly, no firm conclusions can prudently be drawn on the basis of such a limited study, which does nevertheless provide the first indication of the pool's general thrust.

The creation of the Nonaligned News Agencies Pool is a great source of pride for Third World journalists—and the reaction to it in the West a great source of irritation (see the chapters by Olasope and Aggarwala).

D. V. Nathan, an Indian journalist, writing in the magazine *Indian Press* for August 1976 shortly after the New Delhi conference of nonaligned nations, said: "The New Delhi Declaration on a news pool will go down in history as the magna carta of developing nations to throw out the foreign yoke of transnational communication monopoly." But the Third World is not without doubts. Aggarwala is doubtful that the pool will meet the desired objective of promoting a "counterflow of world news which will be Southern-oriented, both in content as well as perspective."

For their part, the Western agencies have reacted with understanding to the development of national news agencies and to the Nonaligned Pool, subject to a single reservation: They hope it does not become a device to block them from reporting independently from the areas involved.

Stanley M. Swinton, vice-president and assistant general manager of AP, saw nothing harmful or dangerous in the pool as it presently operated:

> That doesn't mean it could not in the future become a threat to transnational news distribution. However my basic theory is that the more news the better, so long as news from one source is not permitted to squeeze out news from the international agencies in a twisted Gresham's law way.

Claude Roussel, president and director general of AFP, said his agency felt that free competition was the best guarantee for free and honest information and that the desire of the Third World countries to develop news agencies "seems to us legitimate. . . . On the other hand," he added, "we do not think at AFP that any improvement in the free flow of news can be achieved through the destruction of existing channels, attacks against existing news agencies or the establishment of a system of state or interstate controls."

H. L. Stevenson, editor-in-chief of UPI, and Gerald Long, general manager of Reuters, also felt that the announced aspirations of the pool members were reasonable. Long observed that the pool should not be confused with an "objective" system of news dissemination. The pool, he said, will reflect views of governments; and while views of governments are necessary views, he said, they remain government views.

For all the Western agencies, as indeed for all outside media, the overriding concern is that the pool not become a device to deny access to foreign correspondents. There is thus far no evidence that it has. Western preoccupation with access was accentuated by the fact that the birth of the pool coincided with the battle in UNESCO over the Soviet declaration on the use of news and information, investing the atmosphere with a touch of the Cold War. There was some overlap in support for the Soviet and the Nonaligned Pool initiatives, even though they were unrelated—and one year later, it is fair to concede that there was also some overreaction in the West.

Access is not an academic question, particularly in Africa. David Lamb, writing from Nairobi for the *Los Angeles Times,* says that as of September 1977, "more than one-quarter of Black Africa's 44 governments now ban foreign correspondents entirely or admit them so infrequently and under such controlled conditions that news, in effect, is managed to be blacked out. . . .

"Others admit journalists only for self-serving tours, then send them on their way," Lamb says. "In the Central African Empire, the rare journalist granted a visa must post a $400 cash bond, 80 percent of which is refundable upon departure."

While the facts cited by Lamb cannot be altered, the perspective can be changed by observing that three-quarters of the black African countries do *not* engage in such extreme practices, and that therefore there is room for some accommodation and understanding. It should also be noted that none of the restrictions cited by Lamb are linked in any way with the pool.

Western media can mourn or denounce internal press restrictions by any country, but they cannot challenge it as a legitimate exercise of sovereign power. What is of more legitimate concern is that such internal policies not spill over and restrict the right of access by journalists of other countries.

THIRD WORLD CRITICISMS: POINT AND COUNTERPOINT

Whether they emerge from Asia, Africa, or Latin America, the Third World indictments of the Western agencies strike almost identical themes, modified occasionally to reflect regional differences.

Latin America, for example, has a highly developed press compared with the other areas, and the Western agencies are covering Latin
America far more thoroughly than any other part of the Third World.
The criticism there consequently is aimed less at the volume than at
the quality of the coverage and the predominance of what is felt to be
foreign perspectives or alien cultural values [see the chapter by Guido
Fernandez].

African comment reflects among other things the relatively mea-
ger communication facilities across the continent, an undeniable leg-
acy of the colonial period. The emphasis in colonial communications
was between colony and home, not between this colony and that. The
result is that even today a telephone call from francophone Africa must
sometimes be routed via Paris and London to connect with English-
speaking Africa [see the chapters by Olasope and Hilary Ng'weno].
Satellites and other new technologies have sharply reduced the same
problems in Latin America and to a lesser extent in Asia, but Africa
lags further behind.

Third World journalists and governments naturally provide the
bulk of the comment critical of the Western agencies. But a particularly
instructive vein is also provided by the academics and ideologues
whose argumentation puts the Third World case in a broader intellectual context in a manner that is sometimes incisive, sometimes facile,
sometimes naive, and almost always based on the conviction that the
profit motive explains most existing ills.

The Journalistic View

Olasope, the director of news and current affairs for the Nigerian
Broadcasting System, reflects the views of many Third World journalists in his chapter in this book. One key passage follows:

> Another aspect of the problem is the attitude, the preferences,
> and the prejudices of foreign newsmen. The new states of Africa and
> the rest of the Third World are today preoccupied with social and
> economic development. They are building hospitals, schools, roads,
> skyscrapers. To them, but not to the Western correspondents, this
> development is what is new and relevant. . . . The development and,
> indeed, transformation that is going on all around is hardly ever
> noticed while events or issues that are insignificant or that in no way
> contribute to the progress of the nation, but rather create a bad image,
> get interpreted from the Western point of view and are blown up out
> of all proportion. African countries receive the attention of the West-
> ern mass media only when they are involved in coups or rebellions
> or when those of their leaders who are not considered pro-Western

engage in outrageous or embarrasing acts. . . . The sense of news value and the editorial judgment of the correspondents of the Western news agencies are therefore a distinct impediment to the free flow of news from the African point of view.

Olasope makes much the same indictment of the Soviet Union's TASS and other communist agencies whose correspondents "have been trained to recognize what their employers and their clients want to know about Africa." East and West thus get different images of Africa, he says, each reflecting different ideological orientations. But for African newspapers and radios, Olasope says, the situation is even worse because the agencies of the advanced countries are their only sources of news about themselves—sources that are "controlled, inadequate, and distorted" and hardly an endorsement of the "free flow of information."

Aggarwala, in his chapter, gives yet another Third World perspective by a journalist. There are far more strident comments from the journalistic community in the Third World. Libya's Arab Revolution News Agency (ARNA) for example, accuses the Western agencies of outright "fabrication of news hostile to Third World countries" and a "conspiracy of silence regarding anything advantageous to Third World countries." The Olasope and Aggarwala commentaries, however, are a fairer representation of the case being made against the Western news services by fellow journalists.

The View of Government

Political and economic overtones are naturally sharper in the criticism from Third World officialdom with regard to Western media in general and to the news agencies in particular. This was reflected in the many statements that emerged from the New Delhi ministerial conference in July 1976 when the Nonaligned News Agencies Pool was being formed.

Gandhi, then in the midst of her emergency rule as prime minister, keynoted the conference, hailing the pool as a concept that would help rectify "another lingering consequence of colonialism." She said *inter alia:*

In spite of our political sovereignty, most of us who have emerged from a colonial and semi-colonial past continue to have a rather unequal cultural and economic relationship with our respective former overlords. Even our image of ourselves, not to speak of the view of other countries, tends to conform to theirs. . .

The media of the powerful countries want to depict the governments of their erstwhile colonies as inept and corrupt and yearning for the good old days. This cannot be attributed to the common human failing of nostalgia. To a larger extent there is a deliberate purpose. . . . We want to hear Africans on Africa. You should similarly be able to get an Indian explanation of events in India.

Daniel Mutunda, Minister of Information of Kenya, told the New Delhi conference:

The fact that Kenya News Agency was given a franchise of all foreign news agencies has enabled our government to have access and evaluate the kind of news which these agencies thrive in disseminating to their readership. Indeed, the Prime Minister of India, Mrs. Indira Gandhi, spoke for the rest of us when she remarked that these agencies were only interested in reporting disasters and ignored the efforts and achievements made by the individual developing countries at any given national catastrophe.

A sampling of other government comment follows:
• President Carlos Andres Perez of Venezuela, to the UNESCO Latin American Intergovernmental Conference in San Jose, Costa Rica, July 13, 1976:

Our peoples are continuously subject to the uncontrolled invasion of news that inculcates in our masses alien values which threaten our own national identity.
I firmly believe that international regulation of communication is required to ensure the sacred right to information by guaranteeing that only the truth will be reported and to safeguard the unrestricted right to express opinion. The communication industry cannot have priority over public and social order.
The international press only reports such news as is harmful to the image of our peoples while the powerful press and audio-visual media of the industrialized world completely ignore our struggles, our efforts, our just demands for a new and more equitable international order.

• final report on the UNESCO Latin American Intergovernmental Conference San Jose, Costa Rica, July 12 to 21, 1976:

Specifically, some delegates expressed the view that the communication media (certain types of printed matter, radio, television, and cinema) and certain transnational organs or agencies belonging to the industrialized nations, had contributed a sort of cultural aggression which kept, or tried to keep, the developing countries in a state of dependence with respect to the nations where economic and political power was concentrated. Such a situation, they pointed out, threatened the peace and security of all nations and prevented the advent of a more just and peaceful economic order.

- statement by the Tunisian Secretariat of State for Information:

By offering the Third World only those items they have themselves broken down, filtered, expurgated and distorted, the big supranational news systems constrict the developing nations into having the same subjective vision of the world, and principally certain parts of the world, as themselves. Consequently, some areas even though they are close to one another, only know of one another through the interposition of those supranational systems and have only vague notions, gathered haphazardly from the international news agencies, of their respective life styles, problems and aspirations.

The Intellectual View

The intellectual formulation of the Third World case takes place not only in various United Nations arenas but also in such forums as the Dag Hammarskjold Foundation and publications such as *Development Dialogue,* published in Sweden, and *Socialist Thought and Practice,* published in Belgrade. Nowhere, however, is it done more articulately than at the Latin American Institute for Transnational Studies [ILET] in Mexico City, a research organization directed by a Chilean intellectual named Juan Somavia.

Somavia's analyses can at various moments be called trenchant, piercing, brilliant, or overblown. His own ideological bias shows clearly, although in fairness it must be said that he makes no attempt to hide it. Even so, his analysis of the industrial world's domination of communication channels, with particular reference to the work of the four major news agencies, is perhaps the best single source to capture the essence of the Third World rationale.

What follows are key points of a paper by Somavia entitled "The Transnational Power Structure and International Information" and subtitled "Elements for policy definitions with respect to transnational news agencies." It was prepared in collaboration with the Dag Hammarskjold Foundation in 1976.

Somavia begins by positing the existence in the world of a central power structure dominated by various entities from the developed world. In defining the power structure's makeup, he omits any reference to the Soviet Union. The North Atlantic Treaty Organization

(NATO) and the South East Asian Treaty Organization (SEATO) are elements of it, for example, but not the Warsaw Pact.

In addition to this military element, the transnational power structure has political, economic, industrial, trade-union, and intelligence aspects, all playing accepted roles in a system that operates in almost every Third World country.

The "transnational instrumentality" also has a "communications-advertising-culture dimension," an essential part of the system "which affords the control of that key instrument of contemporary society: Information." He adds:

> It is the vehicle for transmitting values and life styles to Third World countries which stimulate the type of consumption and the type of society necessary to the transnational system as a whole. . . . Loss of control over the communication structure by the transnational system would mean the loss of one of its most powerful weapons; this is why it is so difficult to bring about change in this field.

Somavia apparently does not regard the Soviet Union's TASS either as a news agency or as one of any importance; he lists the "main agencies of importance" as UPI, AP, Reuters, and AFP. He insists that they are not really "international" but "transnational" entities whose operations are "interlinked with other branches of the transnational production system, advertising, magazine and television-program production in particular and also transnational enterprises."

> Their structure and links with the rest of the transnational system, their ownership, their private-enterprise rationale of seeking constant expansion and long-term optimization of profits, together with the values that govern the present training of communicators, lead these agencies to treat information as a commodity and to regard their main aim as that of "selling" their product more successfully than their competitors. The "logic" of the market becomes the criterion for their conduct.

Somavia then presents an argument against the traditional concept of freedom of information that is figuring more and more prominently in Third World rhetoric and which may well have been inspired by the works of Herbert I. Schiller of the University of California at San Diego.

Somavia says the principle of "free flow of information" was approved by the United Nations Geneva Conference in 1948 under the strongest urging of the United States and especially of AP and UPI, which were best positioned immediately after the war to launch international operations. Schiller makes this same point more bitingly in his

"Genesis of the Free Flow of Information Principles," calling the free-flow concept a part of the "outward thrust" of American postwar business. According to Somavia:

> This concept has been used as the conceptual cornerstone to justify their [Western news agencies] "independence" and to enable them to carry on their activities without national or international social accountability of any kind. In this way, the seal of legitimacy has been placed on their right to act exclusively in their own interests, transmitting their particular view of events according to the political and economic determinants of the transnational system of which they form part. As a result of the failure to question in practical and conceptual terms the manner in which the principle of "free flow" has been applied, the agencies are currently neither socially nor juridically responsible for their acts, either to the foreign countries in which they operate, or to the international community. [These points then follow:] In practice, the principle of "free flow" means the agencies can determine what is news. . . . They are thus made into arbiters of existing reality.

Because of their background, the agencies apply criteria to news selection that often reflects "neither the interests nor the social realities of many Third World countries."

The agencies tend to use labels and adjectives to "stigmatize targets of the system." They can refer to "Marxist" President Salvador Allende in Chile but never to "capitalist" President Richard Nixon. "Progressive political leaders in the Third World are described as 'extremists' or 'rebels' but conservative or reactionary politicians are unlabelled."

From all this Somavia comes to his central point, that "information is a social good, not a commodity," and that it should be subject to some control.

> Providing information is a social function; it should not be a business transaction. Like all other social functions carried out on behalf of and for the service of community, its exercise should not be left to the exclusive judgment of those involved in the activity in question. For the transmission of information confers power and every society should be organized so that those holding power are socially responsible for its use. . . .
>
> [Somavia finds in the] commercial concept of news a built-in systematic discrimination against those events that cannot be "sold," which therefore in accordance with this rationale, are not "news" because the controlling market has no interest in them. At the same time there is a tendency to distortion by the projection of those aspects of events that make them more marketable.

Somavia proclaims that the old concept of "free flow" of information must be replaced by "an *equilibrated* free flow of *responsible* information" (emphasis added).

"We are not," he says, "advocating government control over the agencies' news flow." Yet he goes on to call for a "structure of legal and social responsibility" without making clear how "legal" measures can be taken without governmental action. What is clear, however, is that Somavia's entire rationale would place him four-square on the side of the Soviet declaration in UNESCO on the "uses" of information by the state.

Somavia says that in establishing a "framework for legal and social accountability" for the information disseminated by the agencies, governments should consider asking them for information concerning their central ownership and control structure, "the nature of the operational policy orientation received from the main office," full financial disclosure, and "banking connections, links with advertising and transnational communications enterprises." Nowhere does his conviction that the agencies are tools of some faceless power broker appear more clearly than in this passage.

He would also have the agencies satisfy governments as to their readiness to "cooperate in a positive way with studies undertaken by official and academic organizations with respect to the content, forms and characteristics of their activities." With this, Somavia's disclaimer of wanting government "control" of the agencies takes on a new light. If he does not want to impose control from above, he surely seeks to promote submission from below. This is further indicated by his suggestion that news agencies also be asked to explain the professional standards and journalistic criteria on the basis of which they "intend" to carry on their work in a given country. The implication is plain that if the explanations are not satisfactory, the intention need not materialize.

A point-by-point response to Somavia would be tedious and not likely to win converts. But a few specific observations would serve to throw some of his observations into better balance.

He asserts at one point that U.S. nationals dominate the choice of news that the AP and UPI circulate within Latin America. This finds little support in a study prepared by John T. McNelly of the University of Wisconsin School of Journalism and Mass Communication for the meeting of UNESCO experts in Quito, Ecuador, June 24 to 30, 1975.

McNelly's study of Latin American news patterns found that "much of the regional news transmitted by the global agencies is produced by Latin Americans. Some of them serve as bureau chiefs, others

Moscow is one of the world's two great power centers. The West-as staff correspondents in the bureaus or as part-time correspondents or 'stringers' in smaller capitals or provincial cities."

In the case of UPI, the 1977 bureau directory for Latin America lists five offices headed by U.S. citizens, one by a Canadian, and 12 by Latin Americans. Two of UPI's corporate officers are not U.S. nationals. The vice-president in charge of the agency's European, Middle Eastern, and African division is Julius B. Humi, a British citizen. The vice-president of its international operations is Claude Hippeau, a French citizen.

Somavia can also be challenged for his assertion that coverage patterns of the Western agencies are dictated overwhelmingly if not solely by the needs of their home markets. He clearly is unaware that the UPI and AP staffs in Latin America collect thousands of words daily that circulate only within Latin America and are of no interest whatever to Cleveland, Reno, or Miami.

McNelly's report also indicates the role of Latin-Americans in influencing the content of the news reports. He found that Latin American newspaper and broadcast media not only provided much of the news for agency reports but further influenced the flow with their requests for coverage in other areas. There is thus no single "controlling" market, as Somavia seems to feel, but a multiplicity of them.

This point is made forcefully by Long, general manager of Reuters, in his estimate that the British market is the source of less than 20 percent of his agency's revenues. Says Long:

> We are addressing ourselves to markets outside the country of our headquarters all over the world. For example, for us, the whole of Africa is a very important market indeed. We supply news services to government information services, very often in Africa, in Southeast Asia, also Japan and Latin America, so to say we at Reuters are addressing ourselves primarily to a western audience is quite simply wrong.

Reuters clearly is far less dependent for income in its home market than are AP, UPI, and AFP, although all have a worldwide clientele. But it does not follow, and in fact is not true, that these worldwide operations are always profitable or undertaken only in search of foreign profit, as Somavia seems to feel.

The agencies do not disdain profit. It is only profit that permits them to function independently of government. It is only profit from point A that permits them to undertake coverage in point B where there may be much news but no possibility of selling it, either because the agency is forbidden to sell the information, as in the Soviet Union, or the clientele is limited or nonexistent.

ern agencies maintain as many correspondents there as the Soviet government will permit. But they cannot sell their news to *Pravda*, *Izvestia*, or *Trud*. The best they can do is a trade of service with TASS, which is the filter through which any non-Soviet dispatch must pass to get to the Soviet press. TASS, on the other hand, is free to sell its service to any Western newspaper that wants to buy it.

Critics like Somavia and Schiller do violence to reality when they try to equate the news agencies with profit-making corporate entities such as International Business Machines (IBM) or Unilever. IBM and Unilever exist to make profits. When they go abroad, it is only in search of profit. The agencies go abroad in search of news. If they can also profit along the way, it is welcome to their always hard-pressed coffers. IBM and Unilever can abandon an unprofitable foreign field without a thought. Not so the news agencies. They were running vast deficitary operations in Vietnam during the war but had no alternative to continuing coverage. It is not likely that any agency is earning enough in Israel or Lebanon, for example, to pay even its local bills, but the agencies cannot as a consequence abandon coverage.

It would be equally naive and unrealistic to say that the balance sheet has no effect whatever on coverage patterns of the four Western agencies. Like individuals or governments, the agencies can do only what their total resources permit. If they indeed were the handmaidens of giant profit-making international enterprises, finances could hardly be a problem. But the situation is otherwise, and executives of all four agencies are frank to admit that they lack resources to cover the world as they would like to cover it.

What resources they have are deployed with the best interest of their overall service in mind and this results in coverage that is uneven. There is a concentration of staff in areas that produce the most news of most interest to most of their subscribers. They do, as has been seen, provide some especially tailored news services for specific regions. In this regard, Latin America is no doubt best served. But to take the Third World as a whole, it is simply a fact that agency operations there are more skeletal than they are elsewhere, which is another way of acknowledging that deficiencies exist.

What cannot be acknowledged, because it is simply not the case, is that these deficiencies reflect either contempt for the Third World or the dictate of some vague transnational apparatus aimed at keeping the peoples of the Third World in a state of economic and cultural subjugation. Suspicions like those can only hinder any initiative for greater cooperation between Western and Third World media.

Critics such as Somavia quarrel with more than the performance of the international agencies. His institute is also critical of the Latin

American press for its apparent satisfaction with the work of the agencies and its failure to undertake more intracontinental coverage itself. Fernando Reyes Matta, an associate of Somavia, reflects this attitude in an analysis published in *Development Dialogue* (1976:2) under the title, "The Information Bedazzlement of Latin America." Essentially, his point is that newspapers of the region are so conditioned to the news judgments and tastes of the big Western agencies that they too are incapable of recognizing stories of great regional importance even when they present themselves.

While the agencies covered the birth of the Surinam Republic on November 25, 1975, Reyes Matta said, not a single one of the Latin American newspapers sent its own correspondent, and a few even failed to use the agency accounts. "The Surinam case," he said, "exposes the continent's inability to look at itself, and its failure at self-interpretation. The easy option was taken, to reproduce a version of the news whose political character was obviously different from that which motivates the Third World countries."

He cited other cases of developmental news where, he said, the agencies provided coverage but "the act of rejection came from the media, from those in charge of selecting international news."

The combined thrust of the Somavia-Reyes Matta critiques is thus a call for reorientation not only of the Western agencies but also of the overwhelming privately owned press of Latin America. Like Somavia, Reyes Matta believes correctives to agency domination must come from governments, although he couches his formula in somewhat softer terms. "This," he said, "is a problem which cannot be dealt with at the level of action and decision of the agencies that operate in Latin America. It has to be faced at a political level, with a serious attempt to break the atomization and dependence." Again, a call for governmental intervention.

From these statements by Third World journalists, officials, and intellectuals, there begin to emerge the far-reaching implications of the insistent call for a "new order" of international news and information. More is involved than a mere quantitative balancing of the flow of words between nations on the global circuits of the big Western news agencies. It calls for the acceptance of new norms and attitudes toward news and information by journalists as well as governments.

Nothing, including abstract concepts of personal freedoms, is more important to most Third World commentators than national development. This is bringing growing emphasis on the perceived need for governments to interest themselves in news and information in the name of national development.

THE AGENCIES: PLUS AND MINUS

The Third World case against the Western agencies is not difficult to assemble. It is far more difficult to make an objective assessment of it. It is even more difficult to make any really accurate comparison of the relative strength and coverage patterns of the big agencies in various parts of the Third World (see the chapter by Mort Rosenblum on how the agencies work).

Because of the intense competition between them for the mantle of being the biggest and most comprehensive, the agencies tend to be wary of releasing too many of their operating secrets when it comes to size of staff, number of bureaus, and the like. William Hachten, when writing *Muffled Drums,* published in 1971, remarked, "All news services appear to exaggerate their manpower figures." He is not the first researcher to wonder.

Independent checks on some aspects of agency operations and coverage networks have been made, although all seem to leave something to be desired. One study may touch on the news filed by all four agencies to North Africa—but not to the rest of Africa. Another may measure the work of all four in Latin America but nowhere else. Still another may tabulate all countries where three of the four—but not the fourth—maintain correspondents.

Even this piecemeal data, however, can serve to bolster observations and assessments made by students of the various areas. It is, for example, widely taken as fact among journalists with international experience that so far as their foreign operations are concerned in the Third World countries, AFP and Reuters are dominant in Africa, and UPI and AP in Latin America. There is nothing as clear-cut about Asia. All four are active there, but on balance Reuters—largely because of its historic ties with the press of India, Ceylon, Singapore, and Malaysia—is likely to be ahead of the field in its news distribution operations.

An interesting perspective on agency domination in Latin America is provided in the previously cited article by Reyes Matta. To measure agency coverage of Latin America, Reyes Matta analyzed the sources of outside news published in 16 Latin American newspapers in 14 countries in a four-day period in 1975. Among them were some of the most prominent newspapers in Latin America—*Excelsior* and *El Heraldo* of Mexico City, *O Estado* of Sao Paulo, *La Prensa* and *Clarin* of Buenos Aires. The list also included *La Prensa* of Lima, which, together with Peru's five other big dailies, was nationalized by the country's socialist military government in 1974.

Reyes Matta's study indicated that the two American agencies were preeminent as news suppliers in Latin America. UPI was found to have provided 39 percent of the published material; AP 21 percent; AFP 10 percent; Reuters-LATIN (a joint operation between Reuters and a group of Latin American newspapers) 9 percent; EFE (Spain) 8 percent; ANSA (Italy) 4 percent; LATIN (a news agency operated by several larger Latin American papers) 4 percent; the New York Times Service, 2 percent; and the rest by *Le Monde* of Paris, the Post-Times service, Cuba's Prensa Latina, and others.

For Reyes Matta, a positive finding was that dependence on the two U.S. agencies had dropped from 80 percent to 60 in a decade. He noted that much of the difference, however, was provided by other non-Latin American sources.

Another positive finding was that some large papers had access to far more international news sources than ever. *O Estado* was found to have not only AP and UPI but also AFP, ANSA, DPA (Germany), LATIN, and Reuters. *Excelsior* of Mexico City had seven sources.

But despite all this, Reyes Matta said, "We find *old shortcomings of dependence* [emphasis his] still persisting in the rest of the papers." With few exceptions, he said, the papers published dispatches as they were received from the big agencies with no attempt to rewrite or edit them. Reyes Matta expressed special disappointment with the performance of the nationalized *La Prensa* of Lima and of the Chilean newspapers that had supported the late President Salvador Allende.

"The latter," he said, "continued to draw most of their world news material from the transnational agencies, UPI in particular, without any processing or real perspective.

"Both the choice and important news themes and the focus on the fact have followed the market-inspired criteria laid down by the agencies that for decades have dominated information in the region" he said.

"With such criteria," Reyes Matta commented, "the agency and media wire-men do not hesitate to give greater importance to the New York opening of an exhibition of 80 photographs by Caroline Kennedy than to the oil agreement [between oil-producing and Third World countries by which the former agreed to help cushion the latter against rising prices demanded for oil]."

Most journalists would agree that the press of Latin America is far better, and also far better served by the agencies, than is indicated by Reyes Matta and his colleague at ILET, Somavia.

What can be stated without hesitation is that of all the regions of the world, Africa, especially black Africa, is the most undercovered and that agency operations there are the most vulnerable to criticism.

When it comes to coverage of Africa, AFP and Reuters are ahead of the field in terms of full-time staff correspondents. The runners-up are not only AP and UPI but also West Germany's DPA and—as a reminder that Africa is an ideological battleground—the Soviet Union's TASS, the PRC's Hsinhua, Czechoslovakia's CTK [CesKoslovenska Piskova Kancelar], and some of the other communist agencies.

For all their talk of international brotherhood, the agencies of the communist countries rarely employ locals as their correspondents. They prefer their own home-trained nationals for reasons that hardly require elaboration. The Western agencies are more inclined to rely on local journalists either as full-time representatives or as part-time stringers—a practice that incidentally has subjected them to a different kind of criticism. The U.S. agencies have frequently been taken to task in professional and academic journals in the United States for not having more U.S. nationals as correspondents overseas. This reflects the attitude that Americans can best report for Americans—which is precisely the principle that Africans, Asians, and Latin Americans are now invoking for themselves.

The employment of local journalists by the Western agencies might be cited as a positive attribute if it reflected only a desire to get a multinational perspective. In fact, the decision is often taken on grounds that a local employee costs less than someone from the home office.

Several available studies on the scope of agency operations in Africa indicate they are doing more than their critics indicate but that on the whole they have much to be defensive about. What these studies do in common is to identify AFP and Reuters as the dominant services in Africa, both in terms of covering Africa for the rest of the world and of providing world and African news to Africa.

AFP emerged as the agency with the largest number of staff correspondents in Africa in a study conducted in 1973 by Robert L. Bishop of the University of Michigan. This study was sponsored in part by the Center for Research on Economic Development at Ann Arbor and was published in the Winter 1975 issue of *Journalism Quarterly*.

Reuters was second in the Bishop survey with AP and UPI behind in terms of staff representation. Bishop said the heavier representation by AFP and Reuters reflected the fact that the two European agencies had larger clientele in Africa since both of them provided services in both French and English.

"The American agencies do not feel that they can really compete in Africa because few media in Africa can afford them, and no one outside of Africa will pay the bill," Bishop said.

TASS, which gives away its material, has not made much headway because ideology prevents it from operating as a true news agency. Reuters may break even because it runs a very lean operation

and because it was able to sign up a great many clients before independence. AFP survives because of the more than $12,000,000 it re-
ceives for subscriptions from French governmental agencies. It
calculates that it might break even on its African service if its clients
paid their bills—but some are two and three years in arrears.

A somewhat earlier study by Hachten, cited in *Muffled Drums,*
also found AFP to have more staff correspondents (24) in Africa than
Reuters (22). The comparable figure for AP was given as six, UPI five,
and DPA four.

A United States Information Agency [USIA] survey cited by
Hachten indicated that Reuters sold its service in more places in Africa
than any other Western agency. "Reuters was received in 39 African
countries while AFP had clients in 33," Hachten wrote. "AP was received in only 14 and UPI in 19. TASS, which is not sold but is given
away free, was received in 19 countries."

The position of the two U.S. agencies appears to have deteriorated
sharply since 1971 to judge from an April 1977 study cited by Pinch in
his analysis for the U.S. State Department's Senior Seminar in Foreign
Policy. This indicated that AP was now going into eight countries as
against 14 in the earlier study and UPI into five as compared with 19.
Reuters appeared to be holding its own. AFP's current operations were
not reflected in Pinch's study.

This study went beyond Africa, measuring two phases of agency
activity in 85 nonaligned countries (13 in the Arab region, 41 in Africa,
14 in Asia, nine in the Americas, and three in Europe). One objective
was to determine how AP, Reuters, and UPI services were going into
these countries—whether directly to the news media, or by way of a
national news agency or government information service. The other
was to ascertain how widely the agencies were represented for coverage in the 85 countries.

In the three-way comparison (AFP having been excluded) AP was
found to have some type of coverage in 71 countries, Reuters in 69, and
UPI in 46. The Reuters service was found to be entering 68 of the 85
countries compared to 31 for AP and 27 for UPI. Some countries had
more than one service. Of the 126 agency contracts in 85 countries, 70,
or 56 percent, were with official news agencies or government offices.
This pattern was most dominant in Africa where in 30 of 38 cases, the
agency news reports were delivered via official channels. Even where
services were sold direct, the contracting newspaper or broadcaster was
most often subject to government regulation of some kind.

These findings simply illustrate that in most developing countries,
the governments already have available mechanisms that can exercise
internal news control by filtering out of agency offerings anything that

is felt to be inimical to cultural or national traditions or to official policies.

While it is impossible to measure the extent, it is a fact that overt ideological editing of agency news is going on every day. Ghanian newspapers refer to Rhodesian Prime Minister Ian Smith as "the rebel Smith." Radio Ethiopia, according to the *Manchester Guardian* of November 9, 1976, invariably changes "South African Government" to "the Fascist government of South Africa."

Clearly, the Western agencies cannot accommodate themselves to that sort of instruction, but they must provide an answer when the Third World asks why, if it is proper to say "Marxist President Allende" or "Strongman" Idi Amin, it is improper to call Smith a rebel or the South African government fascist? It is a fruitless debate, proving only that simplistic labels can work much mischief.

Bishop, as part of his previously mentioned study, checked the AFP and Reuter files for a two-week period to determine what picture, what impression, one African country might get of another on the basis of this Western reportage. The study was limited to AFP and Reuters dispatches from Kenya and the Ivory Coast. Bearing in mind that AFP and Reuters were the most active of the Western agencies, Bishop concluded that "the wire services are failing in interpreting African nations to other Africans and to the outside world"—the same point, of course, that Third World commentators are making.

Another complaint made by these commentators finds a measure of support from Aaron Segal, former editor of *Africa Report,* in an article published in the 1976 Summer-Fall edition of *Issue,* a magazine specializing in African matters. This complaint is that Western coverage is prone to using simplistic labels like pro-Soviet or pro-American to describe movements or governments that cannot accurately fit into those stereotypes.

Segal says that political events "by and large" do get reported by Western media although, he says, the coverage is "often distorted, negligible or nonexistent (witness the failure to explain to Americans the extraordinary changes during the last five years in Madagascar, including the ousting of a U.S. ambassador)." Segal continues:

> The problems with political coverage are usually a failure to present events within an African context or setting, emphasis on personalities rather than on problems (characterized by treatment of Uganda and Idi Amin) and the search for simple explanations of complex problems, e.g., tribalism, racism, colonialism.

The shrillest Third World rhetoric is fond of charging that Western agencies are sounding boards if not official undercover arms for their governments. This suspicion was unfortunately only reinforced by recent disclosures of the CIA's infiltration of some U.S. news media. No amount of denial can undo the damage that the CIA has done to U.S. journalists overseas.

In this connection, notice must be taken of a study indicating that when the AP and UPI do reflect bias with regard to the United States in their operations abroad, it is more likely to be bias against than bias for. L. John Martin of the University of Maryland analyzed U.S.-related items supplied to the Near East and North Africa from July 7 to 13, 1975, by six sources—the four global agencies plus TASS and the USIA daily wireless file.

It could not have surprised Martin that TASS manifested the most bias against the United States in terms of percentages. But it was the French agency AFP and not either of the two U.S. agencies that carried the largest number of items reflecting pro-United States bias.

Martin concluded that Reuters and UPI showed the least bias, "Reuters (Near East) having no biased items, while Reuters (North Africa) carried one favorably biased item. . . . UPI's one biased item was classified as unfavorable to the United States," Martin said. "On the other hand, the AP wires carried 9 (2% biased items—three favorable and six unfavorable)."

This study also brought a measure of support for still another Third World complaint—that news flow is too heavily weighed with news about the industrialized world. During the one week test period of Martin's study, the AP filed about twice the wordage of UPI, but both devoted an almost identical percentage to news about the United States —42 percent for UPI, 43 percent for AP. AFP devoted 29 percent and Reuters 32 percent of their transmissions to items related to the United States but lesser amounts to North Africa where the figures were 22 percent for AFP and 15 percent for Reuters.

The intensity of the Third World condemnation of the agencies might have suggested that their services were far more heavily weighted with news of the industrialized world than the Martin study indicates. Indeed, UNESCO's own studies credit the world agencies with efforts to do more in and for the Third World, although these occasional credits are lost in the more general criticism.

Sommerlad, the chief of UNESCO's division of communication research and policies, said in his 1975 paper that some of the major world agencies "at least tailor-make special services in an endeavor to respond to client demands in particular regions. The result is a signifi-cant reduction in the dominance of the news from the industrialized world." He cited a UNESCO-commissioned study of the Reuters West

Africa service on 11 selected days in 1973 which showed 42 percent of the news stories originated in advanced countries, 32 percent originated in Africa, 18 percent originated in other Third World countries, and 7 percent originated elsewhere. "This," Sommerlad added, "may not be typical for all regions, and one reason why much attention is now being paid to news pooling and exchange arrangements between national news agencies is to ensure a much greater availability of news of regional interest."

Assessing the validity of Third World complaints against the four Western agencies on any objective basis is, as noted at the beginning of this section, almost an impossible task. Facts are not too plentiful and subjective judgments can not be eliminated. Yet with all of these caveats, it does not seem unreasonable to point to some conclusions.

In defense of the agencies, it can be said that some of the criticism against them is undeserved and some of it is overblown. Charges of deliberate bias against Third World countries or governments are rooted not in fact but in emotion. Charges that the agencies respond only to demands of their home markets are demonstrably untrue. So are charges that Third World news is filed only in time of crisis or disaster; it is only the volume that can be questioned. The fact remains, however, that there is a great disparity between coverage patterns in the developed world as a whole, and the Third World as a whole. These general conclusions can be made:

There is a distinct imbalance in the flow of news both in content and volume from the developed to the developing countries. The disposition of agency correspondents say eloquently where the emphasis is. AP and UPI probably have more staff correspondents in their London offices than they have in all of Africa. And for all of their preemenince in Africa, Reuters and AFP probably have more regular staff in the United States.

There is a vast gap in the quality of regional coverage provided by the Western agencies to the Third World. While Latin America may be relatively well covered, it is not covered as well as Western Europe. But even so, it is vastly better covered than Asia, and immeasurably better than Africa.

Agency coverage in the Third World tends to seek simplistic solutions or Cold War ramifications in situations that are typically Asian, African, or Latin American. Labels like "anti-American" or "pro-Soviet" can and do mislead. This can result as much from professional as from ideological attitudes. Regardless of nationality, news agency people understandably adapt writing styles, choice of "lead" material—

indeed, an entire definition of news—to conform with what they see dominating their respective teleprinters. This results in a homogenization of outlook by which subtle nuances of extreme local importance are leveled out in the interests of a distant and unsophisticated reader.

There is an acknowledged tendency among Western media, including the news agencies, to devote the greatest attention to the Third World in times of disaster, crisis, and confrontation. Correspondents are airlifted in to cope with the emergency and depart when it is over. Coverage then reverts to the status quo ante, which means, in many places, little if any coverage at all.

There is an obvious shortage on agency wires of what can only be called regional developmental news. The completion of a new highway near Bamako does not fit the traditional definition of news by the agencies. It is too parochial, too local, unseemly faro for the foreign correspondent. And yet, that is what is being demanded by many Third World commentators. Clearly the feeling of community in the Third World is more than what is called civic pride in the United States. It goes beyond city limits and beyond national boundaries. To the editor in Nigeria, the highway outside Bamako could be very big news indeed.

DEVELOPMENT: A NEW ROLE FOR THE JOURNALIST

Nothing is more important to the Third World than national development. Even among many Third World journalists who prize free press traditions, it is widely acknowledged that a higher priority must often, and perhaps usually, go to national development—the monumental, uphill struggle to weld often disparate ethnic, tribal, or religious groups into cohesive new nations while bettering their social well-being through economic progress.

Because development is the obvious task of government and because news and communication are considered so vital in promoting it, the Third World journalist is being increasingly regarded as a junior partner in guiding and fostering his nation's growth. The new role can be assigned him as much by himself as by his government. It is known variously as "development" or "developmental" journalism and often finds the journalistic practitioner called a "soldier of development."

The journalist and government in the Third World have somewhat different rationales for this new journalistic role but in the end they wind up with much common ground.

Dilip Mukerjee, an Indian journalist writing in the *Illustrated Weekly of India* on October 10, 1976, said it was time for journalists in developing countries to question the applicability to their countries of the Western journalist's philosophy that news is the unusual, the abnormal, or the aberrant. He wrote:

> Our need is urgent and acute: we belong to societies which are in the process of restructuring and reshaping themselves. In our environment there is, and will be for a long time to come, much that is ugly and distasteful. If we follow the western norm, we will be playing up only these dark spots, and thus helping unwittingly to erode the faith and confidence without which growth and development are impossible.
> And we will be guilty of a misrepresentation of reality as well, because the spots would look less dark without the bright spots to provide a contrast. In other words, we need a new style of journalism which asserts that good news is just as newsworthy as bad ... I am not suggesting that we overlook bad news or whitewash misdeeds. If we did this, we shall quickly destroy our credibility.

The rationale of Third World governments is less tolerant or less understanding of the need to illuminate what Mukerjee calls the "dark spots." The official argument is that many young states are still too fragile, too deficient in literacy and established institutions, and their people more loyal to racial, religious, or tribal communities than to the new concept of statehood, to risk the controversy and confrontation produced by the full exercise of personal freedoms. The Third World journalist is thus advised not to try to emulate the probing, investigatory role of the Western journalist until his own society attains the cohesion and common purpose of the more highly developed countries.

The developmental journalist, then, has a sociopolitical role. The question he must ask himself before he writes is whether it is in keeping with national policy. The Western journalist, in contrast, must ask only if it is of interest or consequence.

The gap between these two concepts is great. But what needs to be understood in the West is that the commitment to development journalism is widespread and that the question is not whether or how to oppose it but how to coexist with it while at the same time doing everything possible to foster freer press traditions over the long term.

Aggarwala says in his chapter in this book that this form of journalism "is not much different from what usually appears in Western newspapers in community or general news sections." In other words, the local story proudly reporting the completion of a new freeway or the opening of a vast new shopping complex. "But an international counterpart of community news is missing from Western media files," Aggarwala says. "The market for this kind of journalism is expanding at a relatively rapid pace in the Third World."

Aggarwala, it should be noted, calls this "development" rather than "developmental journalism," a distinction that can be crucial in the North-South debate. Freedom House defines "developmental journalism" more darkly. The March-April 1977 issue of its journal, *Freedom at Issue,* portrays developmental journalism as part of the UNESCO-influenced thrust toward government policies inimical to free flow of information (also see the chapter by Sussman on developmental journalism in this book).

Governments, of course, are prime movers in prescribing this new role for journalists and the media, but it is difficult to dismiss the official rationale as utterly devoid of validity. A case in point was the speech by Prime Minister Lee Kuan Yew of Singapore to the IPI in Helsinki in 1971. IPI had attacked Lee for suppressing a Singapore newspaper for publishing material he felt to be against the national interest. He agreed to appear before IPI to say why.

Lee outlined the great ethnic and religious differences and tensions within his country, described the relatively low level of education and the bombardment of the people with new ideas and appeals from East and West. "In such a situation," he said, "freedom of the press, freedom of the news media, must be subordinated to the overriding needs of the integrity of Singapore, and to the primary purpose of an elected government."

He said the mass media must "reinforce, not undermine" the cultural values and the social attitudes being taught in schools and universities in Singapore. "If they are to develop," Lee said, "people in new countries cannot afford to imitate the fads and fetishes of the contemporary west. The strange behavior of demonstration and violence-prone young men and women in wealthy America, seen on TV and the newspapers, are not relevant to the social and economic circumstances of new, underdeveloped countries."

The African attitude toward the role of the developmental journalist was well stated by Malam Turi Muhammadu, editor of the *New Nigerian* in an article in the IPI *Report* for July 1975. He was summing up a meeting of African journalists in Zaire where ministers of various governments lectured them on their roles:

> Most of the ministers were concerned lest the journalists equate their role with that of their counterparts in developed countries. Their argument is that Africa, being underdeveloped, needs to concentrate

all available resources in development. Investigative journalism, aimed at picking flaws in the policies and actions of African governments, is therefore not advisable at present since it is unhelpful.

Information, the argument continues, should be in the service of African interest. Thus, the notions of press freedom and access to information as practiced in Europe and America are not relevant. African journalists should be imbued with the urgency of serving the people of Africa as a whole and should not become slaves of non-African interests. They should accept the need to conform to the political exigencies of Africa, which include the fight against the colonialist and racist regimes and the promotion of African unity and personality.

In relationships with governments, the ministers admonished the journalists not to adopt the posture of critical observers. Rather, that African journalists should draw inspiration from African civilization. Journalists, being the second power in any country, have an obligation to become soldiers of development.

It is difficult for many in the West to grasp the enormous complexity of nation building and for them, nothing perhaps can be more instructive than a narrative by Ezena Ogbonna, a Nigerian journalist, in the IPI *Report* (April-May 1975). It deals with the task of trying to get the townspeople of Abakaliki in the East Central State of Nigeria to accept the idea that there is now a remote central government in their lives and that they are subject to it. Ogbonna writes:

The people refuse to pay tax, and any attempt to persuade them or apply a bit of coercion results in confusion. Such attempts have always been violently repulsed by this community [which] does not see itself as part of the changing Nigerian society. The rigidity with which it clings to traditional methods has not made things easier.

Development methods, no matter how incomplete, are frustrated because they touch on the people's way of life and nobody wants a change from the old beliefs. If community newspapers were encouraged, it would be a first step in involving everybody in the business of government. It would encourage learning and peaceful coexistence between neighborhoods.

Clearly, if community newspapers are to be established in places like Abakaliki, it will have to be done by government. There is no advertising base in Abakaliki to enable a newspaper to exist without official funds—and therefore official control. Abakaliki is thus symptomatic of a genuine problem that exists in the Third World.

PRESS AND GOVERNMENT: A FORMULA FOR COEXISTENCE

The Third World concept of developmental journalism clashes with the arm's-length relationship between press and government that is cherished in the West and brings expressions of concern about the direction that some Third World countries are taking.

Dislike it as they will, however, media of the West and particularly of the United States must accept two truths if there is to be any successful joint approach toward adjusting international news-flow patterns. The first is that developmental journalism is a fact of life in the Third World. The second is that Western outcries against government involvement in news must be more selectively made because the search for remedies in many places must inevitably involve governments.

It is not difficult to proclaim that developmental journalism is essentially the same system that prevails in the Soviet Union, the PRC, or other communist states. The point can be made, although it does little but confuse the debate. Parallels though there may be, it does not necessarily follow that the trends in the Third World are engineered by Moscow or are even Marxist in origin.* There are, after all, other authoritarian ideologies. Restrictive press practices can also be found in the Third World countries that can hardly be called communist or Marxist: Chile, South Korea, and the Philippines are cases in point.

A free press reflects more than a philosophical preference. It is in the last analysis based on societal conditions that are exceedingly hard to find in the Third World. One is a combination of high literacy and sufficient political consciousness to make news and information an essential ingredient of life. The second is the presence of the economic requisities for private and independent operation of newspapers, magazines, or broadcasting—in short, risk capital and advertising.

These conditions do exist to some degree in bigger cities of the Third World—Singapore, Manila, New Delhi, Nairobi, Colombo, and Lagos, to name a few. Independent newspapers can survive there when

---

*It may be time for some Western commentators to reexamine the practice of referring to the Soviet Union as representative of the Marxist theory or system of the press. Leninist would be more to the point in keeping with Lenin's famous quotation of 1924: "Why should a government which is doing what it believes to be right allow itself to be criticized? It would not allow opposition by lethal weapons. Ideas are much more fatal than guns." Marx would surely find it difficult to reconcile the Soviet press system with his attack on the Prussian censorship in 1842 when he was editor of the *Rheinische Zeitung.* With censorship, Marx said, "the government hears only its own voice. It knows that it hears only its own voice. And yet it fixes itself in the delusion that it hears the voice of the people, and demands from the people that it likewise fix itself in this delusion."

permitted. But they are not always permitted. Even when they are, they can still reach only a fraction of the Third World's millions. In India, with a population around 600 million, newspaper circulations rarely surpass 200,000 and daily circulation nationwide is only about one copy per 100 inhabitants. The comparable figure in the United States is 32.6 per 100 according to UNESCO estimates in 1964.

In Africa, Ghana, with a population of some 7 million, averaged 3.2 copies per 100. Ghana's achievement might seem a holy grail to Chad; it achieved 0.03 per 100 inhabitants on the basis of a single daily news bulletin with a circulation of 700.

In all of Africa, exclusive of the Republic of South Africa, there are fewer than 150 daily newspapers. In black Africa, where there are about 70 dailies, all but a few are controlled either by government or by the ruling political party. Even where private ownership exists, as in Kenya (three privately owned papers) or Tanzania (one), for example, the newspapers carefully adjust themselves to government policies.

While they face no overt censorship, Kenyan journalists, according to David Lamb of the *Los Angeles Times* (November 27, 1977) "understand how far they can go. . . . They know what ministers can be attacked without governmental repercussions." Lamb writes, "They know they cannot question foreign policy or suggest that the government is not working or criticise the president and his family."

Given all of these conditions—illiteracy, authoritarian governments, the lack of private capital, the lack of advertising or other unofficial sources of revenue—it is indulging in fantasy to think that Western-type press institutions can take root, let alone flourish. The sole alternative in most of the Third World, if all media forms are considered, is government financing and therefore, government control. To inveigh against government intervention without weighing these factors is tantamount to telling these nations that they must forego development of national media and make do with what they have.

In fairness to UNESCO, it must be acknowledged that it is this very realization that has for years led it to foster government media development. UNESCO must not be faulted if it accepts the inevitability of some governmental role in media development. Where it is vulnerable to criticism is in the tendency of its staff or its experts to hold up state regulation of content as a social imperative, even in areas such as Latin America, for example, where independent press systems are well established.

In the absence of other options, a government-supported or controlled press is surely better than no press at all. With a press system controlled by government, there is at least the long-term possibility that it will transform itself into a more independent system. Precisely that sort of a metamorphosis led to the free press institutions in the West. It is not too fanciful to suggest that it could be helped to happen elsewhere.

It is not likely to happen in rigidly regimented societies like that of the Soviet Union where control is part of the organic plan. In most of the Third World, news and newspapers have not yet been formally and irrevocably declared to be state monopolies on the Soviet model. Nigeria and the Philippines, for example, have constitutional free press guarantees that are equal to the First Amendment. They have been suspended for the time being by what are described as emergency conditions. It would require powers of divination to say how long those emergencies will last. But because so many Third World countries are still developing, it remains possible that, given the proper sort of encouragement and assistance from the outside, they will come down in the long term on the libertarian side.

That hope, that possibility, is surely motive enough for Western media to make some constructive response to the critical voices in the Third World. And the Western media, fashioning their reply, must bear in mind that the alternative to cooperation with government-run press systems in many places is alienation and confrontation. That point, unfortunately, is not widely enough acknowledged; editorial voices in the United States in particular pronounce anathema on governmental involvement in news without qualification. Witness one of the resolutions adopted by the IAPA meeting at Williamsburg before the Nairobi conference in 1976. It proclaimed IAPA's "opposition *to any attempt on the part of the state to control ownership of news organs,* any endeavor to interfere with free access to news sources, and to any restriction to the free spread of ideas" (emphasis added).

Or consider the statement issued by the National News Council in New York, September 21, 1976, in calling for the defeat of the Soviet Declaration on news policies at Nairobi: "The National News Council would be unfaithful to its mission if it did not condemn governmental control of news wherever it exists and regardless of the arguments advanced for it."

IAPA and the National News Council would indeed be betraying their trusts if they did not fight for free access or against control wherever a free press does or can exist. But if their intent is to oppose any sort of government involvement with news media anywhere in the world, regardless of local circumstances, they are sentencing many Third World countries to indefinite periods of informational poverty for the simple reason that these countries have no alternative. An acknowledgement of that fact must be the starting point for working out any effective response to the Third World.

Indeed, even some highly developed Western countries are beginning to find that state aid is vital to the preservation of their national press. Hard-pressed dailies in Sweden, Norway, Iceland, and Finland—hardly an authoritarian state in the lot—are even now getting official subvention of various kinds, and subsidies are being debated in Switzerland (IPI Report, April-August 1976). Assistance in Scandinavia is usually extended through exemptions from sales taxes or as direct subsidies tied to the smallest circulations. "In Norway and Sweden, it is now generally accepted, by both press and political authorities, that the life of many newspapers depends on their receiving government aid," according to Einar Ostgaard, a Swedish press consultant in an article for the IPI *Report* (April 1976).

Nor is even the U.S. press, perhaps the most suspicious of government, unwilling to accept government help in the form of lower postal rates, special press tariffs for telecommunications, and exemptions from the antitrust laws to permit certain types of joint operations denied other private enterprises.

This type of official assistance can be defended with the argument that it recognizes the importance of a multiplicity of voices in a democratic society. U.S. publishers have argued eloquently that without preferential postal rates and without special antitrust status, some magazines and newspapers would inevitably die, as some in fact have. In much of the Third World, the question is not so much how to prevent the death of the mass media, but how to give birth to them. The general principle behind preferential press rates or favored antitrust status is not unlike the one involved in the Third World—that in the absence of other remedies, the answer lies with government.

The search for remedies is now under way in symposia, conferences, and seminars in various parts of the world. UNESCO experts are also at work on the basis of the Tunisian resolution approved at Nairobi, although it is questionable whether UNESCO can ever come up with a formula acceptable to all of the conflicting ideologies represented by its membership. There is little common ground between Lenin and Jefferson on free expression.

The first significant Western response to the problem has come from the World Press Freedom Committee, an organization that has some 30 affiliates in the West. This committee was founded as a joint project of IAPA and IPI, largely through the efforts of Beebe, the associate publisher of the *Miami Herald,* who for many years has been a driving force on IAPA's Freedom of the Press Committee.

During the first years of its existence, the World Press Freedom Committee functioned principally as a monitor of global threats to free press practices. In 1977, however, the nature of its work altered dramatically to embrace an ambitious fund-raising project to assist press development in the Third World. The change in emphasis was responsive to events at the UNESCO conferences in San Jose and Nairobi in 1976. But it was also given some impetus by proceedings at a UNESCO colloquium in Florence in April 1977 that was intended to smooth over some of the tensions generated by the angry debate in Nairobi over the Soviet resolution on the uses of the mass media. Beebe, who had been at Nairobi, was also present in Florence as head of the World Press Freedom Committee.

Prior to his departure for Florence, Beebe had been instrumental in forming a special development committee of U.S. publishers and broadcasters for the purpose of raising an initial $1 million for Third World assistance. The launching of this special project was to be announced at the annual conference of the ANPA in San Francisco later in April.

Beebe found the atmosphere at the Florence UNESCO meeting so hostile to Western media traditions that he dispatched a cablegram to the ANPA meeting in San Francisco to add urgency to the fund drive. The announcement of the drive, together with Beebe's cable, was read to the San Francisco meeting on April 25 by *Chicago Tribune* editor and vice-president Kirkpatrick, who also was instrumental in launching the development project.

Beebe's cablegram said, in part, that the talks in Florence had

> convinced delegates from the West that we are fast losing the global war in the field of communications. What was billed as a conference on the "free and balanced flow of information" was largely a series of attacks on U.S. news agencies and the western media. This was led by the communists and leftists who exert great influence on UNESCO.

Beebe's cable reported that Eastern European delegates at Florence were making much of the training programs being offered to Third World journalists by Hungary, East Germany, Romania, and Bulgaria. He said that when he mentioned the World Press Freedom Committee's new program in Florence, "it threw the Soviet bloc members into a flurry of concerned activity" and that it was "obvious the Soviets are bothered that an organization of the private sector might start offsetting their brainwashing programs. . . . This is a major crisis," Beebe's cablegram to the San Francisco meeting concluded. "Please take it seriously."

By late 1977, the World Press Freedom Committee had elicited the support of 28 organizations or publications in North and South America, Europe, Australia, Hong Kong, and Japan. Its special fund-raising program, headed by Jack R. Howard of the Scripps-Howard newspapers, had reached $300,000 by the end of the year, by far most of it from U.S. media.

The committee describes itself as "dedicated to: A media free of government interference. A full and free flow of international news. A responsible and objective media. Providing technical assistance to those media needing it." Its initial grants included such things as $20,-000 to the University of Nairobi School of Journalism for equipment for a weekly laboratory newspaper and scholarships; $10,000 for organizing and conducting a training school for print and broadcast reporters in Trinidad; and $10,000 to the IPI to help underwrite an African seminar in Nairobi on economic and financial reporting.

The importance of this program is that it is tangible evidence of the desire of major Western media, notably in the United States, to help. But it is obvious from the committee's stated goal, and its emphasis on private, nongovernmental initiative and funding, that it can at best deal with only select parts of the problem. The recipients of the initial grants are mostly countries with relatively well-developed press systems; even so, repeated grants of $10,000 or $20,000 or $30,000 are likely to be required. And still larger amounts on a continuing basis will be needed to help the less developed countries even to approach the relatively more developed. The question must be asked whether private media—and more specifically and realistically speaking, private U.S. media—can alone provide the millions that will probably be required over a protracted period.

In any case, nothing that has yet been done from any quarter touches the central part of the problem—the loud dissatisfaction with the global news provided by the four big Western-based agencies. Although the four are a common target and might be thought natural allies in seeking a response, the intense competition between them rules out any concerned, consortium-type approach.

"It's awfully dangerous in a situation like this to organize the battalions on both sides," Gerald Long, general manager of Reuters, told an interviewer from the *IPI Report* in 1967. "You then confirm that there is some sort of a fight. I don't see any fight. I see various developments more or less welcome to various people. But I do not want to organize the thing into a battle."

All four of the Western agencies have proclaimed their readiness to work on a bilateral basis with any national agency to provide training and assistance. But all are quick to add that they themselve lack the resources to finance such projects. These economic limitations deepen the dilemma. All four are concerned lest the trend toward national and regional agencies eventually militates against them and restricts their range of access and coverage. And yet they are unable to do much about the conditions that are contributing to this concern.

Clearly, the initiative will have to come from elsewhere, and so will the financing. In view of all the complexities and all the obvious limitations, it is difficult to escape the conclusion that official monies from a variety of governments may have to be a part of the answer. It is equally clear that any successful program must be truly multinational and its direction based on equal partnership of diverse interests.

What is needed at the outset is a multinational umbrella organization to start a program aimed at overcoming the admitted deficiencies in Third World news coverage. The components of such an organization can be found in the membership of the Nonaligned Pool on one hand and among the media represented by the World Free Press Development Committee on the other. What follows is one conceivable way that a beginning might be made.

Interested press groups in the West might join with interested Third World agencies to form an entity that could, for illustration's sake, be called the Multinational Pool. The pool would have a 12-seat directorate. Six seats would be assigned to members of the Nonaligned Pool. The other six would be filled by elements of the World Press Freedom Committee. The directorate would thus be made up of 12 separate nationalities.

One possible lineup would be Egypt, India, Mexico, Kenya, Nigeria, and the Philippines on the one hand, and the United States, Britain, France, West Germany, Sweden, and Japan on the other. Agency membership in the directorate itself would be limited to the nonaligned bloc. AP and UPI would, for example, be represented by their supporting media.

Once organized with one of its members as chairman, the Multinational Pool would begin assembling a staff by asking the principal agencies represented by each grouping to make available to it the services of one experienced correspondent for a fixed period. Salaries for the period of service would be borne by the regular employers as their contribution to the Multinational Pool. For practical purposes, the number might be limited at the outset to 10 reporters from each grouping, with the understanding that the big four Western agencies always participate. The West German DPA and Japan's Kyodo could round out this grouping with them.

The provision of a single correspondent (perhaps with his expenses paid for the first year or so) would place no onerous burden on any one organization.

In addition to agency reporters, the Multinational Pool could also invite major newspapers represented in the two groupings to loan experienced correspondents to its special international reporting corps, again with their salary and expenses underwritten by the regular employer. The number of participating reporters from any one country would need to be limited to prevent any domination.

Correspondents assigned to the Multinational Pool would be assigned by it to geographical areas of concentration. They would visit countries within those areas on a systematic basis, working closely with local journalists in the process, and report on economic, cultural, and industrial development projects underway. Their dispatches generally could be airmailed to a central office whence they would be made available simultaneously to all world media over the distribution facilities of all of the participating agencies, including, of course, the Nonaligned Pool. The practical effect of this process, because of the multinational nature of the proposed pool, would be, for example, a dispatch by an Indian journalist on a Nigerian event for the U.S. press or one by a French journalist on an Indian event for the Japanese press. Because of the intricate, crisscross exchange agreements among world agencies, the reportage of the Multinational Pool would automatically be available to nonparticipants such as TASS or Hsinhua over the wires of any of the participating agencies, and they should be free to use it if they desired.

The major agencies might be asked to provide the use of their leased communications facilities to the Multinational Pool correspondents on the limited occasions when a correspondent in the field felt a dispatch could not await airmail service to the central office.

While the four Western agencies would all have equal and simultaneous access to the output of the Multinational Pool, their own competitive operations in any area would in no way be affected.

The Multinational Pool would be financed by funds raised by the directorate through national committees working in their own characteristic and preferred manner. Funds raised by the Nonaligned Pool members would obviously be from government treasuries. In this form of cooperation, there could hardly be any serious objection to accepting funds from other interested governments represented in the directorate. Private contributions from any quarter would be welcome.

The pool would be directed by an editor selected by the directorate. There would be three deputy editors from other geographical regions to assist in directing the corps of correspondents and carrying out other functions of the central office. It could, among other things, act as an international clearinghouse for exchange programs and scholarships for training of journalists or in providing technical assistance. The training of journalists would embrace the training of journalists from the United States, for example, in African problems as well as Africans in U.S. problems and procedures.

The mechanics for such an umbrella organization would not be difficult to work out if this approach were felt to have merit and, more importantly, if the concept of mixed multigovernmental funding were acceptable to U.S. media.

The advantages of a centralized, multinational approach are both practical and psychological. Its cooperative nature would be in keeping with the essential principle of partnership. Priorities would be set jointly, not predetermined by a foreign interest. In the area of finance, the pooling of monies from all sources in a multinational treasury could relieve the misgivings of U.S. government. Grants from private and/or governmental sources would be so intermingled that no participating newspaper or agency could be said to be in the pay of any particular government.

The editor of the Multinational Pool service would clearly have to be a figure of stature, a journalistic equivalent of the United Nations secretary general. Happily such journalists exist. An enterprise along these lines could hardly be launched more propitiously than under the direction of such journalists as Mohamed Abdel Gawad of Egypt, director of the Middle East News Agency (MENA) or George Verghese of India, to name only two.

The mission of the Multinational Pool would be to provide, on a cooperative basis and under the direction of professional journalists, the type of news reportage now felt to be missing in and from the Third World. It would avoid day-to-day "hard" news, especially that concerning national or international politics, areas that are more properly left to existing news sources. Instead, the Multinational Pool would place its emphasis on the projects and programs in the Third World for national economic, cultural, and social development. Most important, it would do this by fostering cross-cultural transfers of news and information.

2. INTERNATIONAL LAW ASPECTS OF THE FREEDOM OF INFORMATION AND THE RIGHT TO COMMUNICATE

LEO GROSS

THE SOVEREIGNTY OF STATES AND THE TWO BASES OF INTERNATIONAL LAW

Increasingly, with the onset of the industrial revolution and the rapid increase in the movement of persons and goods across national boundaries, international law has become the medium through which states attempt to facilitate transnational activities. It could not be otherwise since states have exclusive authority only within their territory. If transactions going beyond the territory of a state are to be regulated at all, the cooperation of two or more states is required. This is also true with respect to activities within the territory of a state that are intended to produce or that in fact do produce an effect in the territory of another state. Thus, international law develops with and depends on the consent of two or more states and takes the form of a bilateral or multilateral treaty that usually requires ratification. This is called conventional international law.

There is, however, also customary international law that emerges from the practice of states and their acceptance of such practice as binding. The origin and evolution of customary international law has never been explained satisfactorily. While it may be a matter of controversy whether a certain principle or rule is or is not part of customary international law, there is no doubt that a body of customary international law exists. Thus in case of a dispute submitted to the International Court of Justice, the court, "whose function is to decide in accordance with international law such disputes as are submitted to it," is directed to apply international conventions and "international custom, as evidence of a general practice accepted as law."[1]

It is important to bear in mind that since international law depends upon the consent or practice of two or more states, the agreement of the states concerned is necessary in order to determine the meaning of a written or unwritten (customary) principle or rule and its applicability in a given situation. By common agreement this function may be conferred by the states at variance on a tribunal of arbitration or the International Court of Justice, which renders a binding decision. Just as the rules require common consent for their creation, so they require common consent for their interpretation and application. Of course, states do hold views, sometimes very firm views, about their own rights and obligations and those of other states, but such views must be taken for what they are: views of interested parties. As such, they have no binding force for other states, they are autointerpretations. Before a tribunal or the court they become allegations as to the facts and the law and are treated as such. It should be noted, however, that resort to a tribunal or the court is the exception and that states prefer to seek settlement of disputed facts or principles by diplomatic negotiations or to postpone solutions or, in some cases, to resort to unilateral action, which may aggravate or stalemate the dispute.

One of the characteristics of states in modern international law is their independence or sovereignty. This term has been much debated and frequently misunderstood. But as defined by a distinguished jurist, sovereignty means "that the State has over it no other authority than that of international law."[2] States, though sovereign, are not above the law but are bound by it. This may seem like a truism but in the rhetoric of states one frequently encounters the mistaken notion that the limitations that international law inevitably imposes upon states are somehow contrary to or incompatible with their sovereignty. But compliance with the law is inseparable from the very notion of international law. Thus the Charter of the United Nations, which declares in paragraph 1 of Article 2 that "the Organization is based on the principle of the sovereign equality of all its Members," also declares in paragraph 2 of the same article, "All Members, in order to ensure to all of them the rights and benefits resulting from membership, shall fulfill in good faith the obligations assumed by them in accordance with the present Charter."

The duty to fulfill obligations in good faith applies, of course, not merely to the charter but to all conventional and customary international law. The 1969 Vienna Convention on the Law of Treaties incorporates in Article 26 the customary rule of international law of *pacta sunt servanda:* "Every treaty in force is binding upon the parties to it and must be performed by them in good faith."

In the same vein, Section X of the Declaration on Principles Guiding Relations between Participating States in the Final Act of the 1975

Helsinki Conference on Security and Cooperation in Europe, provides that

> the participating States will fulfill in good faith their obligations under international law, both those obligations arising from the generally recognized principles and rules of international law and those obligations arising from treaties or other agreements, in conformity with international law, to which they are parties. In exercising their sovereign rights, including the right to determine their laws and regulations, they will conform with their legal obligations under international law; they will furthermore pay due regard to and implement the provisions in the Final Act of the Conference on Security and Co-operation in Europe.[3]

It may be both useful and necessary to refer to two additional basic principles that may have a bearing on the freedom of information and the right to communicate. It is generally accepted that states may not invoke provisions of their internal law as justification for their failure to perform their obligations under treaties or under customary international law. This principle hardly needs elaboration or justification. Were it otherwise, it would always be open to states to escape their obligations under international law by the simple act of changing their constitution or amending their legislation. This would spell the end of international law and usher in an era of anarchy. It is, therefore, of vital importance for all states that prefer international order to international anarchy to act in accordance with the "generally accepted principle of international law that in the relations between Powers who are contracting Parties to a treaty, the provisions of municipal law cannot prevail over those of the treaty."[4]

The other principle of equal importance is known as domestic jurisdiction: states are free to exercise their sovereignty within their territory. The principle of domestic jurisdiction is reinforced by the principle of nonintervention, which found expression in too many instruments to be examined here, including the Final Act of the Helsinki conference.[5]

It is a frequent error, in the rhetoric of governments and jurists, to refer to domestic jurisdiction as "inherent" or "indivisible" or "inalienable." There is nothing inherent or indivisible about it. On the contrary, it is a relative principle. As the development of conventional law demonstrates, the area of domestic jurisdiction has been dramatically reduced. Suffice it to recall matters of security and finance, economics and communications, health and sanitation, and finally of human rights that have become matters of international concern and regulation by treaty and even, as some argue with respect to human rights, by customary international law. The Permanent Court of International Justice (the predecessor of the International Court of Justice) stated the principle saying, "The question whether a matter is or is not solely within the jurisdiction of a State is an essentially relative question; it depends upon the development of international relations."[6]

What is or is not within the domestic, that is, discretionary, jurisdiction depends not merely upon the state of development of international relations but upon the states concerned. Thus, two or more states may enter into an agreement concerning freedom of the press, the gathering and transmission of news through specified media, or concerning the admission or exchange of radio or television broadcasts. Between parties to such an agreement, these matters are no longer within their respective domestic jurisdiction. But the same matters remain within the domestic jurisdiction of states that have assumed no commitments in relation to other states. In short, it is not the nature of the subject matter that is decisive for answering the question whether it is or is not within domestic jurisdiction but rather the existence or absence of treaty commitments or of a principle or rule of customary law.

It may not be amiss to emphasize, since there is some confusion on this point, that absent an obligation derived from customary or conventional international law, the state is "sole judge" even though the subject matter is of concern to other states or of international concern. It is always open to states to enter into agreements that serve their mutual interests. If there is no principle or rule by which a state binds itself in relation to another state, it may admit or exclude reporters or radio or television broadcasts as it may exclude any aliens or books or newspapers or raw materials or manufactured goods.

It may be noted that there were periods in the development of international relations where freedom of persons and goods prevailed in a substantial part of the world. In such time periods, it was not only a fact of international life but one that was regarded as mutually beneficial. But increasingly, laissez-faire gave way to assertions of control and regulations, to what may be called *"dirigisme."* This has certainly been so since the end of World War I and has become dominant since World War II in spite of the unprecedented interdependence between the states and peoples of the world. The freedoms that were once taken for granted have become part and parcel of a continuing bargaining process between pairs of states, between groups of states, and between all states in the international system.

In this process, international organizations play a vital part. They offer a convenient forum for large-scale conferences. This is particularly true of the United Nations and, in matters of culture and education, the United Nations Educational, Scientific and Cultural Organization (UNESCO). When deliberations in the United Nations or in UNESCO yield a convention or a treaty, such a convention or treaty will become binding on the states that sign and ratify or accept them in the usual way. But on occasion, as a first step to a treaty, such as the 1967 Outer Space Treaty, the organization concerned merely adopts a resolution or declaration by the requisite majority or unanimously. The question then arises whether such resolutions or declarations are binding on members generally or on those who voted for them. There is also the question whether resolutions, such as the 1948 Universal Declaration of Human Rights, are or have become part of customary international law and therefore binding on all states. This question is of fundamental importance as Article 19 of the Universal Declaration of Human Rights proclaims the freedom of information and, perhaps, even the right to communicate, and is regarded as the legal basis for the "free flow" of information through all media and across national boundaries.

TOWARD AN INTERNATIONAL BILL OF RIGHTS

In the current debate about freedom of information, Article 19 of the 1948 Universal Declaration of Human Rights occupies a central place. It states: "Everyone has the right to freedom of opinion and expression; this right includes freedom to hold opinions without interference and to seek, receive and impart information and ideas through any media and regardless of frontiers." Read in its ordinary meaning, this clause establishes one world for the purpose of receiving and imparting information as an individual right. It is clear, from the text, that there was no intent here to promote a one-way flow of information. On the contrary, flow in all directions and regardless of frontiers was the aim. That the flow of information has become in some parts of the world and in relation between a number of states one-sided, is not due to Article 19 but to other factors that are well known. Article 19 was not designed to generate information but merely to ensure its unobstructed flow in accordance with the law of the sending and receiving states. This condition laid down in Article 29 of the declaration is frequently overlooked but it is as much a part of the declaration as is Article 19. This is not surprising, considering that the text of the preamble proclaims the declaration as "a common standard of achievement" and that the rights and freedoms enumerated in the declaration should be secured "by their universal and effective recognition and observance" among the peoples of the member states. Thus, the states are to provide for these freedoms, including Article 19, and the individuals enjoy them in virtue of and within the limits of national constitutions, laws, and legal traditions.*

But did the declaration impose a legal obligation on the states to adopt its rights and freedoms into their legal systems? If it did not, or if the states failed to enact implementing legislation, can individuals claim these rights directly from the declaration? The latter question can be answered in the negative, although there were some cases in which it was invoked in a domestic court. But in principle such resolutions or declarations are not self-executing.

The former question has been much debated in the literature and the declaration has often been described as binding in the discussions in the United Nations and elsewhere. Much has been made of the fact that the 1948 declaration was re-cited in countless subsequent resolutions of the General Assembly. It has also been pointed out that it was adopted in the constitutions and the legislation of many states. Obviously this argument can equally well be turned around: the adoptions would indicate that the states concerned considered them necessary in order to make the declaration applicable within their territories. It has also been argued that the declaration implements the general provisions of the UN Charter that are binding on members. This argument begs the question: do the provisions of the Charter relating to human rights impose obligations or are they, particularly Article 55, merely statements of objectives and purposes for achievement of which the

---

*In a recent Soviet textbook the following view on Article 19 is to be found:

For over a quarter of a century legal scholars have now been arguing as to whether there is a universally recognized principle of the freedom of information in international law. The main argument of those who claim that there is such a principle is the fact that some declarations and conventions on protecting human rights contain provisions concerning the right of everyone freely "to seek, receive and import information and ideas through any media and regardless of frontiers."

These provisions, however, have a different meaning than that attributed to them by some legal experts and diplomats. To begin with, human rights are not in the full sense of the word international. The rights of citizens are regulated by the legislation of every state on a sovereign basis and independently of any external authority. Acts of international law relating to human rights merely imply the acceptance by states of certain general principles, which are to be reflected in their national legislation. The degree to which these general principles are taken into account and the form this takes can vary according to national, historical and other features. Article 28 of the Universal Declaration of Human Rights states that "everyone is entitled to a social and international order in which the rights and freedoms set forth in this Declaration can be fully realised." Obviously only each state itself can ensure a proper social order on its territory, and this applies to the mass media too [A. S. Piradov, ed., *International Space Law* (Moscow: Progress, 1976), p. 190].

members, in Article 56, "pledge themselves to take joint and separate action in cooperation with the Organization."? The text supports an affirmative response to the latter interpretation.

Moreover, the Charter does not confer a legislative function or competence on the General Assembly. Apart from resolutions relating to the internal functions of the organization, such as admission of states to membership, adoption of the budget, and some similar matters, resolutions, even when they are called declarations in order to underscore their significance, are recommendations which do not bind the members legally.

Responding to an assertion by the former director of the Human Rights Division in the UN Secretariat, John P. Humphrey, that the Universal Declaration of Human Rights has "now become (insofar as the norms enunciated in it are justiciable) part of the customary law of nations and is therefore binding on all States,"[7] Eric Suy, the Legal Counsel and Under-Secretary of the UN, expressed what in the present submission appears as the better view: that "while it is clear that a General Assembly declaration does not have the force of law by the mere fact of adoption, it is possible that in the course of time such a declaration, if it reflects the legal conviction of states, may acquire the force of customary international law through state practice."[8] It is what states do in the internal forum that counts and not what they say in the international forum.

The 1948 declaration was intended as the first stage in the process of formulating an obligatory international bill of rights. This process was completed in 1966 by the adoption of two instruments: the International Covenant on Economic, Social, and Cultural Rights and the International Covenant on Civil and Political Rights to which is attached an optional protocol. These covenants and the protocol entered into force on January 3, 1976, and on March 23, 1976, respectively. As of April 1977, 42 states had become bound by the economic rights covenant and 40 states by the civil and political rights covenant and protocol.

The protocol contains provisions for examining "communications from individuals claiming to be victims of violations of any of the rights set forth in the Covenant." Such communications and comments from the governments alleged to have committed violations will be considered by the Human Rights Committee established pursuant to Article 28 of the civil and political rights covenant. The committee is to report on its activities to the General Assembly through the ECOSOC. The oversight provisions under this protocol do not go very far and their effectiveness remains to be tested. This covenant also opens the way to state-to-state complaints for those parties to it that have made a declaration under Article 41. Such complaints are to be considered by the Human Rights Committee, which will endeavor to resolve the matter. In case no solution is reached, the committee may, pursuant to Article 42 and with the prior consent of the states parties to the dispute establish a conciliation commission. The commission will seek a solution, but if no solution is reached, the commission will make a report. This will include the findings on all questions of fact and the commission's views "on the possibilities of an amicable solution of the matter" (Article 42(7(c)). It is then open to the parties to accept the contents of the report. The effectiveness of this procedure is yet to be tested.

The International Covenant on Economic, Social and Cultural Rights is generally considered the "softer" of the two covenants for two reasons. First, it lacks any enforcement procedure whatsoever and, second, it formulates rights that are to be secured by the action of the states that are parties to the covenant. In the current discussion on freedom of information, however, Article 15 should not be overlooked.*

The contents of Article 19 of the Universal Declaration of Human Rights, in a somewhat modified form, appear in Article 19 of the civil and political rights covenant, and this article includes some of the content of Article 29 of the declaration. Article 20 of the covenant is also relevant as it appears to qualify the right to freedom of information laid down in Article 19. The text of these two articles of the covenant is as follows:

Article 19
1. Everyone shall have the right to hold opinions without interference.
2. Everyone shall have the right to freedom of expression; this right shall include freedom to seek, receive and impart information and ideas of all kinds, regardless of frontiers, either orally,

---

Article 15
1. The States Parties to the present Covenant recognize the right of everyone:
   (a) To take part in cultural life;
   (b) To enjoy the benefits of scientific progress and its applications;
   (c) To benefit from the protection of the moral and material interests resulting from any scientific, literary or artistic production of which he is the author.
2. The steps to be taken by the States Parties to the present Covenant to achieve the full realization of this right shall include those necessary for the conservation, the development and the diffusion of science and culture.
3. The States Parties to the present Covenant undertake to respect the freedom indispensable for scientific research and creative activity.
4. The States Parties to the present Covenant recognize the benefits to be derived from the encouragement and development of international contacts and co-operation in the scientific and cultural fields.

in writing or in print, in the form of art, or through any media of his choice.

3. The exercise of the rights provided for in paragraph 2 of this Article carries with it special duties and responsibilities. It may therefore be subject to certain restrictions, but these shall only be such as are provided by law and are necessary:

    (a) For respect of the rights or reputations of others;

    (b) For the protection of national security or of public order (ordre public), or of public health or morals.

Article 20

1. Any propaganda for war shall be prohibited by law.

2. Any advocacy of national, racial or religious hatred that constitutes incitement to discrimination, hostility or violence shall be prohibited by law.

Two observations are in order: First, the right to freedom of information has now become part of a legally binding treaty for states that have or will become parties to the covenant. Second, like Article 19 of the universal declaration, it offers a legal basis for a two-way flow of information. On the other hand, it is to be noted that, first, it establishes the right for individuals and it is not clear how far, if at all, it confers rights upon the *media themselves.* Second, the net of possible legal restrictions—Article 19, paragraph 3(b) and Article 20—is cast very wide. The fact that a state such as the Soviet Union, which has not been regarded in the West as a champion of the right to freedom of information, has become a party to the covenant may indicate the Soviet Union's belief that it can live comfortably with Article 19. On the other hand, this fact may also be seen as a token of willingness of the past Soviet leaders to bring their Nation closer to the basic requirements of the right to freedom of information.

Clearly Article 19 offers, if no more, a legal basis for promoting the freedom of information on the international plane. How useful it will prove to be depends on the number of states that ratify or accede to the covenant. If the United States takes the freedom of information and other rights seriously and desires to play a significant role in their application, it must ratify the covenant and protocol and also make the optional declaration under Article 41 of the former.

The 1966 civil and political covenant was in the works for nearly two decades and does not reflect the emerging concern with one- or two- or multiple-way flow of information in its wider sense. Notably absent is a specific reference to what is called the "right to communicate." It has already been suggested that this right may conveniently be seen as included in the formulation given to the right to freedom of information in Article 19 of the covenant.

It is interesting to note that the right to communicate is also absent from the more recent Final Act of the Helsinki conference. To be sure, there is nothing in the "Third Basket" [the final section of the Helsinki agreement, which is on human rights] that could be construed as an endorsement of the one-way flow of information. Nor is there anything that could be construed as an endorsement of the two-way flow. Like the 1948 universal declaration, the "Third Basket" is a statement of aims and objectives and, as such, it lacks the specificity normally associated with legal prescriptions. There is, however, no doubt that Parts 2 and 3, entitled "Information" and "Co-operation and Exchanges in the Field of Culture" respectively, are imbued with the spirit of mutuality and mutual agreement. They offer some guidance for the future collaboration between states represented at the Helsinki conference as well as between states in all parts of the world.

TERRITORIAL RIGHTS: EVOLVING DEFINITIONS AND *DIRIGISME*

The proposition that has been basic to the argument presented so far is that in principle states are sovereign under international law. The area of their discretionary jurisdiction depends upon the development of customary and conventional international law. A state does not have to prove that it is free to act in certain matters but it has to prove that there are no limitations placed upon its freedom to act either by customary international law or by conventions to which it is a party. It is important to recall that a state's view on its legal rights or obligations is not conclusive. Freedom to receive and impart information across national boundaries, even if it were established as a principle of customary international law, would still be subject to regulation by states. It has been admitted that the limitations imposed by international law upon a state's regulatory authority are ill-defined, so that in practice the freedom may be reduced to the vanishing point. Without pretending to a detailed analysis, some general observations may be suggested, especially with respect to radio and television broadcasts.

It has been said already that states are sovereign over their territory. It has to be added now that states are also sovereign in the air space above their territory and their territorial waters.* This principle was first formulated by the Paris Convention for the Regulation of Aerial Navigation of October 13, 1919. It provides that "every State has com-

---

*There is a good deal of controversy about the extent of territorial waters, which ranges from three to 12 miles and more. The Third Law of the Sea Conference, in progress since 1974, may produce an agreement on this matter.

plete and exclusive sovereignty in the air space above its territory and territorial waters." The principle was restated in the Chicago Convention on International Civil Aviation of 1944 as follows:

Article 1
The contracting States recognize that every State has complete and exclusive sovereignty over the airspace above its territory.

Article 2
For the purposes of this Convention the territory of a State shall be deemed to be the land areas and territorial waters adjacent thereto under the sovereignty, suzerainty, protection or mandate of such State.

The effect of these principles has been summed up in a leading treatise as follows:

> The principle of exclusive sovereignty in the air space for the subjacent State, which has received general approval in connection with aerial navigation, enables that State to prohibit the disturbance of the air space over its territory by means of Herzian waves caused for the purpose of wireless communication and emanating from a foreign source.[9]

But this principle has been limited by several telecommunication conventions and by radio regulations of a general and regional character.

Controversies have arisen over the right of a state to "jam" broadcasts emanating from other countries. The U.S. Department of State considered the jamming of the Voice of America "unlawful" as such because it was contrary to Article 44 of the Atlantic City Telecommunications Convention of 1947 (Article 48 of the 1965 Montreux Convention) and Article 3 of the Radio Regulations, which prohibit "harmful interference" to radio services of members. Referring to the USSR jamming, however, the State Department stated that "an additional factor enters into the problem, namely, the nature and the extent of the right of a sovereign government to prevent the broadcasting into its territory of information which, for reasons of its own, that government deems harmful to its national interest." The department went on to say:

> On this question there appears to exist no specific or formal limitations under international law to the action which a sovereign government can take.
>
> Where a government resorts to jamming of incoming radio signals to prevent such "harmful" information from reaching its territory, it is theoretically confined in that process to the use of signals

which will cause no harmful interference *outside its territory.* I use the expression "theoretically confined" because it is obviously not possible technically to generate a radio signal which will completely blanket incoming radio broadcasts up to a point coinciding exactly with the national boundaries, and yet will have no appreciable effect immediately beyond that point. But it is possible to limit the geographical range of the jamming radiations to a fairly well defined distance beyond the borders, while still accomplishing the desired purpose within the national territory.[10]

It is unnecesary for the purpose of this article to examine the technical provisions of the Radio Regulations on "unnecessary tranmission" and "harmful interference." It is sufficient to note the admission that there are no "formal limitations" on the action that a sovereign government may take against transmissions that it deems to constitute "unnecessary transmission" and "harmful interference" or just plain propaganda. It may well be that further technological progress will enable jamming to be carried out in a "theoretically confined" area, that is, within the confines of its territory. In any event, the United States was not required to accept the Soviet view on the matter any more than the Soviet Union was required to accept as correct the U.S. view.

In this particular case, the United States found ample support in the United Nations. First, the ECOSOC Subcommittee on Freedom of Information, then ECOSOC, and finally the General Assembly adopted resolutions in which mention was made of General Assembly Resolution 59(I),* Article 19 of the 1948 Universal Declaration of Human Rights, and Article 44 of the Atlantic City Telecommunications Convention.

---

*This resolution, adopted on December 14, 1946, called for the convocation of a conference on freedom of information. The preamble, however, is still of interest and is as follows:

THE GENERAL ASSEMBLY,

WHEREAS

Freedom of information is a fundamental human right and is the touchstone of all the freedoms to which the United Nations is consecrated. . . .

Freedom of information implies the right to gather, transmit and publish news anywhere and everywhere without fetters. As such it is an essential factor in any serious effort to promote the peace and progress of the world;

Freedom of information requires as an indispensable element the willingness and capacity to employ its privileges without abuse. It requires as a basic discipline the moral obligation to seek the facts without prejudice and to spread knowledge without malicious intent;

Understanding and co-operation among nations are impossible without an alert and sound world opinion, which, in turn, is wholly dependent upon freedom of information . . .

The General Assembly resolution 424(V) of December 14, 1950, continued as follows:

> Considering that the duly authorized radio operating agencies in some countries are deliberately interfering with the reception by the people of those countries of certain radio signals originating beyond their territories, and bearing in mind the discussion which took place in the Economic and Social Council and in the Sub-Commission on Freedom of Information and of the Press on this subject,
>
> Considering that peace among nations rests on the goodwill of all peoples and governments and that tolerance and understanding are prerequisites for establishing goodwill in the international field,
>
> 1. Adopts the declaration of the Economic and Social Council contained in its resolution 306 B (XI) of 9 August 1950 to the effect that this type of interference constitutes a violation of the accepted principles of freedom of information;
>
> 2. Condemns measures of this nature as a denial of the right of all persons to be fully informed concerning news, opinions and ideas regardless of frontiers;
>
> 3. Invites the governments of all Member States to refrain from such interference with the right of their peoples to freedom of information;
>
> 4. Invites all governments to refrain from radio broadcasts that would mean unfair attacks or slanders against other peoples anywhere and in so doing to conform strictly to an ethical conduct in the interest of world peace by reporting facts truly and objectively;
>
> 5. Invites also Member States to give every possible facility so that their peoples may know objectively the activities of the United Nations in promoting peace and, in particular, to facilitate the reception and transmission of the United Nations official broadcasts.

This vigorous endorsement of the principles of freedom of information is somewhat qualified by paragraph 4. Who is to judge the contents of the broadcasts? "Unfair attacks or slanders" and "ethical conduct" are rather broad concepts lacking objective definitions. And, as suggested above, General Assembly resolutions do not make law. Moreover, the assembly, marching to a different drummer, adopted in 1972 Resolution 2916 (XXVII), which is much more restrictive and will be discussed later in this chapter.

Be that as it may, the attempt to base the illegality of jamming on, and to derive support for the free flow of information into the territory of another state without its consent from, telecommunication conventions does not appear persuasive. In the first place, these conventions are designed to ensure the enjoyment of radio broadcasts *within* a state's territory. Second, the reliance on the prohibition of harmful interference that pervades applicable conventions begs the question, for this principle, as defined in Article 35 of the 1973 Telecommunications Convention of Madrid-Torremolinos, protects only states that themselves "operate in accordance with the provisions of the Radio Regulations."*

The most recent area of international regulation is outer space. This will be briefly examined in order to determine whether the space law provides a new basis for freedom or free flow of information irrespective of state sovereignty and the right of excluding harmful or undesirable messages.

The Treaty on Principles Governing the Activities of States in the Exploration and Use of Outer Space, Including the Moon and Other Celestial Bodies, was adopted by General Assembly resolution 2222 (XXI) on January 25, 1967. Unlike the conventions on air discussed above, the space treaty proclaims the freedom of outer space in Article 1(2): "Outer space, including the Moon and other celestial bodies, shall be free for exploration and use by all States without discrimination of any kind, on a basis of equality and in accordance with international law, and there shall be free access to all areas of celestial bodies." Although there is no provision in the space treaty relating directly to the current controversy about satellite broadcasting, the reference to international law in Article 1 is probably significant. Of potential significance are several other provisions in Articles 3, 6, and 9.

Article 3 stipulates a duty for states that are parties to the treaty that the use of outer space shall be carried out "in accordance with international law, including the Charter of the United Nations, in the interest of maintaining peace and security and promoting international co-operation and understanding."

Article 6 stipulates the international responsibility of states that are parties to the treaty for the activities carried out "by governmental agencies or by non-governmental entities, and for assuring that national activities are carried out in conformity with the provisions set forth in the present Treaty." The activities of nongovernmental entities "in outer space . . . shall require authorization and continuing supervision by the appropriate State Party to the Treaty."

---

*Annex 2 of this convention defines "harmful interference" as "any emission, radiation or induction which endangers the functioning of a radio navigation service or of any safety service, or seriously degrades, obstructs or repeatedly interrupts a radio communication service operating in accordance with the Radio Regulations." In Article 19 of the convention, members reserve the right to stop any private telegram and "to cut off any other private telecommunications which appear dangerous to the security of the State or contrary to their laws, to public order or to decency."

Article 9 requires that all activities in outer space be conducted "with due regard to the corresponding interests of all other States Parties to the Treaty." It then goes on to lay down the requirement of consultation in case of harmful interference in these words:

> If a State Party to the Treaty has reason to believe that an activity or experiment planned by it or its nationals in outer space, including the moon and other celestial bodies, would cause potentially harmful interference with activities of other States Parties in the peaceful exploration and use of outer space, including the moon and other celestial bodies, it shall undertake appropriate international consultations before proceeding with any such activity or experiment. A State Party to the Treaty which has reason to believe that an activity or experiment planned by another State Party in outer space, including the moon and other celestial bodies, would cause potentially harmful interference with activities in the peaceful exploration and use of outer space, including the moon and other celestial bodies, may request consultation concerning the activity of experiment.

The provision for consultations does not ensure that agreement will be reached, but if none is reached, the states concerned will act in accordance with their own conception of their rights and obligations. It must, of course, be clearly understood that such autointerpretations have no binding force.

The references to international law and the Charter of the United Nations may include both formal and substantive principles. Insofar as the content of television or radio transmission is concerned, it is well to recall that under international law states have the right of self-determination. Pursuant to it, the states are free to adopt political, economic, social, and cultural policies and systems of their own choosing. This is expressly incorporated in Article 1(1) of both international covenants of 1966.*

The principle of freedom of outer space like the freedom of the high seas has its limits. Just as the freedom of the high seas ends where the territorial sea begins, so does the freedom of outer space end where the territorial air space begins. But whereas there is a right of innocent passage through the territorial sea, there is no such right through territorial air space. The right of innocent passage does not include,

---

*The text is as follows: "All peoples have the right of self-determination. By virtue of that right they freely determine their political status and freely pursue their economic, social and cultural development." It would have been more appropriate to say that "States" have this right as international law deals with states and not peoples. The right of self-determination of states is not to be confused with the controversial right to self-determination of peoples.

apart from some exceptions, the right for ships to enter ports without the consent of the territorial state. Similarly, the use of outer space for satellite broadcasting does not include the right to enter the territorial air space or the territory of the subjacent state. If this is conceded as, in the present submission, then it must be that a state may exclude television broadcasts. It is always open to states to negotiate agreements for opening up access to their territories for radio and for television broadcasts. Some states have done so, other states have not opposed it but without any sense of legal obligation. There is as yet no general agreement on the subject.

The usual procedure, however, of preparing the ground for a binding treaty on satellite broadcasting through nonbinding resolutions has been under way for several years. Without any pretense at comprehensiveness, one or two resolutions will be mentioned. One is the "Declaration of Guiding Principles on the Use of Satellite Broadcasting for the Free Flow of Information, the Spread of Education and Greater Cultural Exchange" adopted on November 15, 1972, by the general conference of UNESCO.

This 1972 UNESCO declaration, while recognizing in Article V "the free flow of information" as the objective for satellite broadcasting and the principle of freedom of information in Article IX, also calls for respect for "the sovereignty and equality of all States." It contains suggestions for greater attention to the culture and degree of development of different countries. Article VI stresses "the right" of each country "to decide on the content of the educational programmes broadcast by satellite to its people." Article IX(1), not surprisingly, spells out the requirement of consent: "In order to further the objectives set out in the preceding articles, it is necessary that States, taking into account the principle of freedom of information, reach or promote prior agreements concerning satellite broadcasting to the population of countries other than the country of origin of the transmission."

This may be utterly unacceptable to advocates of "freedom of trade" and freedom of competition but it is merely an application to new technology of a well-settled principle of international law. As noted earlier, since World War I there has been a trend away from free trade to protectionism and at most, "freer trade." Protectionism has frequently been justified in terms of the need to protect "infant industries." Today, cultural protectionism may similarly be supported by developing countries in terms of the perceived need to protect "infant cultures." Saying this is not necessarily approving. It is certainly arguable that all states and peoples stand to gain from a balanced multilevel exchange of programs that respects national susceptibilities, perhaps even idiosyncracies.

In the United Nations, the Soviet Union on August 9, 1972, introduced a "Draft Convention on principles governing the use by States of
artificial earth satellites for direct television broadcasting." The outcome of the debate was resolution 2916 (XXVII) of November 9, 1972,
which noted the draft convention and in its operative part requested
the Committee on the Peaceful Uses of Outer Space to undertake the
elaboration of principles for a convention on direct television broadcasting. In the preamble the General Assembly expressed its belief that
such broadcasting "must be based on the principles of mutual respect
for sovereignty, non-interference in domestic affairs, equality, co-operation and mutual benefit." It also considered that satellite broadcasting
"could raise significant problems connected with the need to ensure the
free flow of communications on a basis of strict respect for the sovereign rights of States." In this connection it is important to note that
Article IX of the Soviet draft convention extended the protective principle from the air to outerspace in providing that

> 1. any state party to this convention may employ the means at its disposal
> to counteract illegal television broadcasting of which it is the object, not
> only in its own territory but also in outer space and other areas beyond
> the limits of the national jurisdiction of any state.
> 2. states parties to this convention agree to give every assistance in stop-
> ping illegal television broadcasting. Under Article V of the proposed
> Soviet convention direct television broadcasting would be illegal if carried
> out without the consent of the state concerned. Any transmission of televi-
> sion broadcasts would also be illegal if contrary to substantive limitations
> on content which are indicated in broadly inclusive terms in Articles IV
> and VI.

The United States, which cast the only negative vote against the
resolution insisted in the debate that the resolution "does not put sufficient emphasis on the central importance of the free flow of information and ideas in the modern world," and that "in actual practice the
sovereignty of States and the unimpeded flow of information and ideas
should complement rather than conflict with one another."
The most recent document in this series is the "Draft Declaration
on Fundamental Principles Governing the Use of the Mass Media in
Strengthening Peace and International Understanding and in Combating War, Propaganda, Racism and Apartheid," submitted to the
UNESCO General Conference at its Nineteenth Session in Nairobi in
1976. The consideration of this draft declaration was postponed. It is a
politicized draft including pronouncements and cross-references to
highly objectionable resolutions of the General Assembly of the United
Nations. Its emphasis is particularly strong on national sovereignty,

noninterference, "the existing disequilibrium in the circulation of information" from developing countries and the achievement of "a balanced exchange of information" (Article IV). It also would make it a duty for mass media to promote the realization "of a new international economic order" (Article VII). It calls on "professional organizations in the field of mass communication to define and promote standards of professional ethics on a national and international level" (Article XI). Finally, it declares in Article XII: "States are responsible for the activities in the international sphere of all mass media under their jurisdiction."

Obviously this declaration, even if adopted, would have no binding force, and it may be possible that it is *ultra vires* the competence of UNESCO. Nonetheless, while in some parts the draft declaration may reflect, albeit in a somewhat exaggerated form, the principles of international law discussed above, it is indicative of a strong tendency in the direction of *dirigisme,* or state control. The principle of state responsibility is well known in international law and the space treaty incorporates it in Article 6 but only with reference to activities by nongovernmental entities. The proposed Article XII would extend it to activities of all media, notably the press, an extension that is bound to meet with strong opposition from the proponents of the free press. The intended objective of the draft declaration may well be the controlled flow of controlled information. States are free to choose the sociopolitical system under which they wish to live, but there is no reason why states attached to the principles of freedom of thought and of expression and of the free flow of information should participate in attempts to subvert them.

NOTES

1. Article 38(1) of the Statute of the Court, which is an integral part of the Charter of the United Nations. The Court is also directed to apply "the general principles of law recognized by civilized nations" and, as subsidiary means, the teachings "of the most highly qualified publicists of the various nations."

2. Separate Opinion of Judge Anzilotti in the Austro-German Customs Union case, [1931] P.C.I.J., ser. A/B, No. 41, p. 57.

3. U.S. Department of State, Publication 8826, General Foreign Policy Series, no. 298, p. 82.

4. The Greco-Bulgarian "Communities" case, Advisory Opinion of the P.C.I.J. [1930] P.C.I.J., ser. B, No. 17, p. 32.

5. It provides in Section VI:

The participating States will refrain from any intervention, direct or indirect, individual or collective, in the internal or external affairs falling within the domestic jurisdiction of another participating State, regardless of their mutual relation....

Accordingly, they will, *inter alia,* refrain from direct or indirect assistance to terrorist activities, or to subversive of other activities directed toward the violent overthrow of the regime of another participating State.

It is not clear what is meant by "external affairs" falling within domestic jurisdiction. For a recent study of domestic jurisdiction see J. S. Watson, "Autointerpretation, Competence, and the continuing Validity of Article 2(1) of the Charter" 71 *American Journal of International Law* 60-84 (1977).

6. Tunis-Morocco Nationality Decrees case, Advisory Opinion, [1923] P.C.I.J., ser. B, No. 4, p. 24. In the same case, the Court held that the clause in Article 15(8) of the Covenant of the League of Nations concerning matters "solely within the domestic jurisdiction" relates to "certain matters which, though they may very closely concern the interests of more than one State, are not, in principle, regulated by international law. As regards such matters, each State is sole judge."

7. Letter to the Editor, *New York Times,* March 20, 1977, p. E16.

8. Letter to the Editor, *New York Times,* April 1, 1977, p. A28.

9. L. Oppenheim, *International Law I* (8th ed. by H. Lauterpacht, 1955), Longmans, Green p. 529.

10. Letter by Assistant Chief of Telecommunications Policy Staff (Lebel), Department of State, of August 30, 1950. 13 Whiteman, *Digest of International Law,* pp. 1031–32.

3. DEVELOPMENTAL JOURNALISM:
The Ideological Factor

LEONARD R. SUSSMAN

Ideology ... the body of doctrine, myth, symbol, etc., of a social movement, institution, class ... with reference to some political and cultural plan, along with the devices for putting it into operation.

Random House College Dictionary

The fundamental doctrines of Western journalism are being challenged as never before by Third World governments and news media. Despite their own widely divergent philosophies of governance, the developing nations display near unanimity in attacking the transnational news services. This challenge to Western journalism has been encouraged by two intergovernmental organizations: the United Nations Educational, Scientific and Cultural Organization (UNESCO) and the Ministerial Conference of Nonaligned Countries on the Press Agencies Pool, and by a number of private, or quasi-private organizations—such as the Dag Hammarskjold Foundation (Sweden) and the Latin American Institute for Transnational Studies (ILET, in Mexico City).

The doctrine is premised on a critique of existing systems and doctrines (not unusual for new ideologies). Generally speaking, the Third World tends to assume that there is an ideology that directs Western journalism. Indeed there is. The four major Western news services—Associated Press (AP), United Press International (UPI), Reuters, Agence France-Presse (AFP)—are progenies of the competitive free-market systems in their respective countries. Each in its own way reflects an established tradition of reportorial and managerial independence from governmental controls, direction, and reprisals. The U.S. news services trace their independence to the First Amendment to the

Constitution of the United States. That fundamental law emphasizes the rights of the individual citizen in competition with the state—in sharp distinction to most Third World philosophies of government. Indeed the freedom of the U.S. press (meaning all the mass media) has inspired the development of a sizable body of doctrine in itself. The jealous guarding of this independence from all forms of government encroachment may be regarded as a fully institutionalized ideology. Indeed this concept is embodied in UNESCO's constitution as the "free flow of ideas by word and image."

No matter where news reports originate—whether in a poor, highly illiterate, traditional society or in an industrialized nation of the East or the West—the Western journalistic criteria are virtually the same. The distant event, trend, or personality is described essentially with the ultimate "consumer" in mind. Overwhelmingly, the audience is in the Western and Northern worlds where the free-market or the mixed, capitalist-socialist economy prevails; and where, at least in principle, most of the news customers live within the Western tradition in which citizens have clearly defined rights.

Within the United States, the "free flow" doctrine is further bolstered by the concept of the "free marketplace of ideas." The wide diversity of reports and viewpoints offered the public is deemed to guarantee that no one view, no singly purveyor of news, and no one medium will monopolize the channels of communication. In such a system, errors or imbalance projected by one medium can be corrected or balanced by others. Newspaper readers in one-paper or chain-dominated cities can turn to radio and television for alternate reports. The people of the United States, moreover, have become critical consumers. (They question advertising claims, politicians, and press reports, as well as established institutions.)

In the less sophisticated societies of the Third World there has been no such established tradition for questioning the communications media. Most important, the Western news media, viewed from abroad, do not reflect the diversity that is available to U.S. citizens at home. To be sure, AP and UPI may carry somewhat different versions of the same event, and both may report the conflicting charges made by principals in a news story, but the fundamental range of subjects covered and the reportorial point of view will generally differ only slightly.

Thus the Western news media are perceived quite differently by the leaders of developing countries in Asia, Africa, and Latin America. They declare that the pervasive impact on their societies of Western news and life-styles tends to destroy their indigenous cultures. They call it "cultural imperialism," and profess to see in the phenomenon a neocolonialist effort to prevent the economic development of their countries. To remedy matters, they call for new arrangements that will "balance" the flow of news between the developing and the developed worlds. Most news reaching the Third World now concerns events in the industrialized countries. They therefore regard the "free flow of information" doctrine imbedded in UNESCO's 1945 constitution as outmoded. It must be replaced, they say, by the balancing of the volume of news moved North and South and by changes in news budgets to provide in equal measure reports of the Third World's economic development.

Development journalism has been a factor in the Third World for nearly 15 years. It began as an inspiration of professional journalists, not government information directors. It recognized a nation's need for economic development. This, in turn, required reporters and editors capable of understanding and transmitting increasingly complex economic, scientific, and related information. Similar efforts had been made in the United States decades earlier to encourage better scientific and economic reporting. Juan Mercado, director of the Philippines Press Institute, first sponsored seminars on economic development. In one test, the Philippine News Service cooperated by sending reporters to libraries to abstract in popular language the scholarly findings of development researchers. John Lent notes the efforts of other editors in Asia:

> Chanchal Sarkar, director of the Press Institute of India; Amitabha Chowdhury, head of the Asian Programme of IPI; Maasaki Kasagi of Nihon Shinbun Kyokai; and Mochtar Lubis, editor of *Indonesia Raya,* recognized that new directions were necessary in reporting Asia because of the "cumulative effect of the growth of national economies, changes in the character and profile of the audience and, above all, the results of the peoples' experiments and frustrations with new political systems."[1]

The Press Foundation of Asia (PFA), created in 1967, regards the training of development journalists as its major function (see the chapter by S. M. Ali). The PFA claims to have trained 250 newsmen in three years as "Asia's first corps of development journalists." The PFA, like similar professional groups in Asia and Africa, was founded mainly by U.S., British, and German foundations, with some indigenous nongovernmental support. The Third World journalists who inspired these programs employed Western news media ideology—including the rough separation of press and state—to advance their profession and, in turn, the development of their countries.

The worldwide economic and political turmoil of the late 1960s had one unifying effect on the Third World. Although its national interests and ideologies remained diverse, the Western news media became a common target for almost all the governments and news media in the developing nations. The doctrine common to all—through the ideological spectrum from right to left—was the assertion of a development litany: economic development is essential to assure the well-being of a society and the sovereignty of the state. Effective communications to all sectors of the citizenry is a principal instrument of economic development. Only the government is responsible for, and can assure, the proper use of communication for this purpose. Therefore, governments must control the mass media in the name of economic development.

I call this "developmental journalism," as distinct from the earlier development journalism, which was essentially nongovernmental in origin and practice. Developmental journalism has become a widely shared concept and objective among Third World countries, crossing all lines of political and economic doctrine. While national differences frequently arise with respect to issues of economics, trade, and monetary arrangements, near unanimity over the basic Third World Challenge to Western journalism persists.

THIRD WORLD "USES" OF NEWS MEDIA IDEOLOGY: AN OVERVIEW

> Ideology! This is what gives the evil deed its sought-for justification and the villain the lasting callousness he needs. This is the social theory which helps him vindicate his deeds in his own eyes and those of others, to hear not reproaches and curses, but praise and honor.
>
> Aleksandr Solzhenitsyn
> *Gulag Archipelago*

Despite its many ideological orientations, the Third World is generally responsive to the simplistic analysis that, in the media controversy as in economic development, it is "us" against "them."

Our purpose, therefore, is to explore the limited but effective area of agreement on news media questions in the Third World and the far broader spectrum of ideological differentiation. The aim is neither to underestimate the degree of dissatisfaction with the Western press, which is real, runs deep, and is growing; nor to exaggerate Third World complaints so that constructive adjustments are inhibited. Negotiations are urgently needed and, within the principled limit which a free press sets in maintaining its ethical standards, eminently desirable. We will try to identify the ideological factors and to explore those areas where negotiation is possible.

The news media confrontation is rooted in colonial realities. For the West, colonialism ended 15 years ago when scores of dominated peoples secured political sovereignty. For the Third World, the economic effects of earlier political domination remain: Human needs are as badly fulfilled as human rights. It has taken the industrialized nations another 15 years to acknowledge the economic plight of their poorer neighbors. Meanwhile, the Third World has discovered that Western journalism, despite its impressive technology and vast power, may be a vulnerable giant. The West has learned, since the Nineteenth Biennial General Conference of UNESCO at Nairobi, in October-November 1976, that Third World complaints are widespread and intended to generate serious responses—and will not disappear if ignored.

Just as political action and some terrorism has spearheaded the political assault on colonialism and oil price-setting has sparked the attack in the economic sphere, so government influence over the information media underlies current demands for "decolonization" of the Western mass news media.

One may observe three broad ideological aspects of the Third World's struggle against the Western news media. Opposition is based upon one or more of these.

1. *Complaints that have readily perceived validity in the Third World.* The new sovereignties believe they remain economically subservient to the developed nations and see the gap growing wider as North-South communication increases. Even the developing countries that export oil and exert great economic pressure on the industrialized nations believe themselves embattled and not progressing sufficiently. Third World leaders, standing with one foot in a traditional culture and the other in a vastly different and intrinsically overpowering one, see their peoples, values, and social structures in transition—always a sensitive time for those intent on holding power. Often, the domestic tradition carries no guarantee of personal freedom, only the tolerance of closely-knit tribal or cultural groups. There is generally no basis in law for the independence of the press from the government. The pervasive Western media tend to exacerbate all these tensions in the society.

2. *Nationalist ideologies intended to install or maintain a regime in power, or achieve influence for the nation beyond its own borders.* These ideologies are widely diverse in their political and economic

orientations. They all tend to elaborate on the "readily perceived validity" of complaints against the Western news media. They thus share the premise that developmental journalism is a useful concept to assure the availability of mass communications for mobilizational or integrational purposes.* These ideologies have a defensive objective as well. The tendency in most developing countries is to regard control of internal communication as an assurance of the regime's security. This is patently unverifiable. The frequency of coups in many of them is a matter of record. Successful regimes often take control of domestic broadcasting stations and printing presses. Yet, more often than not, it appears that the defeated regimes succumbed not primarily to communication power, but to gun power.

3. *Marxist ideology, which provides a ready-made explanation—the class struggle—for all the complaints of the developing nations in the field of communication.* It is the rich nations against the poor: those rich in organized wire services, communications technology, support from corporate financing, and associations with political and military power structures. The rich-poor gap is real. Almost every aspect of the news media controversy lends itself readily to this analysis. It should not be surprising, therefore, that even non-Marxist states in the Third World are susceptible to Marxist argumentation.

The Soviet Union, for its own nationalist purposes, is the principal purveyor of Marxist ideology as the model for replacing the free flow of information with tightly knit, centralized control of all information media in the pattern of a communist society.

Solzhenitsyn sees ideology as the antithesis of truth, used to justify "the evil deed," enabling the "villain" to "vindicate his deeds in his own eyes and those of others." Not all ideology, of course, is untruth; indeed, the best propaganda blends some obvious truth with the propagandists' own views, which may depart significantly from demonstrable fact. Thus, the Soviet Union's highly controversial draft declaration prepared for UNESCO's biennial conference at Nairobi, October-November 1976, proclaimed a series of high purposes: "Declaration on Fundamental Principles Governing the Use of the Mass Media in Strengthening Peace and International Understanding and in Combating War Propaganda, Racism and Apartheid."

*Propaganda is mobilizational when it uses the press, radio, film, even word of mouth, to alert or to incite the citizenry to perform particular actions: cultivate the land, populate the country or practice birth control, prepare for war. State communication is integrational when, generally over the longer term, it promotes the reading of certain literature, learning particular vocations, strengthening specific cultural traditions, and following or reinforcing the national leadership.

The numerous stated aims of the declaration were unobjectionable even to the Western delegates. The "villainy" entered, however, in the key procedural word "use"—the implicit use of the mass media by governments. This was elaborated in the highly publicized Article XII of the Soviet draft (approved by an intergovernmental UNESCO conference at Paris in December 1975): "States are responsible for the activities in the international sphere of all mass media under their jurisdiction."

This was the most extreme statement of the Third World's concept of developmental journalism. With the considerable assistance of mainly black African states at Nairobi, the Soviet declaration was set aside.

It is a highly differentiated Third World. The nations cover four continents and several archipelagos and are characterized by numerous ideologies and social and economic structures, ranging from the primitive to the sophisticated. Generally speaking, their one point of agreement is the belief that they are dominated and exploited by the industrial countries. The radical states attribute to the developed nations a conscious ideological hostility. The more moderate believe the developed countries may *unwittingly* support a system that perpetuates social and economic injustice. In the informational field, therefore, for the West to ignore or underestimate the intensity of feeling about long-continuing news media domination can only further encourage the governmental control and harassment implicit in many communications policies discussed at UNESCO and the conferences of the nonaligned nations.

The radical governments, through their press and radio, project the extreme solution—authoritarian control of communications and all other aspects of society. The Soviet Union and its satellites have succeeded in penetrating the press of the Third World, often by invitation, as a counterbalance to pervasive Western influences, and often by offering communications assistance as part of a larger deal generally involving sale or loan of military equipment. The Soviet Union and the People's Republic of China (PRC) in the 1960s liberally endowed the African liberation movements with arms and supplies and, not incidentally, with radio equipment and in some cases, printing presses and newsprint.* Present and former recipients of Soviet or PRC aid are less

---

*In 1961, Guinea received $110 million in credits from communist nations: a radio station from the USSR, a printing plant from East Germany and Poland, and technical aid and a radio transmitter from Czechoslovakia. That same year, Ghana was given $182 million in credits for communications, a printing plant and film technicians. Tanzania got a party newspaper plant from East Germany and (in 1966) a radio station from the Chinese. There are examples of other extensive credits and gifts through the years.

likely to attack the donors. Moreover, the endless Soviet charges of Western "imperialism" provide ideological specificity to support the Third World's complaints against the West.

It is not sufficient to differentiate the historic experience of the developing countries. It is also necessary to separate the real from contrived or ideologized issues, and to identify those substantive inequities traceable to Western news media policies or procedures. Western media managers, therefore, face an assignment as difficult as one they often give their journalists: to discover not only the "what?" but the "why?"—the reasons for the Third World charges and demands against the Western news media, and as well, how the various adversaries *think.*

This requires an awareness of the role of communications in diverse societies, taking into account vastly different cultural values, a lack of security in a still-dangerous world, and varying degrees of indigenous authoritarianism, with or without a highly developed social, political, or economic ideology. This means, too, a pragmatic sense of when authoritarianism of whatever stripe precludes good-faith cooperation. This should enable Western media managers themselves to differentiate among those demands and countries that deserve only a rhetorical response and those that merit serious, cooperative efforts to improve not only our news service to them, but theirs to themselves, and to the advanced nations generally.

THE PERVASIVE MARXIST IDEOLOGY

An Exponent from the United States

[Cooperation between Western news media managers and their Third World counterparts may be feasible, however, only after North and South strip away the pervasive ideological factors that distort the valid issues. Many of the background papers prepared for recent UNESCO conferences on news media issues call for the formulation of a "national communications policy," implicitly supporting governmental control of all communications media, generally in the name of national economic development. These same papers also include Marxist arguments calling for the "use" of mass media to end economic and cultural "imperialism." It is not surprising that Marxist analysis and the USSR's outright support of press control in its UNESCO declaration have permeated every level of international discussion of the mass news media. The Soviet objective is to insinuate its charges of the West's "cultural imperialism" into all Third World examinations of news media issues. To the extent that the non-Marxist nations accept this analysis, they become that much more susceptible to authoritarian controls within their own countries.

It is clear that in the Third World there exist many forms of Marxist, Marxist-oriented, or socialist states, whether nonparty, one-party, or multiparty, that are in varying degrees susceptible to the Soviet exploitation of news-media issues. It is important, therefore, to examine closely the prevalent Marxist analysis. A clear formulation is provided by U.S. protagonist, Herbert I. Schiller,[2] who is frequently cited in Third World news media documents. His papers are often published by the Soviet-dominated organization that dispenses Marxist ideology cum media technology to the Third World.[3] Apparently, Marxist bureaucrats and scholars regard Schiller as living U.S. proof that Marxism accurately exposes the diabolical objectives attributed to Western news media. After all, a U.S. citizen admits it!

Schiller maintains that multinational corporations, mainly those from the United States, organize the world economy. The news media and communications are vital parts of their system of administration and control. They define social reality and influence the organization of work, the character and uses of technology, and the curriculum of the educational system. This domination from the center (the U.S. multinationals and their adjunct, the news media) to the periphery (the Third World) is only now being revealed, says Schiller. This process, he says, is "cultural imperialism," a term frequently found in Marxist literature and in UNESCO "expert" documents. As this realization increases, there "will surely be a period of growing cultural-communications struggle—*intra*- and *inter*-nationally—between those seeking the end of domination and those striving to maintain it."[4]

Schiller holds that "a largely one-directional flow of information from core to periphery represents the reality of power," as does the promotion of a single language, English.[5] The impulse originates with "commercial imperatives" producing the "cultural takeover of the penetrated society."[6] To achieve this end, "public media" become the primary target of penetration.*

He describes international broadcasting as the spearhead for capturing the indigenous media of developing countries. The very professionalism of Western broadcasters, Schiller says, precludes masses of Third World citizens from participation in broadcasting. He calls for "despecialization, open admission to recruitment"—clearly, he adds, "in opposition to the general structural and ideational requirements of the modern, capitalist, world economy."[7]

---

*Schiller uses "public" rather than "mass" or "news" media to emphasize the use of a social instrument for purposes he apparently would not describe as the dissemination of news or objective reportage.

Schiller charges that there is now, if there was not always, "deliberate management" of the Third World, "a large measure of intention in contemporary, American, cultural domination."[8]

He says that "conspiracy need not be invoked" to demonstrate intentional domination, yet he goes on to denigrate even the following unobjectionable goal attributed to a United States Information Agency (USIA) official: "We must now shape our operation in a much more sophisticated manner, with greater attention to the sensitivities of our audience than ever before."[9] Schiller terms this "exhortation" to "sensitize" policymakers as simply further proof of "the global involvement of U.S. capitalism and its urgent need for reliable information about the climate of opinion in the areas in which it is active."[10] Sensitivity thus becomes a pejorative.

Turning to the growing controversy within UNESCO and elsewhere in the Third World, Schiller attacks "the policy of free flow of information" as a form of Western, mainly American, domination and corruption of other people and their cultures. The policy, he says, coincided with the "imperial ascendancy of the United States" because free flow was an "indispensable prerequisite" for U.S. imperialism.[11] Schiller elaborates:

A remarkable political campaign was organized [circa 1945] by the big press associations and publishers, with the support of industry in general, to elevate the issue of free flow of information to the highest level of national and international principle. This served a handsome pair of objectives. It rallied public opinion to the support of a commercial goal expressed as an ethical imperative. Simultaneously, it provided a highly effective ideological club against the Soviet Union and its newly created neighboring zone of anticapitalist influence.

It was obvious that the fundamental premise of free enterprise —access to capital governs access to message dissemination—would be intolerable to societies that had eliminated private ownership of decisive forms of property, such as mass communications facilities. Therefore, the issue of free flow of information provided American policy managers with a powerful cultural argument for creating suspicion about an alternate form of social organization.[12]

Schiller suggests that the free-flow issue and indeed the larger question of personal freedom were merely gimmicks advanced by the likes of John Foster Dulles to initiate the Cold War and achieve commercial markets. Schiller also disparages the late William Benton, chairman of the U.S. delegation to the 1958 UN Conference on Freedom of Information. Benton said of the conferees that "the free are thus face to face with those whose ideology drives them toward the destruction of freedom." Schiller accuses Benton of partisanship because the U.S.

delegate sought an agreement that would "keep world attention focused on the vital subject of freedom of expression within and among nations."[13]

Clearly, Schiller's analysis provides little or no place for freedom of expression within or among nations. He regards the freedom doctrine as passé, as do the Soviet Union and the majorities voting at UNESCO's San Jose conference on communications policies in Latin America in 1976. They call for a "balanced" as well as a "free flow" of information and imply that governments are expected to provide the balancing or supervisory councils of ministers by means of government-run agencies or supervisory councils of ministers of information.

Schiller adds this pragmatic test: "When there is an uneven distribution of power among individuals or groups *within* nations or *among* nations, a free hand freedom to continue doing what led to the existing conditions—serves to strengthen the already-powerful and weaken further the already-frail."[14]

The poor countries have no chance, he adds, because modern technology overwhelms them. Technology, he maintains, determines the fundamental communication patterns: "The mass media—the press, radio, TV—supplement and extend the message the system wants conveyed."[15]

Schiller does not examine the present and future use of the same technology by Marxist states determined to transmit only *their* conception of the universe, with *no* alternative reports conveyed without ideological denigration. Tanjug is, after all, already transmitting daily nonaligned-press-pool reports of the Third World's national news agencies. The massive Soviet press and broadcasting apparatus has been in place nearly as long as the West's mass media. And, as we will see shortly, the vast Soviet-front apparatus directed to the Third World effectively clears the ground for Soviet and Marxist penetration of those countries.

Schiller sets forth his own prescription. He calls it "a policy of self-reliance." Capitalism would be largely eliminated and socialism installed, giving the "highest priority to central planning and strict controls over economic life—arrangements that would strongly influence the flow of technology." He would regulate as well "the level and nature of personal consumption *(including the consumption of information)*" (emphasis added).[16]

It is a short step for him to close his argument with the classic Marxist-Leninist assertion that class conflict determines all manner of human activity. Now, he says, "class conflict has ... moved into the communications-culture sphere in an *explicit* way; and the emergence of national communications policies is the reflection of generally still-unresolved battles between contradictory interests and demands in the cultural-informational sector." For, he says, "the communications system is controlled by or represents the dominating class, externally or internally based."[17]

The cry for "national communications policies" originated in UNESCO some seven years ago. Schiller cites several UNESCO recommendations of these policies but does not indicate the Soviet authorship of the basic resolution.

Schiller turns to the future. He sees the United States increasingly disrupted internally and declining steadily as a power in the world. The issues in communications assume increasing significance in the larger struggle to maintain or change the total system. That system—"the crisis-riddled state capitalist order"—is doomed, he says. "Accordingly, national communications policy making may be regarded as a battleground of the contending forces on the social stage."[18] News, he says, must no longer be "manufactured information." News must be redefined. Schiller gives one yardstick of newsworthiness: "Understanding of and identification with worldwide liberation movements and the struggle against imperialism in all its forms necessitate the elimination of present Western television and radio news formats."[19]

He cites favorably the Cuban and Chinese models of "news" transmittal. He advises against permitting the latest U.S. technology (satellites, computer networks) to function internationally until ideological controls are in place through "communications policies." Otherwise, he says, technology will replace the "free flow doctrine" as the means of imposing U.S. social "imperatives."[20]

The Mexican Connection

Juan Somavia, executive director of ILET, Mexico City, also relies on Schiller for his own analysis and recommendations. A conference at the institute in May 1976 (in collaboration with the Dag Hammarskjold Foundation) on "The Role of Information in the New International Order" concluded that "the development of a new international information order is an integral element in the establishment of a new international order.[21] The present "transnational information structure" must be reformulated because it "makes impossible a real understanding among peoples." Information, Somavia says, underscoring Schiller's terms, "is used as another instrument of domination." The principle of " 'free flow' of information has created an information system that ratifies the structure of transnational power." News is just merchandise to be sold according to the "logic" of the dominant market, says Somavia.

Thus, there must be "profound changes" in the "existing interrelation" between the corporate center and its communications instruments (Somavia uses Schiller's terms "center" and "periphery" to describe the dominating and dominated countries). These changes must include the creation of a new body of law governing international communications. Both the periphery and the center must be "mobilized" to establish "a new framework of international juridical responsibility for the responsible exercise of information activities." This is precisely the intent of the still-pending Soviet resolution delayed in November 1976 at Nairobi. ILET also calls for a journalists' code, presumably set forth by governments. This, too, was recommended at the San José UNESCO conference on communication in Latin America in July 1976. Further, journalists must be "committed to the will for liberation of dominated countries" (another Schiller theme). Presumably, their "will" must be demonstrated in their news reporting and editing, as Schiller urges.

ILET, too, calls for the creation of "national communications policies" leading to "another development"—alternate information agencies. The press agencies pool of the nonaligned pool countries is cited as one part of such development. Underlying all this is a new concept of what is news that must emerge "from the demands of the dominated majorities." The United Nations must reflect these new concepts to begin the "decolonization of news."

The Prague Headquarters

We should not take lightly Schiller's prophecy, underscored by Somavia and ILET, that "national communications policy—the main theme of much UNESCO and Marxist ideology—is the wave of the future. That is not to say that all "national communications policy" stems from or incorporates Marxist doctrine. It does mean, however, that there is an eminently effective movement to shape the "national communications policy" of Third World countries after the Soviet model.

The major apparatus for implementing Soviet media policies in the Third World is the International Organization of Journalists (IOJ) the Soviet-supported and dominated operation that claims to "unite" 150,-000 journalists and mass media specialists in 109 countries. Since 1969, IOJ has had consultative status B at UNESCO. IOJ participates in UNESCO programs and formally addressed the Nairobi biennial. UNESCO officials, in turn, attend IOJ conferences and write often for IOJ publications, reinforcing IOJ's appeals addressed to the Third

World. Indeed, UNESCO provides financial support for IOJ conferences run principally for the indoctrination of Third World news media. The IOJ has an extensive publications program in many languages: pamphlets, guides, periodicals, and full-length books are turned out on regular schedules. This is unquestionably the most extensive outpouring anywhere in the world of technical and analytical publications addressed to journalists, particularly in the Third World.

The Democratic Journalist, a monthly magazine of some 28 pages, published in four languages on quality paper with great professional competence, is a case in point. Its articles discuss every level of news media skill—from that expected of a dean of a journalism school to that of a reporter or photographer. Soviet "journalists" dominate the pages, but there are Finnish, East European, and Third World contributors to add an international flavor. There is, of course, an occasional U.S. contributor, either supporting, or at least not conflicting with, Marxist analysts.

Running through every publication, conference, public statement, or other product of IOJ are strong Marxist themes. IOJ, of course, provides a sounding board for the ideological demands voiced at UNESCO news media conferences, for example, the need for "national communications policies." IOJ serves equally as the dispenser of technological skills and ideological rationales. Its guidebook on how to run a wire service is sound and businesslike—and thoroughly interlaced with Marxist ideology.[22] It is intended to undermine the credibility of Western news media and substitute "socialist" journalism, whose function is mobilizing Third World peoples for the class struggle.

This objective is clearly stated by a Soviet writer in IOJ's *Developing World and Mass Media.* Azad Khadian Talivaya Ibragimov holds that there are only two fundamental kinds of journalism: "communist and capitalist." He recognizes there are "diverse ideological and political streams" within the developing countries. He therefore distinguishes five kinds of press participating in the class struggle:

1. the press of the national bourgeoisie (Mahatma Gandhi's *Harijan* exposed colonial rule but did not go far enough; the national bourgeoisie "have the tendency," says Ibragimov, "to go over the antinational or even pro-imperialist positions")
2. the revolutionary-democratic press (as in Algeria; it strives for noncapitalist development by intensifying the national liberation struggle, but it is not a working-class press.)
3. the communist press, which disseminates antiimperialist ideas, "including those which have now been adopted by revolutionary democrats" (the success of a developing nation's press "frequently depends" on

whether it actively supports the "anti-imperialist struggle for national liberation" in cooperation with the communist press, as in Iraq)

4. the press of local monopolistic capital (such as the *Statesman* of India), which is controlled by capitalistic magnates and "can hardly be listed as national publications"

5. the press of foreign monopolistic corporations, which should be expropriated as soon as possible. Ibragimov maintains that the "nationalization of the mass media" and the "growth of the party and government press" is, "in our view, a progressive development" for all countries. "The basis of the work of the press ... must be the aims of national development—in the political, socio-economic and cultural fields," Ibragimov concludes.[23]

To facilitate the Third World's development of a "progressive" press, IOJ conducts seminars and conferences to train journalists to accept professional and ideological responsibilities. One of the earliest IOJ training programs developed "young cadres—press photographers and photo editors." The training of journalists from developing countries, with particular stress on the creation of a national press, was examined at Djakarta in February 1963. It was decided there to establish the IOJ Center for Journalists' Training in Budapest. That same year, courses were begun by IOJ in East Germany and Czechoslovakia, in addition to Hungary, to train journalists from the developing countries. This soon became the extensive School of Solidarity in East Berlin to which Third World trainees regularly come.

The Budapest center focuses mainly on radio and television while the Berlin school concentrates on developing newspaper and periodical skills. The Berlin school, says IOJ:

directs its activities to the education of democratic, anti-imperialist and anti-colonialist journalists, chiefly from Africa and Asia, to reinforce the ideas of humanistic, honest, truthful and progressive journalism. Its curriculum concentrates on the role and methods of mass media, the history of journalism, the theory and sociology of information planning and administration in mass media work.[24]

IOJ adds that the Berlin school "maintains close links with its students after they have finished their course."

IOJ also conducts training courses in Africa, Asia, and Latin America. The first program in Africa was begun in 1964 in Algiers. Special courses for Arab journalists were begun in 1967. The following year, IOJ initiated training for Latin American journalists. IOJ increasingly concentrated on professional training. IOJ's Seventh Congress, in January 1971 in Havana, gave training programs the highest priority for the next four years. New publications were initiated. More intensive work within UNESCO, and by UNESCO within IOJ's structure, was planned. As a consequence, UNESCO cosponsored with IOJ in June 1974 in Budapest a colloquium on "the development of communication media and new tendencies in the training of journalists." Forty-one specialists from 16 Third World countries took part. A second IOJ colloquium in December 1975, in collaboration with UNESCO, was attended mainly by African journalist-trainees. The subject: "The need for and importance of the study of journalism in developing countries, and the contribution made to the training of journalists by international and national organizations."

IOJ claims to cooperate extensively through its own Paris office with UNESCO and its many programs in the news media field. IOJ also works with the International Labor Organization (ILO) and the Organization of African Unity (OAU) and has associated itself with the Conference on Security and Cooperation in Europe (the Helsinki Accords).

The concluding remarks of IOJ's spokesman at UNESCO's Nairobi conference bear careful examination: "The world's largest journalists' organization is willing to continue its cooperation with UNESCO. . . . The new and more universal approach taken by UNESCO means relinquishing the distinctly Western character that the organization took in the past."[25]

GUIDELINES FOR ADVANCING THE IDEOLOGY OF FREE JOURNALISM

We have had the time to examine the anti-Western news-media rationales at two major conferences of UNESCO,* two historic meetings of the nonaligned nations that created the Third World press pool,† and countless symposia, published analyses, and tactical meetings. At the UNESCO conference in Nairobi, U.S. journalists and officials had a unique opportunity to speak privately with leaders who express the Third World complaints. These Americans also faced the relentless

---

*The Intergovernmental Conference on Communication Policies in Latin America and the Caribbean, San Jose, Costa Rica, July 1976, and the Nineteenth Biennial General Conference at Nairobi, Kenya, October-November 1976.

†Ministerial Conference of Nonaligned Countries on the Press Agencies Pool, New Delhi, July 8 to 13, 1976, and, in August 1976, the Summit Conference of Nonaligned Countries, meeting at Colombo, Sri Lanka, which ratified the New Delhi arrangements.

efforts of Marxist ideologues to turn the media issues into an informational Cold War.

The timing of challenge and response becomes crucial. In this sense, the Nairobi conference raised the Third World media issue to a new level of interaction between the "haves" and the "have-littles." Significantly, while the West tended to claim a victory in the putting off of the Soviet media resolution, the Soviets hailed the serious consideration of the subject, in their terms, as a victory. They now tell their people the resolution is being prepared for "ratification" in 1978.[26]

As so often happens, the Third World, set between the First and Second, waits. It understands that there are now firmly on the agenda such questions as news flow, content, and breadth of Third World coverage; paucity of intraregional reporting; and the general underdevelopment of Third World news media technology. As a consequence of the Nairobi conference, it is likely that Third World officials expect soon to see what they would regard as improvements in the performance of Western news media. Public attacks on the Western press at present are somewhat muffled. Yet it is well to recall our domestic disorders of the 1960s when the revolution of rising expectations outran our record of fulfillment. Without suggesting too rigorous an analogy between the civil rights struggle in the United States and Third World press demands, there are some similarities. The developing nations are convinced they have been victims of historic injustice and that the colonial limitations on their people, their economies, and particularly their communication systems render the development of their countries and their information media impossible without fundamental changes in the worldwide system of communication. The moderates in the Third World, those not dominated by an anti-West, anti-U.S., or Marxist ideology, ask, therefore, for an international program of affirmative action to redress the historic injustices.

The moderates, particularly among the journalists, are an important force. Even in some countries where governments have dominated the press, newspapermen writhed under the controls and sought ways to resist further encroachment. South Vietnam's reporters overcame strict censorship by writing allegorically of events the censors might strike out. Hanoi, of course, wiped out the private press in 1975. India's press, during the 21 months of repression in 1975–77, persistently used the courts to forestall governmental harassment and creeping nationalization (see the chapter by George Verghese). As S. M. Ali points out in his chapter, Asian journalists respond to governmental takeover and control of the press by focusing on the less controversial aspects of national development (similar to community service programs in the United States). And Hilary Ng'weno of Kenya's *Weekly Review* makes clear his differences with national policy in his chapter. He recognizes that "many young countries have fragile political structures that cannot withstand endless scrutiny by the news media of the shortcomings of those in power or the failures of economic and social development programmes." Yet he attacks the Soviet Union's UNESCO proposals. They "will eventually lead to the curtailment of the flow of information," he writes. "Worse, they replace one kind of distorting factor—that of Western bias—with another, that of governmental or bureaucratic bias." He sees the struggle as "between the proponents of governmental control of the mass media and those of an independent press that is not controlled by the government." Says Ng'weno, "There simply happens to be no middle ground between the two approaches to the role of the press."

The moderates such as Ng'weno provide a sobering opportunity. Their patience presupposes a U.S. or Western willingness to respond to Third World needs in a constructive fashion and, moreover, to respond soon. We are, therefore, in a time of testing. It is time for us to determine how, and how far, we can move toward meeting Third World informational demands and to demonstrate whether such changes can be made within our free market and political systems and without compromising the highest ethic of U.S. journalism.

NOTES

1. In an unpublished paper presented at a conference on culture and communication, Temple University, Philadelphia, Pa., March 12, 1977, Lent describes the professional journalists' early efforts to prepare their readers for the issues of economic development; the Mochtar Lubis quotation from "Press Foundation of Asia and Its Evolution," *Statesman Press* (New Delhi) 1973, p. 1, appears in Lent, p. 2.

2. See his *Communication and Cultural Domination* (White Plains, N.Y.: International Arts & Sciences Press, 1976). He is professor of communications, Third College, University of California, San Diego.

3. See *The Democratic Journalist,* March 1976, pp. 14–17; June 1976, pp. 6–9, published by the International Organization of Journalists, Prague.

4. *Communication and Cultural Domination,* p. 3.

5. Ibid., p. 6.

6. ibid., p. 8.

7. ibid., p. 13.

8. ibid., p. 19.

9. ibid., p. 21, quoting Wilson P. Dizard, "Which Way to the Future?", *USIA Communicator,* 1, no. 4 (July 1973) 11–13.

10. ibid., p. 22.

11. Ibid., p. 24.

12. ibid., pp. 29–30.

13. ibid., p. 36, quoting Benton, Department of State Bulletin, April 18, 1948, pp. 518–20.

14. ibid., p. 45.

15. ibid., p. 49.

16. ibid., p. 61.

17. ibid., p. 68.

18. ibid., p. 79.

19. ibid., p. 91.

20. *The Democratic Journalist,* March 1976, p. 17.

21. "Analysis and Conclusions," conference paper, May 24-28, 1976, Instituto Latinamericano de Estudios Transnacionales, Mexico 20, D.F.

22. Salvoj Hskovec and Jaroslav First, *Introduction to News Agency Journalism* (Prague: International Organization of Journalists, 1972).

23. Azad Khadian Talivaya Ibragimov, "The Press in the Developing Countries of Asia and Africa: Its Social and Class Character and Function," *Developing World and Mass Media* (Prague: International Organization of Journalists, 1975), pp. 25–29.

24. *30 Years of the International Organization of Journalists in Action* (Praguo: International Organization of Journalists 1970), pp. 19–20.

25. *Journalists' Affairs,* November 22-24, 1976, p. 9, published by the International Organization of Journalists, Prague.

26. "Adherence to High Ideals," TASS report broadcast by Moscow Pravda in Russian, December 2, 1976.

4. IMPROVING NEWS FLOW IN THE THIRD WORLD

PETER GALLINER

There is little doubt that the grievances of the Third World countries concerning the present news flow system are intelligible and natural to some extent. But the problems cannot be overcome by blaming the West, nor by excluding the West. They can be tackled with a concerted effort on the part of the Third World countries, together with financial, technical, and moral support from the West.

THE CHOICES

It can be assumed that the Third World will not embrace the dogma either of the Soviet Union or of the West. But there are evidently advantages and attractions in each model, with regard to mass media systems. The choice must come from the Third World itself. No decisions can be imposed either by the East, the West, or the United Nations Educational, Scientific and Cultural Organization (UNESCO). The West can only point out the advantages and merits of the Western model, as well as the implicit dangers, as we see them, of the Soviet model. If we want to influence the tide of events, we must offer support for efforts of Third World countries to expand their communication system and encourage them to create a viable independent news agencies pool and to compete openly and on equal terms with existing agencies so that there is an increasingly free flow of information.

Soviet political ideology is based on the premise that the government and the people are one—that the state and the masses have a single, common purpose and that the Soviet government is the only true representative of the people. According to this logic, there is no inconsistency or lack of "freedom" in the fact that the media are owned and controlled exclusively by the government and the Communist party. Newspapers act as instruments of information, propaganda, and education, and journalists as agents of the government.

Although Soviet citizens are free to send letters to government-appointed newspaper editors criticizing certain articles and even the implementation of some government policies, there is no criticism of the policies themselves, nor any questioning of the basis of the Soviet system. In other words, criticism can only be superficial and never fundamental.

The Soviets made no secret of the fact that the mass media in their society are only for the purposes of information, propaganda, and education. Any criticism of the government or of Marxism-Leninism is regarded as anti-Soviet propaganda and counterrevolutionary. A government that believes it is the only true representative of the people has no tolerance for serious critics. Dissidents are locked up; any publication that does not fully accord with the Marxist-Leninist line is forced underground.

Moscow scorns the Western concept of press freedom, asserting that the Western press is in the hands of a few press barons (whose U.S. contingent apparently lives exclusively on Wall Street). Hence there is no press freedom for the masses. Press freedom in the Western sense, that is, the existence of a diversity of newspapers, and therefore of political views, and the freedom to publish anything within broad limits, is irrelevant in a society that considers itself inherently and unarguably right.

It is not difficult to see the attraction this concept of the mass media holds for certain Third World leaders. A few are genuinely Marxist in their outlook and therefore adopt this model on theoretical grounds. Others, such as one-party or one-man dictatorships, take advantage of the Soviet model to impose censorship, imprison journalists, and prevent criticism, subversion, and dissidence within their own societies. Still others adopt this model of state control because they can envisage no other way for the media to operate in the context of national development. It is this latter group that perhaps deserves most sympathy and understanding from the West.

According to Western tradition (which embraces the countries of Western Europe, North America, Japan, and some countries of the Third World), the role of the press is not only to inform people, but also to scrutinize and criticize government policies and the government itself. The emphasis is on truth and accuracy rather than on propaganda for mobilizing the people. The press, which is usually privately owned and independently run, is one of the many checks and balances essential for the functioning of a democratic society.

Freedom of the press is in no sense absolute, but compared with an authoritarian society such as that of the Soviet Union, the press is far freer in the West. It is freer because it is not controlled by one social force, but subject to pressures from several different sources. While the editor must bow to these pressures to some extent, none can dictate what the paper should print.

The pressures on an editor in a typical Western society may come from proprietors, trade unions, readers, the government, or advertisers. Because he must give some satisfaction to all these sectors, the successful, independent editor cannot afford to follow a single political line. In order to create a "marketable package," he must include a diversity of views within his newspaper. Papers that do adopt a single political line or are concerned with one particular subject are generally subsidized by, for example, a political party or a religious group. But the existence of these specialized newspapers is no threat to a free society, but rather enhances the freedom because the public has a wider choice of reading material. Where there is plurality, there is freedom of the press.

In the West there is an extremely wide choice of newspapers starting from the serious opinion-making journals such as the *New York Times,* the *London Times,* and *Le Monde* to the sensational press catering to the lowest common denominator. But this fault is surely less corruptive than government control where truth is distorted and propaganda churned out for political motives.

The attractions of the Western model are the self-evident high standards of reporting, the relative objectivity and accuracy of information, as well as freedom from any particular government line. Even in the eyes of the Third World, the four major western agencies compare favorably with the Soviet agency Telegrafnoye Agentstvo Sovietskovo Soyuza (TASS) and the Hsinhua agency of the People's Republic of China (PRC).

There is a very obvious advantage for Third World leaders in encouraging objective and accurate reporting. If a government controls its media, how can any neighboring government then trust news reports put out by its national news agency? It is hardly beneficial for any state if nations learn about each other only what their leaders allow. Reports from such biased sources can never be fully reliable.

REGIONAL NEWS AGENCIES

Because news tends to flow vertically from advanced nations to developing nations, there is inevitably a need for a wider horizontal news flow between Third World countries, especially those that are neighbors. Regional news agencies could not only fill this gap, but they could also help to integrate the countries of a particular region and facilitate their economic and cultural development. Instead of one central news agency pool, the Third World could be served by three or four regional agencies (at least initially) that could then exchange information with each other.

Latin America

One of the few existing Third World regional agencies is the Caribbean News Agency (CANA), which was established in July 1975 with the help of UNESCO. It began operating in conjunction with the Reuters Carribbean news service, but in January 1976, after a six-month interim period, CANA became an independent agency. (See Guido Fernandez' chapter on the Agencia Centro Americana, Noticias-(ACAN) for a description of another regional news agency functioning in Latin America.)

CANA may serve as a model for other regional news agencies in the Third World. With a worldwide trend toward greater economic interdependence and integration between neighboring countries, there is a vital need to create a regional communication system to facilitate and encourage this integration. Instant reporting on market conditions and prices, for example, is of vital importance for the economic planning of a region. It is therefore in the interest of all to have factual day-to-day information without reference to the preferences of those in power. Quite apart from this development role, regional agencies answer the Third World complaints against the present state of communications and information flow.

There is, however, the danger of a regional agency's becoming purely an instrument of governments and not subject to any objective forces. But in the case of the Caribbean area the press and broadcasting are both state and privately owned. Because of the existence of some privately owned media, there was enough pressure to prevent the creation of a government-controlled news agency.

CANA is owned by 17 media institutions and governed by an elected board of directors from the media world. In 1972, the governments of the region pledged not to exert full control over the proposed news agency. But many continued to argue that by virtue of their ownership of some media organizations, governments could still exert heavy pressure and influence, if not full control, simply as subscribers to the service.

Ken Gordon, chairman of the CANA board, stressed that the news agency would be an independent service guided by the highest professional standards. The Caribbean agency, he added, was committed to regional development. In the three years of planning, he said, problems such as the "fundamental differences and weaknesses" between the Caribbean states had had to be coped with, as well as the "complicated structure of Caribbean media ownership." In answer to the argument that government participation in CANA meant ipso facto government control of the agency, he said that "it is our hope that the quality of the service will provide effective answers."

In the course of its first year of operation, CANA apparently established itself as both an independent and highly professional news agency. It more than doubled its output of regional news, although this is still minute. The number of subscribers has steadily increased and CANA now serves, among others, Cuba, Surinam, the United States, and the PRC.

At the UNESCO-sponsored Intergovernmental Conference on Communication Policies in Latin America and the Caribbean in Costa Rica in July 1976, the meeting recommended the establishment of a Latin American news agency. No concrete follow-up steps have yet been taken but this prospect is far more ominous than the Caribbean scheme because the vast majority of Latin American countries restrict press freedom by government control and interference in the media. The IPI Annual Review of World Press Freedom describes violations of press freedom in Latin America as among the worst in the world, with "government and government-inspired terror campaigns against the freedom of expression" particularly brutal in Argentina, Brazil, Chile, and Uruguay.

The Arab World and Africa

Arab and African countries have recently discussed the possibility of establishing a pan-African news agency. (See Mohamed Abdel Gawad's chapter for the background of this effort.) The latest meeting was held in Tripoli at the end of March 1977. Representatives from 51 Arab and African news agencies decided upon immediate measures for increasing cooperation in the field of information. The conference, which was held under the auspices of the Organization of African Unity (OAU) and the Arab League, called on all agencies concerned to begin exchanging news and photographs with each other. Delegates called for the opening of joint offices in Arab and African capitals to serve as centers for the collection and dissemination of news. The meeting also recommended a study of a proposal for setting up a joint Arab and African news agency.

Asia

There have been no formal proposals to establish a regional news agency in Asia, although news is exchanged between several national agencies, and the Press Foundation of Asia (PFA) has started a weekly news and feature service (Development, Economics, and Population Themes News (DEPTHnews), which transmits news in seven languages and four dialects (see S. M. Ali's chapter on DEPTHnews). This is a beginning, but a very modest one, taking into consideration the vastness of the continent and the enormous variety of languages and dialects.

The Malaysian national news agency, Bernama, exchanges some feature stories with Antara, its Indonesian counterpart. These two news agencies also exchanged some information with the short-lived Indian news agency, Samachar. There have been rumors that the Philippines government, which controls the media in the Philippines, is planning to create an international agency that would be controlled and financed by that government.

In general, news exchange arrangements in Asia are in a state of flux pending the outcome of the news agency pool proposals. But again the outlook is somewhat bleak, because only the press of Japan, Hong Kong, and, now once again, India can be considered free in the whole of Asia. Furthermore, the few remaining Western news agencies and correspondents in Southeast Asia continue to be harrassed and expelled.

UNESCO's ROLE

⌐UNESCO's part in the efforts of Third World countries to have their own independent information network has been well examined and documented. UNESCO on the one hand has provided a platform for the promotion of the state-run media systems and on the other has served as a forum for discussion among member countries.⌐

Up until the UNESCO general conference held in Nairobi in October-November, 1976, the influence of the Soviet Union was pervasive in UNESCO thinking on communication policy. Western nations only woke up to the fact that UNESCO was practically sanctioning state control of the media in the Third World in time to shelve the provocative "Draft Declaration of Fundamental Principles Governing the Use of the Mass Media in Strengthening Peace and International Understanding and in Combating War, Propaganda, Racism and Apartheid." The proposal constituted a serious threat to press freedom even outside the developing countries, particularly with regard to Article X, which urged states be given the right to "correct" news deemed to be "erroneous," and Article XII, which called for each state to be made responsible for the international activities of its own media.

UNESCO's endeavors to formulate a communication policy dates back as far as the late 1960s. Although the free flow of information and the pursuit of objective truth are principles enshrined in its 1945 charter, UNESCO has been made to appear to favor a policy that effectively supports state control of the mass media.

While recognizing UNESCO's general concern with the free flow of information and the freedom of expression, IPI has condemned UNESCO's support for government-controlled news agencies and the extension of state control to the international arena. In its eagerness to assist developing countries in overcoming their dependency on advanced countries, UNESCO has turned a blind eye to the fact that the majority of Third World countries having a government-controlled press constantly violate the laws of press freedom by imposing censorship, imprisoning and harassing local journalists, and expelling foreign correspondents.

UNESCO should act as a forum for discussion so as to bring out the full implications of the Third World proposals for an independent communication system, including the setting up of one or more news agencies pools.

TASK FOR THE WEST AND THE IPI

The need for change in the present system of communications in the Third World is indisputable. Western (and communist) sources of news do not serve the Third World well, and the wish of Third World nations to develop independent news agencies and news agencies pools should be supported. It is in the interests of Western nations and Western-inspired press organizations to respond to this need and to lend all assistance, as well as expertise and advice, to the areas where it is most required. There is ample room for cooperation and exchange of views —the West has a lot to offer in return for high professional standards of reporting by the new Third World agencies and a guarantee that no government or group of governments will attempt to monopolize the Third World media and exclude competition among all agencies.

Third World Coverage

The complaints from the Third World about Western news agencies are largely based on a misunderstanding of the conditions of the Western media. News agencies in the developed countries have no means of forcing their subscribers to publish their reports. They have to rely on the sheer quality of their reporting. The serious press in the West publishes more information on the developing countries than those countries do on important events outside their own frontiers.

But while it is perhaps understandable that Western audiences are not very interested in irrigation schemes in Africa, for example, there is a strong case for arguing that they should be. IPI's founder, Lester Markel, wrote in 1976 about the importance of international news to everyone: "In this interdependent world, we are affected by almost any event almost anywhere. International news is not foreign; it is local, it is immediate, it is highly relevant to the nation and to the people."

Aid

The Western nations can provide technical and financial help as well as expertise in setting up and expanding new channels of communication across the continents of the Third World.

Western agencies are, and have been, making great efforts to make their services available in the Third World. In return, if the Third World ultimately succeeds in building up its own continuous flow of information, arrangements can be made for Western agencies to use these sources. Considering the rising cost of maintaining foreign correspondents abroad, and particularly in the Third World where the market is declining, agreements on these lines could be highly beneficial to the West. But such an exchange could only be viable if news reports came from independent sources and were reliable, accurate, and objective.

Dialogue

At a Tunisia meeting of the heads of about 40 news agencies from Africa, the Middle East, and Europe held at the end of November 1976, the Iraq News Agency representative complained that even when his agency transmitted a large number of words to the West, few were ever used. In the London *Times* of December 2, Kenneth Mackenzie retorted that "one reason why so little Iraq material was used was because it was not presented in an acceptable form." But no one at the conference had had the courage to say this. Evidently, there is a vital need for more conferences and seminars between media representatives from both advanced and developing countries to discuss such problems as these and to work out precisely what each wants and needs from the other. Lack of communication between the different halves of the world is as much a problem as any.

IPI would be willing and able to organize such conferences to encourage greater interaction and understanding between journalists of the West and journalists of the Third World. IPI sponsored two 10-day meetings between Western financial experts and journalists and a number of African journalists, held in Accra and Nairobi, in 1977. The purpose of these meetings was to hold training and working sessions on the problems of reporting on economic and financial affairs for African journalists.

IPI has also sponsored a meeting of journalists from independent black Africa and white-ruled Africa in Nairobi in 1977. The aim of this meeting was not only to bring together professionals in the same field facing broadly similar problems but also to initiate some sort of dialogue between black and white-ruled Africa. Although such a meeting was politically highly sensitive, there were journalists from both areas who were realistic enough to belive that a meeting of like professional minds was a contribution worth attempting.

Training

Apart from technical assistance, financial aid, and conferences, the West can also contribute enormously toward the creation of an independent press in the Third World through training programs. Some Western newspapers, news agencies, and organizations (such as the Commonwealth Press Union) already train interns. These schemes will, it is hoped, be expanded and new ones launched in the next few years.

IPI has launched training programs for journalists both in Asia and Africa in the past, and there are plans for further training programs in the near future. The changeover from colonial status to independence brought with it a certain amount of disorientation. Existing media were taken over by local interests who lacked training, experience, and know-how, but had political power. There was evidently a need for training.

IPI's task in Asia in the early 1960s was to modernize the already existing press at both management and journalistic levels. But while there had been a long-established press in Asia, there was virtually no indigenous press in Africa when IPI ventured there in 1962. The African training program was set up in accordance with certain basic principles: to assist the Africanization of the media in newly independent English-speaking countries, to assist in raising professional standards as Africans took over from Europeans, and to align the media to the task of national development.

Institutions to train journalists were set up at the University of East Africa in Nairobi (serving Central and East Africa), and the University of Lagos, Nigeria. The training schools ran six-month courses for five and a half years, training over 300 African men and women.

Frank Barton, director of IPI's African training program aimed to teach the students some of the basic journalistic skills, such as reporting, interviewing, subediting, layout, and the use of government handouts. On the question of press freedom, Barton found a "clash of loyalties" between nationalism and journalism. The students understood the importance of objectivity and accurate reporting, but most Africans were fiercely nationalistic and their countries came first. "The freedom of the press," said Barton, "is something very low on the list of Africa's priorities." This is a conflict in the African heart that must be understood by the West if training is going to be successful.

Although it could be greatly expanded, the IPI program was extremely successful. The graduates of the training school quickly moved into senior positions in the press and broadcasting organizations of their countries or became information ministers or press officers in their embassies.

The initial training program was followed by the creation of an advisory service to help senior journalists—generally IPI graduates—with specific problems and to respond generally to requests for help from the media in Africa. The service, like the training schools, operated on the basis of strict noninvolvement in national politics and ideologies.

More than 20 seminars and workshops were organized for journalists and broadcasters, normally geared to a specific theme such as the role of the media in nation-building, newspaper production, and the rights and responsibilities of the media.

A quarterly publication, *The African Journalist,* was launched to encourage professionalism among the new African journalists. It also provided information about other countries, thus reducing isolation and allowing comparisons between different countries of the continent. A training manual, *The African Newsroom,* specifically designed for African journalists was also published; it covers reporting techniques, news editing, subediting, feature writing, layout, photo editing, and the running of a newspaper library. It has become an invaluable textbook in schools of journalism and in newspaper offices in Africa.

Apart from past activities in Africa and plans for future ventures there, IPI has been active in other ways with regard to new developments in the Third World media. We have already commissioned research into the whole complex of problems discussed in this article.

Our response to the suggestion that IPI could be used as a vehicle for multinational sponsorship of Third World projects is that we would accept this challenge only on certain conditions. Although the institute can provide the expertise and organization for cooperative ventures with the Third World, it would not accept money from any individual government. We would rather consider accepting funds channeled, for example, through the United Nations or a special trust set up for the purpose of aiding the Third World. Government contributions are already channeled through UNESCO and this organization has promised to aid the Third World both financially (to a very minor extent) and technically. But IPI, and other organizations willing to participate in Third World projects, would sponsor training schemes, advisory services, seminars and conferences, and any other ventures beneficial to the free flow of information throughout the world.

5. THE WESTERN WIRE SERVICES AND THE THIRD WORLD

MORT ROSENBLUM

A first-time visitor to an overseas bureau of any news agency seldom comes away unsurprised, whatever his background in journalism or foreign affairs. If logic suggested that he expect a huge newsroom overflowing with editors and teleprinters, he might find a cubbyhole buried in papers with no one to answer the phone when the correspondent is out collecting bills. If he thought he would find a lone, bewildered reporter, struggling through day-old newspapers, he might encounter a news staff of five locally hired nationals directed by a multilingual veteran with 10 years at his current post. And in neither case would appearances give any clue about the ability of the bureau to accurately reflect realities of the country it covers.

The day-to-day operation of news agencies of all stripes is perhaps the least understood and most discussed aspect of world communications. It eludes analysis by measuring-stick or personnel counts. It confounds—and confirms—the myths; virtually any view can be substantiated or refuted by sufficient searching for examples. Since this holds true even for reporting among the major industrialized countries, the level of misunderstanding about reporting between developed nations and the Third World can scarcely be exaggerated.

This chapter does not challenge the validity of an orderly examination of the failings and strengths of international reporting. But it underscores the need to consider the specific structures and practices of news-gathering organizations in any discussion on the exchange of news and ideas among nations. It will outline the links among the various global, regional and national news agencies—and the international syndicates—that collect and transmit news among Western countries and the Third World.

Before considering how the agencies operate in practice, it is necessary to identify them briefly, by size and purpose.

THREE GROUPS OF NEWS AGENCIES

There are five predominant world news agencies and dozens of smaller agencies that also report news across borders. These transnational news services, in turn, subscribe to scores of national agencies, sometimes using their dispatches with hardly a comma changed, forming a layered global network almost too complex to plot accurately. Some agencies make direct exchanges with one another, with each having the right to use the other's dispatches by only changing the logotype. Often substantial payments are made when exchanges are unequal; contracts generally limit the conditions under which one agency can borrow from another. The lines can be so blurred that, for example, an Indonesian official might complain about a Reuters dispatch from Jakarta that is nothing more than a slightly rewritten version of a story distributed by the government-backed Indonesian agency, Antara. The official might not have seen the original Antara story and, if he had, he might not have interpreted it as being critical because of its source.

It is virtually impossible to establish a clear ranking of agencies by impact on the total system. Statistics and wordage totals are misleading because agencies calculate their figures in a variety of ways. Also, the weight of 100 words from Agency A can be indefinably greater than 100 words from Agency B, depending upon the judgment and prejudice of the reader. Despite these limitations, broad lines can be drawn.

The Associated Press (AP), based in New York, is considered to be the largest and the most influential agency because of the collective import of the newspapers and broadcasters around the world that rely primarily upon it for news and photographs. The combined readers and listeners of AP's 8,500 subscribers approaches a billion people.

There is such a dispute over which agency is the oldest that when the four major Western services set up booths at a Malaysian conference, three of them put up signs reading, ". . . the world's oldest news agency." AP was founded in New York in 1848, three years before Baron Julius von Reuters began his service, but it was a number of years before AP was a full-fledged international agency. Agence France-Presse (AFP), the French agency, traces its founding back to the now defunct Havas agency that began operations in 1835.

AP and Reuters, which is based in London, are both nonprofit cooperatives, owned principally by the newspapers in their home countries. United Press International (UPI), with headquarters in New York, is a privately owned company, but it operates similarly to AP and Reuters. All three are free of government involvement, and their news reports are generally considered to be basically reliable and free of intentional bias. AFP has an equally important impact on global journalism, and it is widely respected. Some editors, however, have expressed a concern that large subscription payments from the French government might cast a shade on its autonomous status. AFP executives say there is no government connection. The fifth global agency, Telegrafnoye Agentstvo Sovietskovo Soyuza (TASS), is the official organ of the Soviet Union, and its highly politicized news report clearly reflects the thinking of the Kremlin.

Some agencies are stronger than others in different parts of the world, reflecting not only national interests but also remnants of a cartel that was not dissolved until 1935. Before AP forced a dissolution of the cartel, three agencies—English, French and German—had divided the world among themselves, with each having exclusive rights for news gathering and distribution in its own area. Even after the cartel ended, agencies tended to concentrate their efforts in regions where their base countries had substantial economic interests or colonial ties. Reuters and AFP are far stronger in Africa, and AP and UPI predominate in Latin America. Many newspapers and radio stations around the world, however, subscribe to several of the big agencies, either directly or through national agencies that distribute limited versions of their full report, and all four agencies have many thousands of subscribers in more than 100 countries. The TASS report goes to 300 subscribers in scores of countries and, counting radio audiences, it could reach hundreds of millions of people.

Staff totals for the major agencies mean little without an understanding of how each agency works in practice. The basic staff of each revolves around bureau chiefs and correspondents hired in the headquarters country and trained in the home office. As a rule, they are citizens of the agency's home country, but each organization has a number of exceptions. The important distinction is that they are rotated from place to place and may return to the home office for desk assignments. This group can be designated "foreign service" newsmen. They are assisted by locally hired newsmen, either citizens of the country in which they are reporting or nationals of a third country who are fluent in the local language. Many of these have spent time at Western universities and have worked at least briefly at the agency's headquarters. Some are U.S. nationals and Europeans with long experience. But if they are hired to work in a specific bureau on a local wage scale, they do not fall into the foreign-service category. Agencies also make wide use of "stringers," part-time newsmen who range from well-trained journalists supporting themselves by covering news for several organizations at a time to government employees earning a few extra dollars by sending an occasional noncontroversial cable.

Overseas, AP has about 80 foreign-service correspondents; UPI has fewer than 70. Each of the two agencies has five to six times as many locally hired newsmen, not counting stringers. Information supplied by Reuters in late 1976 said that that agency had "about 350 full-time correspondents" but it did not break down the figures into nationalities or categories. AFP statistics showed 792 journalists abroad, but no details were given. AFP, aided by what amounts to an indirect subsidy, often keeps staff correspondents in bureaus regarded as uneconomical by the other three agencies. TASS has several hundred Soviet reporters abroad.

Wordage counts are equally confusing because of duplication. Each agency has specialized regional services that provide major general items but also stories of limited interest to the area served. An AFP fact sheet gives the following daily breakdown, which indicates how regional services are organized:

- service in English, French, and German for Europe and America: 230,000 words
- transmissions in Spanish to Latin America: 45,000 words
- transmissions in French to eastern Europe and the Middle East: 25,000 words
- service in English and French to Africa: 21,000–27,000 words
- separate English-language service to North America: 35,000 words
- English-language service to Asia: 30,000; French service to Asia: 5,000 (Additionally, 7,000–9,000 words are collected and redistributed daily within Asia for local subscribers.)
- transmissions in French to the Pacific and the Antilles and for ships at sea

A Reuters fact sheet notes that an average of 1.5 million words are sent out from London each day. Like AFP, the Reuters file is broken down into regional services. AP and UPI each send out well over a million words daily, transmitting in English and Spanish from New York and in other languages from regional translation points. AP is delivered directly in nine languages around the world.

Operating budgets reveal little in a comparison because each agency has a different financial structure. Most agencies lose money on their news-gathering activities and, if possible, make up the difference with supplemental services or, in the case of some, with subsidies. Reuters maintains profitable economic news services and also rents time on some of its communications lines to offset the costs of collecting general news. AP and UPI rely heavily on income from photo sales. AP received and spent about $100 million in 1976. That was the largest reported agency budget.

A second tier of international agencies, largely aided by government funds, competes with the main news services in some major market areas. The most important of these is Deutsche-Presse Agentur (DPA), which is owned by West German newspapers, with each limited to a maximum interest of two percent. DPA also receives substantial payments for services from the West German government that allow it to maintain some prestige services that it could not otherwise afford. In early 1977, DPA had 49 German correspondents abroad, aided by 32 locally hired newsmen, and it distributed news in German, English, and Spanish in 78 countries to 145 subscribers. (Since one-third of those were national news agencies, the number of newspapers served is considerably higher.) Other middle-level agencies are ANSA of Italy, Kyoto and Jiji Press of Japan, and EFE of Spain.

The principal government-controlled agency of the Third World, Yugoslavia's Tanjug, distributes news in a number of countries, with its own correspondents assigned abroad. It also relays news from other national agencies of developing countries as part of the pool arrangement approved at a 58-nation Summit Conference of Nonaligned Countries in Colombo, Sri Lanka, in August 1976. Tanjug had 47 Yugoslav correspondents based abroad in early 1977. Despite widely heard Third World complaints about lack of attention to news in developing areas, most Tanjug correspondents were in industrialized countries.

Tanjug has been carrying unedited dispatches from other national agencies since early 1975; several other Third World agencies have been distributing pooled reports on a limited basis in recent months. Whatever value national agencies might place on receiving such direct, government-controlled reporting from other developing countries, the pool arrangement has meant little to the major agencies' news-gathering processes. The main international agencies monitor national agencies directly in their various bureaus, and news items are read by newsmen familiar with local conditions. By the time the same items are relayed by a pool agency, far from the country of origin, they have already been read and evaluated.

In order to attract and retain subscribers overseas, some of the second-tier agencies make their services available for only a token payment—or for free. Even DPA, which is not a government agency, has maintained an English-language service to Africa for only 10 subscribers. Several years ago, DPA finally cancelled its French service to Africa after, according to DPA executives, most of the remaining six or seven subscribers fell far behind in their payments. The smaller international agencies tend to provide good coverage of sports and entertainment to offer editors something that they may not get from the larger and more news-oriented agencies. These deficit-level rates and costly special features underscore the reliance on government subsidy by some of the smaller agencies, but, at the same time, these organizations often make an effort to report objectively in order to maintain credibility.

A third group of transnational agencies covers news in specific geographic regions, often with political intent. The Middle East News Agency (MENA) of Egypt predominates in the Arab states (see the chapter by Mohamed Abdel Gawad). Libya's Arab Revolution News Agency (ARNA) is seeking greater influence, particularly in North Africa. Zaire is promoting a pan-African news agency in black Africa, and its organizers have resisted efforts by north African nations to join in. Cuba's Prensa Latina is widely distributed in Latin America. There has been talk of forming a transnational agency in Southeast Asia but, although several neighboring national agencies cooperate closely, none yet has been formed.

A different sort of regional agency has been operating with limited success in Latin America since 1971. The agency, LATIN, was organized with assistance from Reuters as a cooperative among 13 member newspapers from Mexico to Chile. It was originally conceived as a way for Latin American newspapers to receive dispatches from Latin American journalists, along with world news from an established international agency. Reuters, at the same time, would cheaply and effectively cover a large geographical area in which it had traditionally been weak. It was set up and put into operation largely by Patrick Cross, a veteran Reuters executive seconded to LATIN.

According to the original plan, LATIN was to remain independent, gathering all Latin American news for its members and for Reuters while it distributed Reuters dispatches from the rest of the world to its own membership. The two agencies shared a large office in Buenos Aires where their respective reports could be shared and relayed. In practice, a number of difficulties arose. Because of the widely varying political viewpoints of LATIN members, some editors felt that LATIN correspondents did not provide what they considered to be complete and objective reporting. Financial problems and pressure from some Latin American governments forced LATIN to cut back service or, at least, tread lightly. There were internal disputes among the original members.

Although Reuters continued to make partial use of LATIN dispatches for its world services, a half dozen Reuters correspondents placed around Latin America provided backup coverage. Reuters remained closely linked to LATIN, administratively and financially; the Reuters manager for Latin America was, in effect, the manager of LATIN, according to private evaluations by executives of the two agencies.

An important source of revenue has been payments by the Venezuelan government to distribute information via Reuters communications network.

By 1977, about a dozen newspapers had governing "member" status and scores of other newspapers and organizations paid a much lower monthly rate as nonvoting subscribers. LATIN maintained 21 correspondents around the Americas, including an excellent bureau in Washington. Some LATIN members expressed strong feelings that the agency should be nurtured to strength—and eventual autonomy—since it was one of the few Latin American transnational enterprises of any type. But it was clear it depended largely on Reuters for survival.

The LATIN experiment appears to suggest that the major agencies can—if willing because of their own interest—help to establish viable regional agencies that are better equipped to provide stories of local interest. But unless the regional agencies are adequately funded, with strong administrative structures to overcome internal dissent, the secondary agencies run a strong risk of becoming awkward appendages of the larger agencies.

At the national level, there are more than 90 officially backed agencies in the world, along with scores of independent agencies that operate within the confines of a single country. These are too diverse to describe in general terms. The smallest, such as Gabon's news service, are little more than brief government information bulletins. The larger ones operate full-time teleprinter service to hundreds of newspapers and radio stations. A number of national agencies in Third World countries have received technical assistance, advice, and help in training journalists from Western agencies, particularly Reuters and AFP.

In states with firm governments and no tradition of free expression —a large percentage of the world's countries—national news agencies are seldom more than official propaganda services. At the same time, some do a good job of covering nonpolitical stories and news from outlying provinces. As a general rule, government-funded agencies spend more money than they take in, and authorities consider the deficit as money well spent to put across the official point of view. In many developing countries, even where there are privately owned newspapers and radio stations, the deficits are enormous because large sums are spent for sophisticated communications systems and networks of correspondents that allow leaders to address their entire nations. These systems often span jungles and connect isolated islands to capital cities. Such coverage might not be possible with the limited means of an independently financed agency. But the government involvement means careful control over the news report. In some Third World countries, independent national news agencies maintain their own means of transmission, but governments exercise pressure by selectively assigning radio frequencies and by allowing the competing official agency to offer subsidized token rates.

Apart from the international news agencies, some major Western newspapers syndicate the reporting of their correspondents, although most of their subscribers are in the United States, Europe, and Japan. The largest such syndicate is The New York Times, which sells its service to about 450 papers in the world. The *Washington Post* and the *Los Angeles Times* have a combined service. The New York Times Service has 33 correspondents abroad; the Post-Times service has 29 together.

HOW THE AGENCIES WORK

The way the various agencies of the world go about covering news bears little relationship to their place in any simplified set of generalities. In any given instance, a small agency with a questionable record of objectivity may do a far better job of reporting than the superagencies. A basic rule of journalism holds that no organization can be any better than its reporter at the original point of contact with the news. If the original information is wrong, no amount of clever editing or packaging can make it right. This is an extremely important factor in international reporting where alternate information is scarce, and editors have little opportunity to compare reports from their correspondents with other sources. Although the major agencies tend to be more careful in hiring and training journalists, and their salaries are generally higher, there is surely no guarantee that every reporter for a superagency is better than every reporter for a smaller agency. And, even though an agency with a reputation for objectivity might be more careful to avoid bias in editing, dispatches from government news agencies can sometimes present a more balanced picture of local developments than those of the independent global agencies.

Obviously, the character of the agency affects what gets covered and what is included in the dispatch. The major agencies concentrate on overriding political and economic issues that might have significance for wide areas of the rest of the world. They will include the dramatic and the emotional, but the main concern is reporting fundamental change. Gerald Long, general manager of Reuters, touched this point in an interview in late 1976, referring to India as an example:

> We are sometimes accused of not doing what we have not set out to do. How can you give a complete picture of India in, say, 3,000 words a day? No, we're not and we can't. . . . We must operate on the principle of news as exception. Reuters tries to give a fair picture, a rounded picture, but we can only send a limited amount, and we must be selective.

Some smaller or specialized agencies might emphasize news of a more specific interest. Obviously, DPA will give more coverage to a German aid project than any other agency will. Tanjug is more likely to write at length about a cooperative agricultural plan that could be applied elsewhere in Third World.

Newspaper correspondents generally take a different approach entirely. They tend to take a more subjective and analytical viewpoint than agency reporters because they write toward one specific market. At the same time, they have greater length in which to explain opposing outlooks and to expound upon what might be considered gratuitous criticism if stated briefly.

Coverage is affected by a number of factors beyond the talents and energies of the individual newsmen involved and the general policy of the agency. Government interference and inaccessibility of sources often play a major role. The time available for each reporter to collect and to verify news is vitally important. The larger agencies frequently have an advantage because they can spare a reporter to track down sources and investigate background material; but in many capitals the smaller agencies actually have more reporters, with fewer administrative duties to occupy their time. The deployment of correspondents is sporadic, with little direct relationship to the size or economic importance of the countries involved. Each agency establishes its priorities according to the intangible criterion of "newsworthiness," based largely upon historic and current interest to the media in the agency's home country. Reuters and AFP, for example, cover Africa closely because of past and present ties. AP and UPI cover Latin America particularly well. EFE of Spain is at its strongest in Latin America, and Japan's Kyoto has major bureaus in Southeast Asia. Sometimes government agencies place correspondents in countries for purely political reasons having little to do with news judgment.

Since no agency can afford to maintain a heavy presence everywhere, each keeps major regional bureaus scattered about the globe from which correspondents keep an eye on breaking news in the neighborhood. That means, however, that peripheral countries may be covered on a day-to-day basis only by part-time stringers, with little training or motivation, while regional-headquarters countries might be overcovered by newsmen with little to do between trips.

An area-by-area look at how the various agencies operate shows the difficulties and distortions involved. A particularly detailed study of Latin America demonstrates how the patterns apply throughout the Third World. These observations will provide, at best, a broad idea of how the news flows to and from the Third World; they are not intended as criticisms or apologia of any specific organizations or sectors.

Latin America

Nearly every transnational agency reporting from Latin America has its major presence in Argentina, often with sizable bureaus in Mexico and Brazil. Buenos Aires, well situated and comfortable, has long been the principal city in Latin America. Rio de Janeiro and Sao Paulo are less important, despite their commercial positions, because Brazil is the only Latin American country where Portuguese is spoken. Caracas or Mexico City may now rival Buenos Aires in impact on the region, but the moving of established news centers is difficult, and agencies tend toward conservatism. Also, most organizations prefer a base well to the south since U.S. based reporters can easily cover the north, if necessary. Apart from Argentina, Mexico, and Brazil, Latin American countries are lightly covered. At best, a lone correspondent is assigned from abroad with local newsmen as assistants. AP, for example, assigns reporters from the United States to Chile, Peru, Venezuela, and the Caribbean, outside of the major three countries. Full-time local newsmen report from Bolivia, Colombia, and Uruguay. In the other countries, AP stringers provide what coverage is needed.

Most agencies transmit a special Latin American report in Spanish intended only for newspapers and broadcasters in the region. It generally contains the lengthy declarations and complete political detail favored by most subscribers. Simultaneously, dispatches in English or the main language of the agency are sent to relay desks for distribution outside the region. These usually have more background and colorful detail for readers who may know little about the local context of the news.

The special regional service is far more extensive. AP and UPI direct an estimated 80 percent of their total wordage from Latin America bureaus to subscribers in Latin America. Although some items are written by U.S. nationals and translated into Spanish in New York, most are originally written in Spanish by local newsmen. While it is true, for example, that Uruguayan newspapers receive regional stories largely via large international agencies, nearly all the stories are written by Latin Americans—often by Uruguayans—with the eventual reader firmly in mind.

The Latin American news destined for worldwide distribution is largely gathered by local newsmen. In the case of the larger agencies, such dispatches are often a combination of facts assembled by national newsmen and by foreign-based reporters, and they may be written originally by either. Since staffs are small and news often breaks in torrents, there are no fixed rules or ironclad procedures.

Reuters and LATIN operate differently from the other agencies. Dispatches from the correspondents of both agencies are received in their shared offices in Buenos Aires. LATIN editors make up one report, relying mostly on LATIN dispatches from the region and on Reuters cables from the rest of the world, for distribution within Latin America. Reuters deskmen edit and relay stories from their own reporters, if available. Otherwise, they translate LATIN dispatches, working in material from the files or from their own knowledge to provide a larger context. The stories leaving Buenos Aires are already translated, edited, and ready for distribution throughout the system.

TASS correspondents in Latin America file in Russian or Spanish to Moscow, sometimes via New York. Soviet editors prepare regionalized reports in various languages along with a basic service for news organizations within the Soviet Union.

Because of its editing operation, Reuters has the most non-Latin American newsmen in Buenos Aires, usually three or four. In early 1977, AP, UPI, and AFP each had two, although UPI had an additional American supervising editor and, over the whole operation, a regional executive of French nationality. The agency staffs do not only collect and transmit news but they also supervise the incoming report. The Buenos Aires bureaus of the major and middle-level agencies employ at least 12 and sometimes more than 20 locally hired editors, operators, clerks, and messengers. The sales, bill collections, technical problems, and related personnel concerns can take up well over half the time of the executives and staff members sent from abroad.

Working conditions vary widely from one country to another and from one government to the next. And each agency has its own way of dealing with the political climate and the physical obstacles; this, too, changes with the bureau chief on the spot and with overall headquarters policy.

Perhaps the most serious continuing problem is direct or subtle government control over what agencies send. Even if restrictive measures are not applied, the fear of them forces many reporters to withhold vital information and to present imbalanced pictures of the countries they cover. In the past few years, Chile and Peru have expelled some reporters and banned the entry of others. During 1975, the AFP correspondent in Santiago, Jacques Kaufmann, was manacled and blindfolded by Chilean security officers who announced that they were going to kill him. He was held 48 hours and when they later returned to harass him again, he sought refuge in the French embassy and fled the country. Death squads linked to sectors of the Argentine government have threatened reporters in Buenos Aires, and some reporters for local newspapers have been killed mysteriously. EFE bureau chief Jose Antonio Rodriguez Couzeiro was arrested in 1976, and authorities accused him of possible links to the left because they found terrorist literature—a common part of any journalist's files—in his apartment. He was later released. In Uruguay, locally hired newsmen are regularly called before military authorities for psychological hazing. All agencies are required to submit copies of their outgoing dispatches to the Uruguayan interior ministry after transmission. Access to Cuba for most newsmen is strictly limited, available only in special cases. A number of Western reporters have been allowed to visit Cuba but only AFP and several smaller agencies have resident correspondents.

Such government interference has played a profound role in distorting news from Latin America, and elsewhere, causing contradictory images that confuse foreign readers. Since each agency reporter reacts to pressures differently, the result is bound to be a series of totally different pictures.

A few newsmen pay no attention to indirect harassment and, if they submit to censorship, they explain the measures fully in their dispatches. If they are competent and fair, the picture they present will be as close to accurate as possible (unless they are expelled and forced to report from outside). Some might pull their punches on negative aspects but attempt to balance their overall reporting by careful selection of topics. For example, if they avoid writing about the harsh treatment of political prisoners, they might also ignore a social program to help the aged. This type of coverage reveals little and seldom conveys the intended impression. And a large number of reporters simply avoid sensitive issues on the theory that it is better to remain out of trouble in order to continue reporting in the future. Several seize upon this reasoning as an excuse to sidestep difficult subjects that they might prefer not to cover because of lethargy, personal feelings, or fear. Some unnecessarily skirt sensitive issues with a clear conscience by unconsciously underestimating the value of their sources and the interest abroad or by overestimating the threat to their agencies. The obvious result is an overly favorable image that contrasts sharply with that reported at the other extreme.

The lesson drawn by many governments is that if enough pressure can be applied to force large numbers of reporters to write favorably, the few hard-hitting reporters can be singled out for special attention. At the same time, some governments find that if they apply no pressure at all, reporters' dispatches tend to be more critical because there is no fear of reprisal.

But experience has also shown that if enough reporters resist government pressure and report the news as they see it, authorities tend to rescind restrictive measures.

An obvious way to alleviate these problems would be for agency correspondents to cooperate among themselves, reporting frankly from all countries whether there is harassment or not. This might not be as difficult as it seems, since reporters tend to compare notes frequently. But the disparate characters of agencies and newsmen make it at least unlikely.

The international agencies in Latin America—as in the rest of the Third World—share the same basic elements for gathering news. National news services, where they exist, are principal sources. Argentina's official agency, Telam, supplies a low-cost teleprinter service around the clock, and its dispatches are tantamount to government statements. Whatever Telam says is news as long as it is clearly attributed as an official agency report. If a reporter cites Telam and then finds that the story is wrong, he can write a second dispatch contrasting his own information to the version put out by the government. Telam executives, aware that they may be embarrassed by distorted news items, tend to protect their credibility when they can. The largest problem is omission of important news. When Isabel Peron was being overthrown, the Telam wire was carrying sports news from the provinces. A second national news agency, Noticias Argentinas, is cooperatively owned by local newspapers. It was formed in 1973 to fill the gap left when the government forced AP and UPI to close down special national services operated within Argentina. Noticias Argentinas cannot be quoted with any official authority, but it is often faster than Telam, with more sensitive information. UPI sells international news to Noticias Argentinas and relies on it heavily for news sent abroad. AP subscribes to it, like other international agencies, but uses it mainly as a tip service for stories to be covered by AP reporters.

The national news agencies are valuable for texts, speeches, economic figures, sports items, and news about natural disasters and common crime. And, because of personal contacts, they are extremely useful even on the most delicate political items. Most reporters for the national agencies are close friends with those working for international services since many went to the same schools and worked on the same newspapers. In some cases, foreign service newsmen for the major agencies have helped to organize national agencies and to train their personnel. Often the reporters of the national agencies pass along information that is too sensitive for the national news agency wire, and, occasionally, they provide revealing insights about their agency's news decisions.

National news agencies and international agencies share another important role in the distribution of world news. In many countries, international agencies may only sell their services through a national agency, which, in turn, relays it to subscribing newspapers. Although the international agencies can attempt to prevent the national agencies from changing the wording of dispatches—thus distorting the content —there is virtually nothing that can be done about arbitrary trimming of the service. Some national agencies cut stories, or eliminate them completely, for political as well as space reasons, and it is often the international agency that is blamed for failure to report more fully.

The other fundamental sources are the local newspapers and radio stations, whether government-controlled or private. Each agency desk-man pays close attention to both. If he is conscientious and well informed, he will keep in mind the individual political leanings of each newspaper or radio station he deals with. There are still privately operated radio stations in Latin America, but most broadcasting facilities in the Third World are controlled directly by governments. Even if the news is one-sided, it is delivered quickly to a correspondent whether he is in his office, at home shaving, or off on a Sunday picnic. The radio can be indispensable when borders are closed—as was the case during the 1973 Chile coup d'etat—and some news agencies hire professional monitoring services to make sure they do not miss key broadcasts from neighboring countries.

Since no agency anywhere has enough reporters to do all the leg-work it might, each uses its own system of shortcuts. Some seldom go beyond the common pool of information. In Peru, for example, one correspondent for a regional news agency regularly picked up items from the local papers without checking, adding only the attribution, "according to official sources," on the grounds that the press was closely controlled by the government. But the local press was so unreliable that when the president turned 55, three of the daily papers got the age wrong.

Frequently, stories are checked out with a quick phone call to whichever source might be available. That guards against obvious falsifications and blatant errors, but it seldom adds important new information to the story. The more responsible reporters call as many sources as possible—often holding up the stories for hours and even days—to determine the accurate version.

The best correspondents make regular rounds of a wide range of government and private sources, which allow them to evaluate information from national news agencies and official spokesmen.

Often reporters cannot get out of the capital cities to see things for themselves, and they must rely on provincial newspapers and radio stations that might have serious biases. When peasants seized some land in northern Mexico late in 1976, some agencies reported the incidents as if they were the prelude to revolution. But U.S. newspaper reporters who visited the area found that the story had been exaggerated by local, landowner-controlled newspapers which had furnished information to the international agencies in Mexico. "We had to travel a day and a half to find the first case of fields being seized," said one *Los Angeles Times* reporter. "The story had been blown far out of shape."

The difficulty for the analyst—or the reader—is that it can be almost impossible to determine what shortcuts a reporter used. Although the major agencies attempt to check everything carefully, adding balance to dispatches, it is always up to the individual reporter. Many smaller agencies try to apply the same standards. But all reporters face similar government pressures and suffer the same failings; policy guidelines from headquarters do not always ensure complete reporting. If a newsman's techniques are not obvious from his writing, the only clue is his past record.

The question of sources is particularly important. A newspaper correspondent who reports to a single editor has greater liberty to use such vague attribution as "informed sources . . ." He is neither worried about a challenge from his copydesk nor an adverse reaction from the government. His paper trusts him to use solid sources, whether he names them or not. If he is expelled, he will be reassigned, and his newspaper at least will be covered in that country by the agencies. A news agency correspondent, however, must answer to thousands of editors who know nothing about him. Any may demand a stronger source identification. If he is ejected from a country, his agency may not only be without coverage, it might also suffer losses of revenue from subscribing local newspapers. Although the major agencies insist that financial considerations are kept separate from news decisions, and many correspondents ignore such pressures, expulsions are seldom looked upon happily. Therefore, if a correspondent is writing about sensitive information, he must provide significant clues about the authority and the diversity of his sources even if he does not name them.

That can be extremely difficult, as noted, and often a story is left unwritten.

Since all agencies are in a similar position in this respect, there is rarely a competitive factor forcing them to be more forthright. Unless one agency clearly establishes a pattern of torture and murder in Argentina, for example, none are constrained to take the initiative. And if an agency turns up its own evidence and attempts to show a pattern, others may choose to soft-pedal the evidence rather than find themselves in the risky position of having to support it or be left beaten by the competition.

After a dispatch is written and transmitted, it may be inadvertently distorted before it is distributed to subscribers. Control desks at agency headquarters are responsible for clear writing, solid attribution, and balance. But a sloppy rewrite man can inadvertently change the cited source, alter verb conditionals, and overstate the facts. Shortening stories can remove vital elements. When stories must be discarded for lack of wire space, the first to go might be the type of economic and social development items that Third World leaders would be happy to see.

The high-speed, overlapping operations of news agencies can compound errors with alarming magnitude. In July 1976, a young Chilean trainee at the UPI bureau in Bogota was practicing on the teletype with an imaginary flash announcing the murder of President Alfonso Lopez Michelsen. A switch was thrown by mistake and the dispatch, instead of remaining in the machine on a closed circuit, was sent through Caracas to New York. The desk translated the false story without rechecking and relayed it in English and Spanish to UPI subscribers. UPI caught the mistake within two minutes and killed the story, but, meanwhile, EFE's desk in Washington had seen the flash on its contracted UPI wire. EFE sent an unattributed story on the imaginary murder, with a Bogota dateline, and the Spanish agency's main office in Madrid embellished it with details not in the original phony dispatch. The news, from two agencies, was broadcast on Colombian radio stations, and the president was not easily convinced that he was not the victim of an international plot.

Sometimes news agency dispatches become entangled with local stories, creating confusion. In Lima, one agency reporter sent a story announcing the purchase of Soviet aircraft. The government denied the story, but soon afterward the correspondent saw a story in an officially controlled Lima daily confirming the purchase. He wrote a second story, quoting the newspaper's confirmation. But it turned out that the confirmation was simply a rewritten and unattributed version of his own original dispatch that the paper had received as part of the agency's regular report. (It made little difference, anyway, since not long after a spokesman denied the report, the Peruvian president confirmed it.)

Africa and the Middle East

The problems of news gathering in the Third World are most acute in Africa and parts of the Middle East. International news agencies concentrate on crisis centers—Lebanon, the Israeli borders, southern Africa—and pay scant attention to most other areas until they become a "story." There is little demand for African news in much of the world, and the costs of maintaining correspondents there are high. Some of those agencies that use government subsidies to offset the cost of keeping reporters in Africa are selective in what they report for the same political considerations that prompt them to deploy correspondents at a loss. The situation is worsened by many African leaders who seal their borders to newsmen, objecting not only to inaccurate reporting but also to honest reporting that might embarrass them.

Although AP and UPI maintain bureaus in southern Africa and along the Mediterranean, each has a single resident correspondent in Nairobi to cover black Africa. Both agencies regularly send correspondents from Johannesburg or from European bureaus to write stories throughout Africa. Some of their reporting is excellent—well rounded and incisive—but visits are brief and infrequent. Reuters, with close Commonwealth ties to much of Africa, has only a few foreign-service correspondents based there. AFP keeps a number of reporters in Africa, but sometimes their stories skirt controversial subjects. Until early 1977, the *New York Times* and the AFP correspondents were the only Western newsmen in Nigeria, which with 55 million inhabitants is by far the largest as well as the richest black nation in the world. (The Reuters man had been expelled earlier in a dugout canoe and left to paddle with his family to neighboring Benin.) After the *Times* man attended a public meeting regarding civil liberties in Nigeria, he was jailed and then put aboard a plane to Kenya, leaving only the AFP man to send a bare minimum of government-approved information.

In the Middle East, some important countries such as Saudi Arabia and Syria are watched over by stringers, for the most part, and even Iran is thinly covered by most agencies.

When agencies have no correspondents in a country—by choice or otherwise—they must rely on part-time stringers who are paid as little as a few dollars per story used. Some are very good, with a keen professional sense. But often these stringers have other jobs and are reluctant to expose themselves to pressure, perhaps even prison or worse. In one major country, a stringer ignored a coup e'etat and messaged his apologies to his editor several days later, saying he had the flu. Some file only a few stories a year. Even when stringers attempt to do a fair, complete job, they are seldom well enough trained to provide the sort of solid, balanced reporting that agencies insist upon elsewhere. An alternative to the use of stringers is the monitoring of government radio or reading reports of official news agencies from neighboring countries, but this amounts to little more than access to government statements. Reporters can also interview refugees and travelers, as is often the case with Uganda, but there is a risk of relaying exaggerated and biased information that agencies seek to avoid, however despotic a government may be.

At times, national news agencies can be of great help in covering events in neighboring countries. Reuters has depended upon the Zaire Press Agency for news from Uganda on several occasions. (Ironically, some of the same deskmen at the Zaire agency who handled the Uganda dispatches had been trained by Reuters correspondents years earlier under a cooperation accord.) Although Western news executives are often grateful for such help, they see indirect coverage as a poor substitute for being able to send their own reporters into closed countries.

Because bureaus are so few—and they may consist of no more than a single correspondent with a household servant to answer the phone —there are few standard practices. Correspondents travel according to the likelihood of major news, hoping to be in the right place if an important story breaks. Although most try to keep visas current and travel to each country in their territory at least once a year, some correspondents go for years without once visiting countries to which they still have access.

There is some sharing. AP is entitled to use AFP stories from French-speaking Africa under a contract arrangement. Often correspondents pool their efforts on an informal basis because there are so few correspondents and the distances are so great. But the system is haphazard, difficult, and basically unreliable.

A somewhat similar situation exists in the more remote parts of the Middle East, although it is easier for regional correspondents to follow developments, at least by long distance, because communications are better and sources are more plentiful.

Asia

The same factors of distortion that affect agency reporting from elsewhere in the Third World are at work in Asia, but additional components worsen the problem. Western reporters and editors, as a

rule, have trouble mastering the languages and the sociopolitical nuances of the diverse Asian cultures. But since their Asian regional
services are in English and French, few local newsmen are hired and
a high percentage of the stories are written by foreign-service correspondents sent from abroad. The problem is exacerbated by severe
limitations on access to wide areas and by direct pressures of governments seeking to control the foreign press.

Agency headquarters in Asia are scattered across the continent,
each with a different structure. AP has a large bureau in Tokyo, with
autonomous, non-Asian bureau chiefs or correspondents in Manila,
Hong Kong, Singapore, Bangkok, and New Delhi. UPI has a similar
deployment but its regional office, in Hong Kong, has a greater responsibility for the area's news reports than the AP Tokyo bureau. Reuters
maintains a large headquarters operation in Singapore. ARP's coverage
is less centralized. All these agencies rely on locally hired newsmen to
cover Indonesia. None has correspondents in Vietnam, Cambodia, or
North Korea. Burma is covered by local stringers who are extremely
cautious about what they transmit, although occasionally correspondents visit Burma for situation reports.

As a result of these problems, overall reporting from Asia is erratic,
and any agency's dispatches from the region may range from excellent
to flatly misleading, however well they may appear to be sourced and
substantiated. It is often almost impossible to know the degree of reliability of any report, although a bureau's basic reputation is at least
some guide.

Correspondents rely heavily on national news agencies and the
government-controlled radio stations in the developing countries of
Asia. In some cases, the only information available is what can be
monitored from the outside. But even in relatively open societies such
as the Philippines, Malaysia, and Indonesia, agencies subscribe to the
national news services, and they use them extensively. The standard
practice is to identify clearly the agency quoted, by its name and political characteristics. Reporters do not like such secondhand attribution,
however, and sometimes information that appears trustworthy is simply lifted from the teleprinter or mimeographed report of a national
agency and, rewritten slightly, relayed onto the wires of an international agency as though it had been obtained firsthand.

Such use of national agencies does not obviate the need for independent reporters, and international agency executives argue with reason that only a well-trained objective newsman can decide what can be
used from a national agency and what must be supplemented with
information from other sources. But it gives an extraordinary importance to the national agency since the global agencies, in many cases,

have no alternative sources. Whatever speech excerpts, or economic statistics, or details of an event a national agency chooses to report are often the only ones relayed to the rest of the world. And if dispatches from international agencies do not specify that the information came from a government news service, the assumption is that the agency's own reporter heard the speech, studied the related statistics, or witnessed the events and selected what he considered to be the important points. This common procedure should be kept in mind when considering the actual role of national news agencies in cooperative exchanges. Whatever an international agency's policy directives, national agencies, particularly in Asia and Africa, are frequently using vague attribution and little independent verification.

International agency correspondents make wide use of local newspapers throughout Asia, but many rely principally on the English-language press. Most bureaus have local newsmen who can read and translate newspapers in other languages, but the process can be slow and haphazard. The reporters tend to talk only with those Asians who have had the motivation to learn English or French. This can eliminate major streams of national thought, since only in the Philippines and the Indian subcontinent are the predominant newspapers in English.

Also, those Asians who have had the motivation to learn English or French may have an atypical approach toward the affairs of their country. And yet if a correspondent speaks such languages as Urdu or Lao, used only in a single country, it usually means that he has had a close personal association with the culture that might affect his overall objectivity. Obviously, it is a question of individuals.

Although reporters in Asia use their own sources to the same varying degree as reporters in Latin America do, there is often a greater need for reporters in Asia to leave their offices and see things for themselves. Insurgent actions, border incursions, refugee movements, agricultural experiments, oil operations, and smuggling must be covered as close to firsthand as possible, but the hinterlands are less accessible in Asia, and accurate word of such developments filters slowly to the cities; facts are often obscured by governments and interested informants. And in Asia, with few local staff reporters and great problems of communications and distance, the necessary investigative trips require agility and energy. Some of the enterprising correspondents attracted to Asian reporting by the Vietnam war have made it a personal challenge to get to remote spots quickly for eyewitness accounts. Others are loath to leave their fixed routines. The result can be disparate reporting of major incidents, such as the confusing versions of the Cambodian incursions in Thai border areas which were never fully explained by international agencies.

CONCLUSIONS

The picture that emerges from looking at news agencies in action does not fit the tidy characterizations of many of their critics and defenders. A number of Third World leaders charge that Western agencies ignore events of importance in their countries and willfully distort the stories they choose to report. Western news executives often counter that the national news agencies that would make up a Third World pool are of no practical use and are a threat to the free flow of information. The important role of smaller international agencies is lost in the flurry of rhetoric.

From a practical standpoint, several conclusions can be drawn. One is that the major international agencies are often guilty of the failings decried by Third World leaders but not necessarily for the reasons cited and not generally to the degree believed. Coverage is erratic because of faulty processes, insufficient independent funds, simple human nature —and pressures from the same governments that complain of bad coverage. The ideological gamut of the thousands of subscribers of each of the major news agencies guards against deliberate bias. No agency that sells the same service to *Maariv* of Israel and *Al Ahram* of Egypt can stray too far from objectivity. There is no conspiracy, but there are faults. As far as coverage is concerned, it is as much a question of political philosophy as of news judgment. Western agencies can be accused of tending toward a shallow treatment of Third World news, but often the accusations are protests against the reporting of unfavorable or embarrassing information. (Doubtlessly, former President Nixon would have liked to have dismissed reports of the Watergate break-in as trivialities.) On the other side, although Third World pools do have the potential of hampering the movement of Western reporters, it is only a potential. Under the current system, the pool arrangement is a worthwhile supplement to international agency reports.

Another conclusion is that much of the actual misunderstanding is the inadvertent or deliberate confusion over practicalities. It is true, for instance, that stories written in Argentina for Uruguay are relayed through New York, but the operation is mainly a mechanical one, and seldom is a word changed. When Indian officials complained that one agency's radio teletype services passed over Pakistan, an agency executive was moved to laughter. "What do they think the Pakistanis do?" he asked. "Go up in the atmosphere and take out some bits and replace them with propaganda?"

It also is possible to conclude that a good deal of the cooperation and exchange proposed at international discussions is already taking place at a practical level. It is unlikely that Western news agencies will use the unedited texts of national news agency dispatches to any greater extent than they do now. Whatever the extenuating circumstances, each agency has its own standards, style, and selection process. But in dozens of countries, international agencies rely heavily on local news services, even in cases where there is an obvious government bias. It is also likely that, whatever functional agreements are drawn, the international agencies will insist on the right of access for their correspondents when necessary, even if no permanent bureau is maintained.

A fourth conclusion to be drawn is that Western news organizations can help narrow the gap by using more care in selecting correspondents and by preparing them more carefully for foreign assignments. Often seemingly small breaches of custom cause as much bad feeling as the wording of a dispatch. Careless words at a cocktail party or tactless questions at a news conference can weigh heavily. Minor facts are terribly important since mistakes impugn whole dispatches. Frequently it is the extra detail in a story that brings trouble. One Western correspondent was expelled from Zaire (then the Congo) because he mentioned that President Mobutu was wearing Israeli paratrooper wings. If such a detail is vital to the story, it must be included. If it is only a gratuitous irritant, it can be dropped. Sensibilities are particularly important now that many Western reporters are writing more about how people live rather than just on politics and economics. That kind of reporting, though more enlightening to the reader and perhaps more valuable to international understanding, is vulnerable to attack as shallow and subjective. By the same token, Third World authorities must understand what Western readers require. Protests and strong reaction are not likely to change the long-established tastes of hundreds of millions in the West. Leaders should be more tolerant of reporting practices, and they should improve their own credibility by allowing their national agencies to inform more factually and fully.

Finally, we can conclude that Third World journalists can train with Western agencies and in Western institutions, but if they learn well, they run the risk of alienation and harassment at home. A foreign correspondent must keep in mind the perspective of those to whom he is reporting. Governments that might excuse a foreigner for what they consider to be ignorance or a lack of sensitivity are likely to be much harder on one of their own citizens. A foreigner who reports too frankly might simply be expelled and reassigned, but a national can face serious and lasting pressures. There should be no bar preventing Third World journalists from assignments outside of their home countries, but, at the same time, there is little specific advantage to such a plan. A single Third World viewpoint does not exist, and there is no reason why an Indian or a Nigerian should be able to report better from Peru than a U.S. national or a Briton. An Argentine covering Bolivia has the advantage of speaking Spanish, but Spanish is an easy language to learn; he also has the disadvantage of long exposure to cultural assumptions about Bolivians that could easily affect his judgment.

The search for common ground might not be as difficult as these conclusions suggest. Attention focused on the problem over the past year has already moved some editors to pay closer attention to Third World concerns. Some governments have relented on restrictive measures, indicating that the trend toward interference is not necessarily general or irreversible. But, as means are sought to improve cooperation and understanding, it is essential that practical aspects of reporting be kept in mind. A great deal of effort can be wasted trying to achieve what has long been a reality—or in trying to change the unchangeable.

6.   ALL FREEDOM IS AT STAKE

HILARY NG'WENO

There are two separate issues at stake in discussions about the role of the press ... One has to do with the flow of information across national boundaries. The more important one, however, deals with the flow of information within national boundaries. Both the western and eastern nations are basically interested in the former issue, with the west ... stressing the need to keep the channels of communication between nations open whilst their eastern counterparts have been calling for government control of newsmen operating across national boundaries. It is an age-old cold war feud. The west would like to have more access to information about eastern-bloc countries as well as the flexibility to send information into the Communist countries, presumably with a view to changing the opinions of the inhabitants of those countries. The eastern nations, mindful of the politically distabilising capacity of radio stations such as Radio Free Europe and similar outfits, resist this claim by western newsmen. Equally vehemently they are opposed to the idea of letting loose foreign newsmen to gather information about Communist nations and send this information back to their respective media at home.

The issue of trans-national communication of ideas is obviously of vital importance to developing countries, but in practical terms it is not half as important as the flow of information within the boundaries of each country. Whether Kenya has the freedom to gather vital informa-

Hilary Ng'weno is Editor of *The Weekly Review,* Nairobi, Kenya. Reprinted from *The Weekly Review* (Nairobi, Kenya), November 8, 1976, and circulated at the conference on "The Third World and Press Freedom," New York, May 11 to 13, 1977, by permission of the author.

tion about China is, for instance, an academic point; given her present resources, Kenya is unlikely to ever do a credible job of gathering news about China directly from Chinese territory. The vast majority of developing nations are in the same predicament; like it or not, they are not in a position to gather meaningful information about the world around them entirely on their own. For this reason freedom to gather such information is not as crucial as it may be for nations with the necessary capacity to collect such information. In fact, transnational news communication is important to developing nations only in their role as receivers, and here they share the same concerns that eastern-bloc or Communist countries have about unfettered freedom of foreign newsmen to gather information about a country and beam it back for the consumption of the inhabitants of those countries.

Many young countries have fragile political structures that cannot withstand endless scrutiny by the news media of the short-comings of those in power or the failures of economic and social development programmes. Unfortunately for the cause of free communication of ideas, it is precisely the negative and unseamly side of life which many western reporters and news media tend to harp upon when dealing with developments in young countries. Coups, corruption, poverty and calamities are the stable diet dished out by many news agencies in their coverage of third world countries. The coverage is often times made more unpalatable by the tendency among western news agencies and newspapers to look at the Third World in cold war terms. Third world leaders are quite often described as Moscow or Peking-leaning whenever no Western label can be pinned on them, and a general ignorance of the complexities of politics in third world countries often leads Western newsmen to invoke the most farfetched theories to explain political events in these countries. All this is done against a historical background in which most of the press in developing countries was at one time or other owned and controlled by expatriate elements with interests which were far from being in harmony with local aspirations. On several occasions, the foreign pressmen who operate in third world countries have turned out to be affiliates of government intelligence organizations of their various countries, the American CIA being the most notorious employer of such journalists. Worst of all, through the power of the western news media, especially the major international agencies, as well as through such media as television and the cinema, third world people have come to feel a great sense of impotence over the cultural influences which permeate their relations with the western world through the mass media. It is an unrelenting one-way traffic in ideas and values from the western countries to the third world with little opportunity given to third world nations to examine the content of the materials which daily flood their own presses and other media fom the west.

Under these circumstances it is understandable that the dangerous views being propagated ... by eastern-bloc countries about the role of the press have gained support among a large number of third world nations. I call these views dangerous because there is no more appropriate description for a program which prescribes government control of the press as the cure for the ills which afflict the press in third world countries. In the words of the delegates of third world countries which have supported the proposed Unesco resolution on the role of the press, the trouble with the present western treatment of news from the third world is that there is not enough coverage of events in the third world and that the little there is is distorted. Instead of increasing the content and therefore improving the scope of coverage, the Unesco proposals in effect suggest a program which will eventually lead to the curtailment of the flow of information. Worse, they wish to replace one kind of distorting factor—that of western bias—for another, that of governmental or bureaucratic bias. While the implication of all this might be unfortunate with respect to trans-national news communication, they are catastrophic as far as communication on the domestic front is concerned.

To be fair to third world governments who have expressed a desire to change the recent relations in international news gathering between themselves and western news media, they often recognise that governmental control would be inimical to the cause of press freedom if it were to be all embracing. In a typical third world approach to dilemmas of this kind, some of them, and Kenya's stand as expressed by the country's permanent secretary to the ministry of information is a case in point, hope that a system can be evolved which combines the best aspects of western and Communist practices in mass communications. The assumption which underlines third world thinking on issues of ideology is that there is a middle ground between western and Communist thinking, an independent system whilst stressing the strong points in each. Whether the third world nations call their systems Islamic Socialism, African Socialism, or positive non-alignment—the assumption is there. Nothing has disproved the wisdom of third world countries persisting in this assumption, but on the issue of the press there simply happens to be no middle ground between the two approaches to the role of the press represented by the opposing views expressed at the Unesco general assembly. The reason is simple: the conflict is not between western and Communist ideology, but rather between the proponents of government control of the mass media and those of an independent press that is not controlled by the government. The fact that the press in Communist countries is invariably controlled by the government, or more accurately, by the ruling party, does not alter the fact. Control of the press by those in authority is inherent in a totalitarian system of government, whether the government is of the right-wing type such as during the Nazi period in Germany or the greater part of Franco's rule in Spain, or a left-wing type such as is found in the Soviet Union, Cuba or China. There is no point in fooling oneself that it is possible to get the good aspects of government control of the press and marry them with the good aspects of an independent press. Good aspects there are in both systems of the press, but they are not attributes of the press which exist independently of the systems in question. They are not like fruit which can be picked from different trees to make up a basket that would be appetizing to a consumer; they are part and parcel of the systems of communications in which they are manifest. For this reason third world nations will have to stop trying to sit on the fence hoping for an opportunity to present itself that would help them establish a half-way house between government control of the media and independent media.

If most third world delegates at the Unesco general assembly should end up endorsing the Unesco media proposals and thus side with the Soviet Union and eastern press freedom, it will be understandable. Most of the delegates at the conference are government functionaries with little or no first-hand working knowledge of the media. Like most government functionaries all over the world, their concern is not with imparting information but with influencing people. For them information is not information until its probable impact on select audiences has been ascertained. There is good information or information fit for human consumption, and there is bad information—that which must not be fed to the public. The truth or untruth of the information is of secondary importance to government officials. Indeed, sometimes the greater the truth the greater the desire on the part of the government functionary to delay its dissemination, especially if the truth happens to be unpalatable. And it matters not whether the functionary is a Haldeman or Erlichman serving a Nixon beleagured by Watergate scandals or a party hack in Moscow trying to conceal the fact that dozens of Soviet citizens may have lost their lives in an Aeroflot air crash somewhere in Siberia.

It will be understandable that such officials will lean towards supporting measures for the greater government control of the Press. Such control makes their job easier, but only temporarily. In the final analysis, government control of the press leads to the kinds of distortions which third world nations are complaining of with regard to the influence and practice of western news agencies. These distortions cloud the vision of leaders and makes them prone to ill-considered decisions with sometimes fatal consequences for a country. A government-controlled press is by its very nature a mouth-piece of those in power. Like the piper it learns to sing those tunes dearest to whoever is paying, and the numerous upheavals in third world nations over the past 10 years prove beyond any shadow of doubt that what is politically fashionable today need have no appeal whatsoever to incoming regimes bent on establishing fresh legitimacy for their illegal seizure of political power.

A nation that relies entirely on a government (or party) controlled press is at the mercy of the quality of its leadership. If it is lucky, a benevolent dictatorship that is also enlightened might for a while assure orderly and meaningful development for a country without frequent recourse to consultations with public opinion. Theoretically a good party system can also gauge public opinion even while controlling the mass media with an iron hand. But in reality, no benevolent dictatorship or party machinery has ever provided any meaningful or credible substitute to freedom of expression, and in the end most such systems have either been replaced by less authoritarian ones or their leaders have made blunders which have led to their losing their jobs, if not their heads.

In his vituperative attack on Kenya's press, the permanent secretary in the ministry of information warned against the third world press trying to emulate the American press. The American press, he said, is a rebel press, because America is a society which was founded on rebellion having declared its independence from Britain two (hundred) years ago. We don't need a rebel press in Africa, he said. I do not hold a brief for the American press, but it is revealing that the permanent secretary should be questioning the principle of rebellion against tyranny upon which the American nation was founded. Kenya, Algeria and a number of African nations rebelled against colonial rule. Rebellion against tyranny is a heritage to be proud of and a press which continues to espouse the principles of freedom which led to the establishment of the American nation more than two hundred years ago is one that deserves praise rather than the condescending remarks which the permanent secretary made about the US press. Rebellion *per se* is dangerous where it is directed against legitimate and popularly elected authority. But a questioning or inquiring spirit is essential for a healthy press. Unfortunately it is this spirit of inquiry which most third world nations today consider to be rebellion.

There are no easy solutions to the problems of communication which third world nations face. Most of the problems stem from the poor economic conditions in which our countries find themselves.

Even the proposed third world news pool is itself an admission of the limitation of resources available to third world countries. It is no substitute for international news agencies. If used properly, it can augment the flow of information now controlled by such agencies as Reuters, Agence France Presse, Associated Press, United Press International and Tass, but the third world nations do not have the resources to replace these agencies at the moment. More important, the news pool must be operated in such a way that it contains more than the usual government pronouncements which make up the standard newscasts of government controlled news agencies of most third world nations. Such newscasts are usually considered boring to nationals of the countries in which they are made. It is unlikely that by merely crossing borders and being disseminated by a third world news pool they will become any more exciting. At the very worst, there is the possibility that governments will feed into the news pool only self-serving information with the end result that there will be a curtailment of the flow of information from one country to another. A country experiencing difficulties of an economic or political nature is not likely to feed into the news pool any meaningful information about such difficulties for fear that its image abroad may be damaged. Given the fact that such difficulties are frequent in the third world, the tendency will be for the contents of the news pool to deteriorate into a litany of achievements and pious resolutions by different national governments—the kind of stuff which pours out of China for foreign consumption even at the height of great political upheavals of far reaching consequences for the rest of the world.

Cooperation with other governments in such matters as the setting up and the operation of a news pool will certainly not solve the problem of the quality of communications within the borders of each country. Here the authorities must do more than pay lip service to the concept of press freedom which graces the constitutions of many countries. They must provide meaningful assistance to the press in a number of ways. The most important is to upgrade the profession of journalists. In most third world countries the status of journalists is very low. Journalists are not only poorly paid, they are poorly regarded by those in authority. When not being treated as glorified messenger boys for those in power, they are shunned as dangerous purveyors of untruth, half-truths or truths which are unpalatable to the powers that be. What is clearly needed in most developing countries is more concerted efforts to train high level manpower in the journalistic field and to offer the necessary inducements that would attract the right calibre of manpower to the profession. Some countries, such as Kenya, have set up schools of journalism which go some way towards meeting this need, but by and large there is still very little understanding by those in authority of the role of the journalist in a developing country. All too often resources are spent training journalists only to have them employed as mere information bureaucrats with little scope of putting their training to good use.

Just as important as providing the right calibre of manpower for the profession is the need to give the press in developing nations better tools with which to do the difficult job of keeping a nation informed. Far too often governments make a lot of noise about how important the business of mass communication is when in the same breath they refuse to provide the necessary funds to make the task possible. When the money is found it often-times goes into prestigious-looking hardware such as colour television systems while little is spent on actual programming or gathering and dissemination of information. Countries spend millions trying to "modernise" their broadcasting facilities and next to nothing trying to produce their own programmes. Then they turn around and complain that outsiders are unduly influencing the content of the mass media in developing countries by providing canned programmes at cheap rates. Unless developing countries take a hard look at what needs to be done to improve the actual content of the media within their own border, they might as well be resigned to an indefinite future of cultural domination by outsiders.

Obviously the same prescription cannot be given to those countries which have decided to control all aspects of their mass media as that which is given to those, such as Kenya, where an independent press exists. Countries which believe in governmental control of the press, and by and large these are in the majority among third world nations, no doubt feel that it is possible to have a government-controlled press which at the same time is free. Here, of course, one gets hopelessly entangled in semantics, and as the history of debates between western countries and communist nations about freedom has proved, there is no way one side can convince the other of the merit of its case. The reason is that though both sides use the same phrase—freedom of the press— they are not talking the same language. I will be willing to admit that it is possible for a government-controlled press to operate freely, by which I mean in an atmosphere which places the interests of the readers, listeners or viewers—in effect, the interests of the public—above the narrower interests of that group which happens to be in power at any one time. In practice, however, this has not been the case anywhere where the press has been entirely controlled by the government or the ruling party. The argument that the government or the ruling party knows what is best for the people, an argument which is often used in defence of systems where the press is controlled, only goes to prove that one cannot have both control and freedom.

Freedom is an indivisible entity. When governments express a wish to control the press, it is more often than not a sign that they wish to control other areas of public life as well. It is no coincidence that governmental control of the press—whether in left-leaning or right-leaning regimes—has frequently been found side by side with governmental control of other institutions such as the trade unions, the universities, the churches, parliaments and the courts. It is not coincidental because the freedom of these other institutions takes meaning only in the extent to which it is expressed through the media.

It is true that freedom is not a value which exists all on its own. In many countries other values—such as unity and stability—often take precedence. But it is unwise for third world nations to blindly support the kinds of resolutions that are currently before the Unesco general assembly without regard to their ultimate impact on the freedoms of millions of inhabitants of third world nations. It is this larger freedom which is at stake, and not only that of journalists.

7 TOWARD A FREER AND MULTIDIMENSIONAL FLOW OF INFORMATION

PERO IVACIC

In choosing a title for this chapter, I sought to sum up the answer to a question we at Tanjug are frequently asked: what do we mean when we speak of a new international order in the field of information? The answer as formulated in the title—a freer and multidimensional flow of information—no longer provokes serious dispute in the world, just as there is now general recognition of the imbalance in news flow between the advanced countries and the developing countries.

Still, many international meetings are currently being held on this subject. In the last few years it has certainly been a much more frequent subject of international discussion than it ever was before in the three decades since the end of World War II. The press and other news media have joined in this discussion as they have begun talking forthrightly about themselves and others and about the role of news reporting and information systems and the flow of information. All this suggests that the international situation in the field of information is ripe for such discussion.

This chapter will present the experience of a medium-developed national news agency—specifically the Yugoslav news agency Tanjug —and its world view of the situation in the field of information and the need for change. At the same time the efforts made by Tanjug to promote a freer and multidimensional flow of news and information are presented. The aim, however, is not to argue the view represented nor to defend it from those who hold different views.

In setting forth this view, there is reference to the experience of the news agencies of the nonaligned countries, but I have drawn only on their jointly adjusted and adopted attitudes and conclusions; to this extent this chapter may be considered as a presentation of their position.

Since this presentation primarily describes the practice of a given news agency—Tanjug—and the views and conclusions contained in it are based on this practice, only the indispensable reference is made to the present-day situation in the international news flow and the conduct of foreign news media. As to what has been said and concluded at many international meetings and written by a multitude of publicists, ample documentation exists on both sides of the question. Tanjug was an active participant at all these meetings, with the exception of the San Jose conference, and we feel that we have helped in a better appreciation being gained both of the issues and of the concrete action being undertaken.

FOREIGN NEWS COVERAGE AND SOURCES IN YUGOSLAVIA

Yugoslavia's commitment to a free, wide, and multidimensional flow of information derives from the essence of the Yugoslav social reality, Yugoslavia's independent and nonaligned foreign policy, and the organization and character of the press and other information media in Yugoslavia.

Yugoslavia is a multinational and multilingual federal community made up of six constituent republics and two autonomous provinces. Just as there is no principal republic or nation nor one official language, so there is no principal or main daily paper nor primary radio or television station. Within this community, the news reporting and information system is based, as it must be, on cooperation among equals. Multidimensional and equal news coverage must be ensured. Tanjug is a professional news agency with editorial offices at its headquarters in Belgrade and in each of the Yugoslav constituent republics and autonomous provinces—each of which enjoys editorial autonomy in preparing the news products it contributes to the joint news service for the entire country. The fundamental principle is a balanced news and information flow among all the constituent parts of the federal community.

The interests of each component of the Yugoslav self-management community are not always identical; it is Tanjug's great responsibility to keep all the republics and provinces informed and up to date about each other. Tanjug stands behind this same principle in the international news flow.

Founded in 1943 on liberated territory in occupied Yugoslavia, with the scant technical resources captured in battle from the enemy and while fascism was still crushing the greater part of Europe, Tanjug has from its outset received and distributed the news of the wire services—the Associated Press (AP), Telegrafnoye Agentstvo Sovietskovo Soyuza (TASS), Reuters—and radio stations of the Allies. These services carried worldwide Tanjug dispatches on the armed struggle of the Yugoslav peoples for freedom and for building a new Yugoslavia. This was a good example of a two-way news flow.

In its postwar development, Tanjug has relied on three main sources for its foreign news coverage:

1. its own staff of foreign correspondents, numbering 47 in April 1977 and present on all continents
2. foreign news agencies, including the five big international services and over 60 national news agencies
3. the foreign press and radio

In no period has there been a predominant source for foreign news coverage. As Tanjug's total foreign news coverage has grown, Tanjug's own dispatches have increased as its network of foreign correspondents has expanded. The relative participation of national, especially nonaligned, news agencies has also grown, most notably since the establishment of the Nonaligned News Agencies Pool. None of the five worldwide services has had a consistent advantage. Tanjug's criteria for selection have always remained quality, factuality, and speed. Acceptance of the reality that content cannot always correspond to our viewpoint is an important factor in the objectivity of Tanjug's foreign news coverage.

In the absence of any analysis of our own of the reception and use of foreign news sources,* we will quote from a study of Tanjug by Gertrude Ruth Robinson.[1]

> Every news agency serves as a major selection screen for the foreign news which is made available to a country's local media. Tanjug is no exception in this respect but differs from the world agencies like the AP in that it does not single-handedly collect all of its foreign news. Limited financial resources, a less extended technological network, and a staff one quarter as large as the AP's place Tanjug eighth in terms of news output, after the five giants. As a subsidiary link in the international news network it must import much of the raw material from which it fashions its daily foreign report.

This study dating from 1968 provides convincing evidence of the severe imbalance in the news and information available at that time to

---

*UNESCO's planned study of news agencies, both international and national, includes a project on Tanjug.

Yugoslav public opinion. Having cited the main sources of Tanjug's foreign news and noted that the four major Western wire services accounted for 60 percent of foreign news input and Tanjug's own foreign correspondents for only 5.5 percent, the author then points to the shift in these proportions when it came to distribution. For the years covered by this study, Tanjug's newscasts were 44.96 percent news from the Western wire services and 23.93 percent news from its own correspondents.

As the number of Tanjug correspondents abroad has increased and as cooperation has developed with national news agencies, and especially since the Nonaligned Pool was started, this proportion has altered gradually until today Tanjug foreign correspondents are the source of 50 percent of the foreign coverage in Tanjug's newscast. The news agencies of the nonaligned countries are present with about 15 percent of the foreign coverage, with their participation increasing slowly but steadily. However, even for the coverage of countries in which Tanjug has its own correspondents, both European and non-European, Tanjug uses the news reports and information transmitted by national news agencies too, considering these valid sources of authentic news on their respective countries. At this point it is important to emphasize the fact that there has been no decrease in the amount of news and information picked up from the international services but that this better, although still insufficient, balance of various sources used has accompanied an overall increase in foreign coverage.

Tanjug's daily newscasts to its network of domestic subscribers include foreign news coverage of its own selection. But neither Tanjug nor its regular newscasts are the only sources of foreign news and information for these subscribers. Because of practical limitations on the regular news flow from Tanjug, any editorial office may and often does ask for additional coverage from foreign sources on any point of particular interest to it. The various Yugoslav television channels have their programming arrangements with Eurovision and Intervision. Many of the daily papers have their own correspondents abroad or are subscribers, especially in the case of periodicals, to the services of major foreign papers such as the *New York Times* and *Le Monde,* and to feature services, photo services, bulletins, and so on. The articles carried in Yugoslav papers and periodicals from the press abroad are in most cases a matter of their own direct selection.

In short, neither law nor practice gives Tanjug a foreign news monopoly in Yugoslavia. Its job of selecting from the newscasts of news agencies abroad and the international press services is primarily a question of operative and economic practicality. It is precisely the interest of each subscriber in having access to the broadest range of news sources that precludes the various newsrooms throughout the country from relying on just one or only a few foreign news agencies or services. Obviously, these newsrooms have neither the material nor staff resources for each to take on direct reception from a large number of sources abroad.

Of particular relevance to this point is the following passage from Robinson's study on the manner in which selection takes place at Tanjug's foreign news desk:

> Two major sets of criteria determine foreign news selection in Yugoslavia. These may be called journalistic and attention priorities.
>
> The distributor eliminates eight categories of information from the incoming foreign copy: (1.) repetitive items, (2.) illegible stories, (3.) sports reports like baseball not known in Yugoslavia, (4.) obviously propagandistic official communications from minor countries, as well as (5.) speeches given *in extenso* by minor politicians, (6.) Western cafe society news, (7.) clothes descriptions of public officials, and (8.) accounts of the private lives of foreign statemen.
>
> The distributor's gross selection, which reduces the input by two thirds, is thus not governed by ideological but by journalistic considerations. These eliminate overlapping material, many human interest stories, and strident propaganda. Though selection patterns are different from the American, they too show a concern for objectivity not usually attributed to national news agencies.[2]

TANJUG, NATIONAL NEWS AGENCIES, AND INTERNATIONAL WIRE SERVICES

Tanjug, like many other news agencies, maintains relations worldwide and with big, medium, and small agencies. These relations are based on contracts, some for a fixed term, others automatically renewable. As a result, the datelines of some 60 news agencies other than Tanjug appear through Tanjug on the pages of the Yugoslav press. Tanjug's relations with these news agencies varies. Aside from newscast exchanges, in some cases on a commercial basis and in others on a cost-free exchange basis, there are many other forms of cooperation. These range from strictly professional exchanges to informal exchanges of technical advice in the field of telecommunications. A focus of particular importance to us is professional training—for journalists, translators, technical staff, and others.

These are not features exclusively Tanjug's. Many national news agencies, and especially those in the nonaligned and other developing countries, include in their newscasts the news reports and other dispatches of the big international wire services. And the international giants in their dispatches cite national news agencies when these are their source. Cooperation also exists to varying degrees in telecommunications.

There are two points, however, on which we are often critical of the big wire services, both at international meetings and in direct contacts. The first is the presentation given our countries by the big wire services and our low profile as news sources in their distribution networks. I will try to explain this first point very simply in terms of my own country.

Yugoslavia certainly cannot complain of a lack of attention on the part of the big international wire services. They all have offices in Belgrade. In fact, there are more than 70 foreign correspondents accredited in Belgrade, to say nothing of the special correspondents who appear for shorter periods. In 1976 alone, Yugoslavia was visited by 2,000 foreign correspondents. There are also foreign correspondents accredited in countries neighboring Yugoslavia who also report on Yugoslavia. The range in quality and quantity of this reporting is wide —depending, of course, on the paper or other media represented by each correspondent.

Let us focus here on the coverage provided by the global wire services. Their newscasts and informative materials reach thousands and thousands of newsrooms on all continents. This makes the responsibility they have to international public opinion even greater.

We neither can nor want to dispute the right of any agency to give precedence in its coverage, even on a long-term basis, to events and subjects that in our view do not merit attention or do not have a bearing on the fundamental questions and problems in the life and development of our country. This, we accept, is a question of the demands made by the home office of any agency. We cannot pretend indifference, however, to the imposition on a large part of the information media worldwide of a news coverage largely of no particular interest to their public and deficient in what public opinion abroad would like to know about Yugoslavia, the development of the distinct features of its social system, its economic life, and its positions on the building of new, equal relations in the world—the new international economic order—just as these are the areas in which we would like to know more about others.

Our own domestic subscribers, who through Tanjug are up to date on the reporting abroad of events in Yugoslavia, frequently voice their doubts to us. How can we, they ask, rely on the objectivity of news reports from abroad if these same sources report about Yugoslavia with an obvious bias and preponderantly with news of minor importance. This criticism would be lessened if the big wire services could, as is so often urged, show a greater ear and understanding for the changes occurring in relations in the world and for the specifics in the developments taking place in the various social systems and remember that their newscasts and services do not go just to the advanced countries of their home offices but penetrate deep into every region of the world.

This criticism of the international giants, however, in no way implies the least interest or intent on our part to see any limitations placed on their presence in our newscasts or other services. Without the presence of Agence France-Presse (AFP), AP, Reuters, TASS, and United Press International (UPI), the Yugoslav press and other news media could never provide the scope and detail of international news coverage that they do, regardless of the development level of the network of own correspondents abroad and the bilateral news exchanges with other national news agencies.

The second point of criticism is the insufficient use of news reports of national agencies as valid sources of authentic news on their respective countries or the selection made in the instances national sources are cited. Obviously, national news agencies would like to have their news reports included in the newscasts of the big press services of both East and West. We feel their inclusion would contribute to a better-informed public opinion in the advanced countries too, at both ideological poles. Nevertheless, we fully understand the explanation provided by the big worldwide services of the limits they must impose on their news volume. But this only heightens the necessity of responsible selection to ensure correct and timely reporting worldwide. We believe this could be achieved through better and regular professional cooperation between the global and national news agencies and frank evaluations from both sides of newscast quality and usefulness, respecting, of course, the full independence of the partners involved.

This all adds up to our support of the denial of any need for confrontation between national news agencies and the big international services. But this support presupposes news coverage on the part of the big services free of tendentiousness in regard to the vital development interests and independence of any country on which they report.

THE NEWS AGENCY AND ITS ROLE

A news agency dispatch is the first signal of an event or the development of events. This dispatch and all the other forms of subsequent news agency coverage are the "products" that impart and develop the first impression and idea of our "consumers" in regard to whatever has occurred. But first in importance as well as in time is the dispatch, that small, at first sight minor, professional product that is the first information to appear on the news market before world public opinion forms. The dispatch may be followed by articles, commentaries, features, perhaps even films or a book. But the news agency dispatch will be the precursor of all these.

This is why we attach particular importance to news reports and other information exchanges among news agencies. At a time when man is traveling interplanetary roads while, at the same time, on this planet men must still live deprived of the possibility of satisfying their most elementary material and spiritual needs, activity in the field of information acquires new social, economic, and cultural dimensions. In fact, this activity, initiating in the news agency dispatch, becomes a factor in social, economic, and cultural development. Meanwhile, people are increasingly vocal in underlining their right to be kept up to date and objectively informed. These demands are entirely reasonable, and news agencies, with the latest in electronic, computerized "vehicles" being increasingly added to their production technology, have, of course, an exceptionally important role herein.

If then the news agency dispatch is the first step toward knowledge of an event or the development of events at some point on our planet, the news agency, as its author and distributor, should be able to do more than it has to date toward creating something new and more adequately in the interest of the world we live in.

The right to political self-determination has been universally recognized but for the few exceptions on the African continent. Why should the right of peoples to receive correct information not be similarly affirmated? There are few who will dispute today that in this sense major gaps have existed for decades. And these gaps are the reflection of a bloc-divided world—colonial and economic interests, endeavors to preserve spheres of interest and influence, attempts at mental and intellectual domination and colonization—and have been maintained through editorial policies founded in these interests and endeavors.

The last few years, however, have demonstrated that such an approach cannot endure. At the same time, the inevitability of recognition and respect for each other's distinctive and autochthonous features has become evident. As an institution "producing" a view of the world through news dispatches, reports, articles, commentaries, photo features, and so on, we come to feel the untenability of a static present belonging to the past. Our imperative is to move ahead with others who share our views toward the future envisaged. There is no problem of choice here for us; our answer is categorical and has been illustrated in concrete undertakings. One of these undertakings was the launching of the Nonaligned News Agencies Pool.

THE POOL: COOPERATION AMONG EQUALS

On January 20, 1975, the flow of news reports and information among several news agencies of the nonaligned countries began. This multilateral news coverage has come to be known as the Nonaligned Pool. The common concept of this new form of cooperation is one of relations among equals; it does not include establishing a new international or supranational nonaligned news agency.

The idea of the pool grew out of the awareness that the news flow about and among the nonaligned countries was insufficient and lagged far behind the relations developing among them at the political and economic levels.

On the basis of recommendations adopted at the Fourth Summit Conference of Nonaligned Countries, held in Algiers in 1973, bilateral consultations took place between the news agencies of some 10 nonaligned countries on possibilities for joint action to change the existing situation. The fundamentals were set forth in the letter of invitation to join the pool, sent December 3, 1974, to the news agencies of the nonaligned world. Full agreement was reached, and in January 1975 the Yugoslav news agency, Tanjug, launched the collection and redistribution of news reports among the nonaligned countries. This was a modest start. Many difficulties lay ahead, and some of them persist even today. One of the greatest is undoubtedly the low level of development of national information media and a corresponding inadequancy in their technical facilities.

The fast growth of the pool very soon made the need felt for multilateral agreement on the further development and consolidation of this undertaking. In less than 18 months, the pool was functioning with over 30 national news agencies reporting on their respective nonaligned country in Asia, the Arab world, Africa, Latin America, and Europe.

The pool was officially constituted at the meeting of information ministers and news agency directors of 62 nonaligned countries held in New Delhi in July 1976. At this meeting, the pool's constitution was adopted and a coordinating committee formed. The constitution is a public document that clearly sets forth the basic aims and dimensions of this new form of cooperation among nonaligned countries. The constitution makes it entirely clear, for instance, that there is no question of creating any form of a supranational news agency or even an attempt to put statist limitations on the news flow or press freedom. The constitution and pool practice to date are clear proof that this undertaking in no way envisages any eventual competitive role aimed against the existing big international wire services. Therefore, there is nothing limiting involved.

Perhaps it would be most effective to let the constitution speak for itself on these and other important aspects of the pool. Which

> is intended to achieve the broad and free circulation among [the nonaligned nations] of news, informative reports, features and photographs about each other, and also provide objective and authentic information relating to nonaligned countries for the rest of the world. . . .
>
> . . . [The pool] is not a supra-national news agency. All Pool-participating news agencies have the same rights in terms of the circulation of the materials each makes available to the Pool. . . . None of the Pool-participating agencies has a dominant role. Cooperation is founded in agreements reached on the basis of full respect for democratic procedure and quality. . . . Objective information is the basic premise of the Pool, with emphasis on progressive, economic, socio political and cultural developments as well as mutual cooperation and action. . . .
>
> The Pool is intended to facilitate dissemination of correct and factual information about non-aligned countries and their policies. News items included in the Pool could also be made available to other News Agencies, mass communication media and other interested organizations. . . .
>
> . . . The modalities of collection and distribution of news among participating Agencies will be worked out through mutual agreement. The Pool does not preclude bilateral arrangements between participating agencies or between them and other agencies consistent with the objectives of the Pool.

The manner in which the pool functions is the best proof of its democratic basis. A news agency is considered as a participant if it transmits its selection of news reports to one or more of the pool's collector-redistributor news agencies. The process involved is simple. Each participant agency transmits by the means at its disposal—teleprinter, telex, airmail—one or more of its news reports daily to a pool redistribution center.

Each agency selects which reports it will send to the pool. A redistributing news agency translates the reports it receives into the languages in which it usually transmits abroad, scrupulously respecting the substance of the news received. Tanjug, for example, redistributes a six-hour daily total of news for the pool in French, English, and Spanish. Its average newscast for the pool contains between 30 and 40 items from the news services of national news agencies of the nonaligned countries and also from the United Nations Educational, Scientific and Cultural Organization (UNESCO) and the Office of Public Information of the United Nations.

The first meeting of the pool's coordinating committee, held in Cairo in January 1977, noted that more than 40 news agencies in Africa, Asia, Latin America, and Europe were already contributing actively to the news flow of the pool, and that, since 1975, national news agencies had been formed for the first time in 16 nonaligned countries. Five news agencies were already functioning as regional or multilateral collectors and redistributors of news reports and information from other agencies participating in the pool.

At the Cairo meeting the coordinating committee was thus able to assess that the pool had rapidly developed during 1976 and that this new form of multilateral cooperation among the nonaligned countries in matters of information had made great strides.

The constantly increasing number of news agencies ready to function as collector-distributors is particularly encouraging. In addition to the five agencies that had accepted this responsibility at the time of the coordinating committee meeting in Cairo, nine more have expressed their readiness to include pool news in their regular foreign newscasts.

The publication rate of items from the pool newscast is still modest, but it is improving daily. The quality, substance, and presentation of the material provided is also constantly improving, while an increasing number of news agencies of nonaligned countries are actively participating in the pool.

Thus, the principle of the pool, widely accepted by the nonaligned countries during the first two years of its existence, is now becoming a reality. Outside the nonaligned world, where the pool is increasingly making its presence felt in the mass media, interest in the pool has been shown by several news agencies and other bodies concerned with information. Can there be any reason, for example, for it not to be of interest to news agencies outside the nonaligned world—even the international giants—to receive a daily newscast of 30 or 40 news items on daily events and activity in the nonaligned countries?

CONTROVERSY AND DIALOGUE

The pool has been met not only by controversy but also by a new dialogue that has gone beyond the pool to encompass the whole field of information and free flow of news. The start of pool operations brought to the surface many aspects of the causes for seeking new forms of international cooperation in the field of information. One example is the reaction of the worldwide services and a part of the press in the highly industrial countries when the news agencies of the nonaligned countries agreed in July 1976 in New Delhi to formally constitute the pool following its initial 18 months of operation. Those who reacted most harshly had never sought to discuss at any earlier moment the reasons these news agencies might decide it was necessary to establish a news pool.

The criticism that erupted at this point can be summed up on the whole as follows. First, the news agencies of the nonaligned countries are in large part state-owned or under the direct control of the state and this means the news they send is censored. Second, the pool will limit the free flow of news and information from other sources, especially the international news media. The third criticism is that the pool is aimed at creating a supranational news agency and a news monopoly in the nonaligned world, and that this monopoly will therefore make it difficult if not impossible to maintain foreign correspondents in nonaligned countries. Last, the critics say, pool news, because it is all from state-controlled sources, will be only positive and therefore cannot provide a true picture of events in any country of the nonaligned world.

The paragraphs cited of the constitution and the course of the pool so far are certainly an ample basis for judging just how unfounded these worries are. Never, either in the original conception of the pool, in its constitution, or in its practice, has there been anything to imply a supranational agency, censorship, a pushing aside of the existing wire services, or a developing of state controls.

We do not consider it a press freedom to voice unjustified doubts concerning those who take a step founded on the jointly adopted objective of doing what they can with the modest possibilities at their disposal to fill a gap undeniably present in the news flow.

A second example of unjustified criticism: I considered it positive and appropriate for the UNESCO General Assembly meeting in Nairobi in the fall of 1976 to have provided the framework for initiating a hard-swinging, open debate on the new order in the field of information. Right away, however, harsh reactions were heard; any discussion on a new order in the field of information was claimed equivalent to an attack on press freedoms. In the end, some declared, they were greatly relieved that no agreement had been reached. But was it a failure to reach an agreement when an agreement was made to continue debate at various meetings and to charge UNESCO with keeping note of this debate and reporting on it to the next conference? One of these continuations was organized by UNESCO in April 1977 in Florence. There 60 prominent journalists and representatives of communication services with differing views on the free flow of news and information between the advanced and developing countries were able to agree in their conclusions that a gap does exist, that it must be filled, and that therefore the quest must continue until results are achieved.

We can only give our active support to a dialogue among equals and a quest for solutions marked by a mutual appreciation of the views exchanged. This approach can help achieve a better understanding of differences deriving from differing sociopolitical backgrounds and prevent these differences from being obstacles to cooperation. If this spirit of equal cooperation is making headway in the United Nations in relations between different social systems, why should it not be possible to accept an equal and free, multidimensional news flow?

Still, there are issues that will undoubtedly remain subjects of debate, conflict, and compromise and the centers of sharpest controversy in the initiated dialogue. One such issue is the dichotomy implied in raising the question of free or state news services. In discussing this issue let me return to my own experience. The big Western wire services, in their not infrequent references to Tanjug, will almost always slip in a label such as the "official Yugoslav news agency," or the "government news agency," the "government-controlled agency." This is all part of persistent efforts by these big services to impose their view of every state-related news service as deprived of freedom and not entirely reliable in its reporting. Even if the labels applied to Tanjug and many other national news agencies (virtually all the news agencies of the nonaligned countries) corresponded to fact, they remain empty labels to us because we know the concept of state and government is not the same in all social systems and that it is quite unique in the Yugoslav society founded on the principles of self-management.

But we consider this insistent labeling unfair in professional relations between news agencies and in a free news flow. It is even less fitting in regard to countries whose recent independence and statehood reflect the indomitable will of their people in recent decades to rid themselves of the chains of colonialism and other forms of domination. Out of this struggle have also come information media authentically their own, among them news agencies, and an expression of their emancipation and an integral part of their sovereignty and independence. Obviously, technical underdevelopment and a lack of professionals have kept decolonization of the news lagging far behind national needs.* But in the last few years, especially since 1975, there has been a marked acceleration as we have seen the formation of some 20 new national news agencies in the nonaligned countries, with several more at present in the process of formation.

But let us return to Tanjug. It is newsworthy that these same international wire services that apply empty labels have themselves on

---

*Much of the world's population (70 percent) still lacks the most elementary means of informing itself about developments at home and abroad (UNESCO, 1961).

numberous occasions paid tribute to Tanjug's foreign news coverage and cited various of its journalists for their high professional qualities. Without risking conceit or the need for additional documentation, numerous instances could be listed of confirmation abroad of Tanjug's success, despite its limited technological and material resources, at moments of extremely important world events. These have been moments when Tanjug's coverage has been equal to that of any of the international giants, and often even more complete and faster. To mention only a few: Cuba and the Bay of Pigs,[3] all stages of events in the People's Republic of China (PRC), 1968 in Czechoslovakia, the assassination of Allende and events in Chile, the fall of Saigon, the activity of the nonaligned and developing countries at the United Nations, many of the critical moments in the Middle East, the first interview with Carillo on his release from prison, the 1976 Berlin Conference of European Communist Parties, all five nonaligned summits but especially the 1976 Colombo summit, and even chess—Bobby Fischer's world championship victory.

We are proud of these successes and the international recognition they have earned, and we certainly hope many more will follow. But they in no way fire any ambition on our part to build up, even at home, a monopoly on foreign news coverage. Our concern as professionals is to preserve and reinforce our reputation.

The examples cited do not exhaust the list. But they all required fast and top quality professional action and, foremost, an objective approach to very sensitive developments. It is hard to believe that this would be possible for an agency under state control whose product must inevitably be, it is claimed, a censored rather than a free news flow. These examples and Tanjug's daily practice are indicative of its full confidence in its correspondents. But, more important, they prove Tanjug's respect for the principle that freedom of the press means each journalist's and every news agency's acceptance of the full responsibilities of providing news coverage, both the responsibilities toward the community whose events or developments are being reported and those toward the public, both at home and abroad, for whom the news reported is intended. Any other principle is for us abuse of a free press. If the shield of a free news flow and monopolistic advantages are used to try and impose any given criteria of news reporting, and even the political or ideological outlooks of those who distribute the news, without allowing the real and objective facts to be heard on all aspects of events, then we must question whether this can really be called a free and balanced flow of news and information.

Let me reiterate; we do not and cannot deny the right of every news medium, above all the highly developed news agencies with worldwide services, to have their own criteria for what is news and how to interpret events. But we do urge and insist on a full respect for the responsibilities in so doing and a still freer news flow, multidimensional and worldwide.

WHY A MULTIDIMENSIONAL NEWS FLOW?

The sharpest criticism of the present situation in the international news flow is its imbalance, its predominantly one-way flow. The criticism is supported by the established fact of the big gap in the news flow between the small number of advanced countries and the developing countries and logically leads to a two-way flow as the solution.

This imbalance is admitted by the big wire services. They have expressed a readiness to join in efforts to increase the news flow from the developing countries, improve telecommunication conditions, contribute to the technical and professional advancement of information media in underdeveloped countries, and so on.

Our vision, however, of the new international order in the field of information goes considerably beyond this. It is founded in our desire and endeavor to see the realization of one of the basic rights of individuals and peoples—the freedom of access to the news, the right to be fully informed and to inform fully. This will require major changes, or better said, the building up of new elements rooted in the very foundations of the existing system.

Therefore it is not at all a question of replacing the existing worldwide wire services. It is not a question either of simply improving the balance in their news products (albeit a welcome first step). What is needed is to elaborate a complete system—at the bilateral, regional, and multilateral levels—that will enable a multidimensional news flow. A multidimensional news flow must mean access to full news coverage of interest to each and in the interest of each. We have no illusion of a distant future with worldwide news services developed for each existing news agency—there are close to 90 already with their number sure to grow in the future. But we are convinced that there are ways for each country and its news agency to realize the right to report the real facts of interest beyond its frontiers about the most important events of its daily life and its sovereign development.

There is interest also in news coverage of common interest at the regional and continental levels, for groups with similar social systems, among allied movements, and so on. All this goes far beyond the possibilities of one or even more global services. The solution, as we see it, must be a free, universal, multidimensional exchange of news and information. One of its many possible forms, we believe, is that of the Nonaligned News Agencies Pool.

Quite understandably, the experience of the nonaligned news agencies has led radio and television in the nonaligned countries to move toward undertaking cooperation similar to the news agencies pool. A First Conference of Radio and Television Representatives of the Nonaligned Countries was held in late 1977.

Many regional groupings already exist. European news agencies cooperate with entire success in the European Alliance despite the different social systems within which these news agencies operate. The Union of Arab News Agencies was established several years ago. The Union of African News Agencies recently became active. The groups forming Caribbean and Central American news agencies have initiated meetings and already decided on explicit measures to improve the news flow between them, such as telecommunication links and exchange programs.

All this, we believe, is part of the movement toward a freer and multidimensional flow of information and that is what we are looking for.

NOTES

1. Gertrude Ruth Robinson, "Tanjug—Yugoslavia's Multifaceted National News Agency" (Ph.D diss., University of Illinois, 1968).

2. Ibid.

3. For the manner in which these events were reported under government influence by AP and UPI, see the statements of *New York Times* Managing Editor Clifton Daniel, as reported in the *New York Times,* June 2, 1966.

8. ACACAN: A Solution to the Problem of News Flow in the Third World

GUIDO FERNANDEZ

When the idea of a Central American news agency was first conceived, it met with skepticism and a marked lack of interest. The two largest U.S. agencies, the Associated Press (AP) and United Press International (UPI), dismissed it as impractical and predicted the agency, if established, would have a short life. Reuters had established an association with LATIN and had thus far found the experience less than satisfactory. Agence France-Presse (AFP), with few clients in Central America, was not interested in what could prove to be a risky and presumably costly operation.

Moreover, the Central Americans themselves were pessimistic. A segment of the news media thought it was not economically feasible, and although a possible solution would be to apply for government subsidies, it was a method of which they disapproved. Others, even more skeptical, believed that no one would subscribe to the agency's services because not even the Central American people were interested in Central American news.

There were, however, sound reasons to persist. One of the principal reasons was that the five Central American countries and Panama constitute a compact geographical area linked by an up-to-date communications system (microwave), by common interests, and by association in a common market that found itself paralyzed by, among other things, an inadequate exchange of information among the members. Language, customs, a common historical background, and the fact that these countries share a narrow geographical area were all solid reasons to endorse the idea.

Each country also felt a basic need to know what was happening in neighboring countries. The war between Salvador and Honduras, shown to the world through the eyes of international news agencies as triggered by a simple disagreement over a soccer game, was in reality the result of misinformation or a lack of information between the two belligerent countries.

Lastly, Central America was a captive market for global news agencies, which could charge their clients oligopoly prices that unduly increased the clients' operational costs.

The Spanish news agency, EFE, found the idea of a Central American agency worthy of its attention. With its support, and its promise of technical assistance and participation in the equity capital, a group of newspapers and television and radio stations of Central America met in Panama with representatives of EFE and incorporated the new agency.

The bylaws of Agencia Centroamericana de Noticias (ACAN) are not complex. The corporation is registered according to Panamanian law, which is more flexible for the operation of a multinational company. The equity capital is set at $300,000 (Balboas); 300 shares of nominative common stock valued at $1,000 each were issued. EFE committed itself to acquire one share for every two purchased by the media enterprises of the isthmus. The board of directors is made up of seven members: one representative from each of the six countries with the position of treasurer reserved for the EFE delegate. Upon ratification by the board of directors, the appointment of the general manager is to be left up to EFE. In addition to the bylaws, it was decided by unwritten agreement that the board position held by each country would rotate among the members from that specific country. This agreement and these simple bylaws allowed ACAN to function immediately.

Of the 300 shares of stock, 138 have been subscribed to: two-thirds (92 shares) by the press, radio, and television of Central America and Panama and one third (46 shares) by EFE.

The agency was incorporated on December 5, 1972, and started operations on June 6, 1973. During the first three years, the president of the board of directors was Fernando Eleta of Panama. He was succeeded by Guido Fernandez of Costa Rica.

Although there could exist, and in fact, has existed, some rivalry, even hostility, among the newspapers and the TV and radio stations of the isthmus for commercial or political reasons or both, there has been no problem of any kind in assigning the rotating responsibilities to each member. The gentleman's agreement has been rigorously observed.

The agency has contracted for a double microwave circuit, stretching from Guatemala to Panama. There are two full-time correspondents in each country. ACAN has offices and transmitters in the six Central American capitals, where the material is sent out to headquarters in

Panama. At the same time, direct telephone lines go out from each capital to the subscribers.

At present the transmission program functions 10 hours a day. This includes some 60 Central American news items, approximately 10 coming from each country. The rest of the service consists of EFE international news.

EFE's international service comes from Madrid via satellite to Panama. There, a résumé of Central American news is made. This summary is sent by satellite to Madrid where it becomes part of EFE's world service.

The EFE news that is incorporated into the Central American news service bears the EFE acronym. The news originating in Central America for Central American consumption carries the letters ACAN/EFE.

The ACAN effort has not been free from difficulties. For one thing, there is an operational deficit. ACAN has not yet arrived at the break-even point and the expenses are still greater than the income. Cash-flow problems have been solved for now by means of a periodic revision of the rates, competition permitting, and with credit obtained by the company with the Bank of Santander, with the collateral of EFE. For 1977 the operational deficit was calculated at $15,000. If, however, one takes into account the fact that the first year's loss was $60,000 and the second year's was $35,000, the financial improvement is evident. The business hopes to pay all its expenses and to begin the amortization of its debt in the near future.

In 1977 ACAN had 50 subscribers: 13 out of 28 dailies, five out of 18 television stations, and 16 out of the most significant 53 radio stations. The remaining 16 subscribers are private enterprises and government institutions. Competition from North American and European news agencies is very strong, those of North America because their world services are difficult to duplicate and some local media cannot afford to pay for more than one service, and those of Europe because they charge very low prices and in some cases even offer services for the token sum of $50 a month. None of the agencies whose services are sold in Central America have full-time correspondents in these countries. In Costa Rica, for example, it is estimated that all the Western agencies together sell about $10,000 worth of services monthly and spend less than $1,000 a month on stringers. The policy of ACAN is that each of its members pays the salaries of its correspondents and the cost of its microwave service with the income gained from the sale of the news services in that country.

One of the sources of income for ACAN is embassy service—daily bulletins collected by messengers from the chancellories and transmitted first by microwave and then satellite to the diplomatic missions of subscribing foreign governments. The sale of this service is actually the only bond, although of a purely commercial nature, ACAN has with the isthmus governments.

ACAN is trying to finance its operations exclusively through the sale of its news services and reporting. Even though it is unlikely that a government would try to use the withdrawal of the embassy service as a means to pressure the agency, it would be quite a setback for its financial operations. The elimination of embassy services could alter the normal functioning of the agency.

On occasions, the governments of certain countries have attempted to interfere in microwave communications. These interferences are possible, because in all Central America the governments control tele-communications directly or indirectly. But this has occurred only when delicate political situations have existed. It is necessary to recognize that the interference in these cases has been motivated by reasons the governments considered to be legitimate national emergencies and have been applied in a transitory form and without discrimination between international agencies and the local news media. Normally the communication is fluid, without foul-ups, and technically better than radio.

Another problem confronting the agency is the selection of qualified personnel for each of its members. Although ACAN salaries equal those of the highest-paid reporters on a nationally circulated newspaper, the stipulation that ACAN reporters may accept other work makes it difficult to find good journalists. The existing group of correspondents, however, is sufficiently competent so that ACAN has not, up until this point, had to resort to stringers.

ACAN subscribers have not, as yet, made the fullest use of the material provided them, although steady improvement is obvious. At the beginning, they used ACAN news only in cases of civil unrest, catastrophies, earthquakes, hurricanes, or sports events. Little by little the presence of two full-time reporters in each Central American country gave ACAN an advantage over other agencies whose stringers file only what has been already printed in local papers, normally a day later. ACAN's economic, cultural, and political coverage is finding a place for itself in the dailies and other news media. The correspondents are invited to make frequent news analyses and the subscribers evidence growing confidence in their skills and good professional judgment.

EFE has understood the character of ACAN and has respected its independence. It is not a subsidiary of EFE, but a Central American company—the first real transnational company in which both the talent and the capital of the six countries are active—in which EFE has a minor participation and only one seat on the board of directors. The managers named by EFE with the authorization of the board of directors have been extremely competent professionals. The technology and the equipment furnished by EFE have given the agency adequate working conditions. As a result of the more democratic orientation of Spanish politics, EFE, as an agency, has acquired greater autonomy and maturity, and this in turn has allowed it to play a more professional role in ACAN's operation.

The advantages of ACAN can be summed up in Five points. First, it is a basic instrument for Central American integration. It provides an information infrastructure that collects and distributes news about the area, strengthening cultural, political, economic, and social ties upon which the development of the area depends. Second, it encourages reciprocal understanding among peoples who, in spite of the characteristics they have in common, maintain separate identities. Third, it fosters a wide diffusion of the news throughout the Spanish-speaking world. The *Diario de las Americas* of Miami, for example, with a circulation reaching the entire Hispanic community in that region, dedicates a whole page daily to Central American news. The Mexican, Venezuelan, and Columbian papers, as subscribers to EFE, now have more and better information about Central America than ever before.

A fourth advantage lies in EFE's international service, which gives Central American countries a better understanding of what is happening in Spain. The political transition in that country since the death of Franco has been observed more accurately, thanks to the impartiality of the news agency.

Last, although ACAN does not aspire to displace any international agency, it is competing efficiently as a second or complementary service indispensable to the Central American press. Long before the idea of a Latin American regional agency was discussed in UNESCO, this agency was born as a typical Third World agency with the advantage of being politically independent and of being self-controlled and self-managed.

9. ESTABLISHING AND MAINTAINING A FREE PRESS: A Latin American Viewpoint

RAUL KRAISELBURD

DEVELOPING AN INDEPENDENT NEWS AGENCY

Nothing is more important for a developing nation right now than that its journalists and newspapers lead the effort to establish permanent communication with the world. If this effort should be left to the government, the consequences would be serious not only for journalism as a profession but also for freedom of expression and for the future of democracy.

In 1972, I formed a commission to study the possibility of forming an independent national news agency in Argentina. After examining all aspects of the project, the commission concluded that the only thing lacking in Argentina was the willingness of the newspapers to act. Many directors of Argentine newspapers considered the idea to be reckless and doubted that such an initiative could ever be carried out. They assumed that the newspapers would not pay the required fees, that they would not have the know-how, and that only a foreigner could head up such a firm. However, when the Peron government announced its intention of establishing an information monopoly, it took only the approval of the smallest and a few of the medium-sized newspapers to establish Noticias Argentinas. Even those who originally opposed the idea now contract the agency's services.

The formula for establishing Noticias Argentinas was very simple. We began by estimating the cost of the most limited services. We then divided this cost among the newspapers that were willing to pay for it. The willingness to risk that amount was little in comparison with what was gained. Our system was very simple; we were going to spend 100 and get 100. At the outset, the service was primitive but we had begun.

Although Argentina is a large country, with over one million square miles (2,776,889 sq km), a third of the country's 23 million citizens live in and around Buenos Aires, the capital city. Our first difficulty in trying to create a national news service was that the large newspapers of Buenos Aires already had their own correspondents in all the important provinces of the country. Furthermore, the newspapers in the provinces were especially interested in news about the federal government. Thus, we ran into the problem of having nothing important to sell to the large newspapers of the capital. Added to this was the fact that only four of our clients had a circulation of over 40,000 copies a day. Our budget was limited by the economic constraints on those who were going to buy our service. We are talking here about newspapers with a circulation of 10,000 or less. In 1973, we were able to spend $15,000 monthly, which barely covered the expense of maintaining some journalists in the capital and paying the high cost of transmission of our news stories. The four daily newspapers with circulation above 40,000 agreed to pay $1,500 each month. The rate for those with lower circulation was $100 per month.

These economic constraints created serious problems in competing with the state news agency, Telam, which also handled the paid advertisements of the state. In a country where at least 40 percent of the economy is administered by the state, the advertisement of its enterprises is very important. Advertising revenues are used as a means of pressuring newspapers to buy Telam's service and not that of Noticias Argentinas. In addition, Telam can spend any amount it cares to and charge very little for its news service because the state covers its losses.

The four large dailies receive our service by wire or by telephone. About 50 other papers receive it by radio. Hardly two months after the agency's creation, the presidential press secretary requested that the communications center not allow Noticias Argentinas to use the state's radio equipment. A great outcry arose from all the newspapers, even those not receiving our services. The opposition party, protested. We were able to continue transmitting, but there were always inconveniences.

In addition, the communications system in Argentina suffers from chronic deficiency. The telephone system often does not function for hours at a time. Our radio transmissions suffer interference. The newspapers have very old radio receivers and have neglected to care for their antennas and teletype equipment. A group of young technicians began advising us. We had to finance the building of receivers and radio-teletypes and sell them to the small newspapers, which could hardly afford them. We also offer free advice regarding antennas and other technical matters. However, there are still problems with transmission. But the high cost of microwave systems and telephone lines forces us to use radio transmission as our primary means of communication. The rates for the other services are much higher in Argentina than in other countries.

We hope that by the time the World Championship of Soccer is held in Buenos Aires in 1978, the communications system in Argentina will have been upgraded in accordance with the government's plan. Even so, Noticias Argentinas will run into problems regarding the purchase of equipment. Besides equipment needed for the central office, we need to install teletype machines and photo transmitters in the principle cities of the interior. Financing this upgrading presents a serious economic problem.

Although our revenues have increased considerably within a short time, operating costs have gone up accordingly, so equipment purchases must be made from other funds. We could raise our clients' rates, but in many cases they do not have the money for radio receivers, and it would be almost impossible for them to consider radiophotograph receivers.

Besides the need for credit, Noticias Argentinas also seeks to acquire equipment that has fallen into disuse in the United States. For example, the acquisition of radiophotograph receivers that North Americans might consider obsolete would be an important advance for us, allowing us to enlarge our limited buyers' market. Even on a strictly commercial basis, such transactions would be advantageous for the U.S. newspapers and news agencies that are now practically throwing the old equipment away. Instead of abandoning the equipment, they could sell it to us at a reasonable price over a period of time.

The operational problems of Noticias Argentinas are similar to the problems of the small and medium-sized newspapers in Argentina. While an American pays about 0.8 percent of his monthly salary to have a newspaper delivered to his home, in Argentina it costs 5 percent of one's salary. Newspapers, then, are very expensive for the general public. Because of the economic crisis, people must pay greater attention to other necessities. In such a situation, Noticias Argentinas must bear in mind that its clients are having economic difficulty. It cannot charge them the full price for its services.

In spite of these problems, during its four years in operation, Noticias Argentinas has made great progress. It has consistently transmitted for 18 hours a day, by radio and teletype, and maintained a radiophotograph service for morning and evening newspapers. From the beginning, the international scene was covered by UPI (United Press International) through a service contract. At the outset, the overseas section occupied almost the same amount of space as the national section. As the months passed, the tendency was to expand the coverage of news within the country; the importance of international news decreased correspondingly.

During the early days, it was thought that the 40 newspapers that were stockholders in Noticias Argentinas would be the agency's correspondents in the country's interior. Because of this, we had journalists only in Buenos Aires. The system began to change once Horacio Tanto took over as the agency's director. Correspondents were appointed for such important Argentine cities as Córdoba and Rosario. As the services increased, so did the number of clients, and the large dailies of Buenos Aires began to contract with Noticias Argentinas. The initial $15,000 in monthly revenues has increased over four years to $35,000, but costs have increased at the same rate. And, in spite of political pressures and the unfair competition waged during the Peron era by Telam, Noticias Argentinas' services have been contracted by almost 100 percent of the private communications media in Argentina.

The stockholders are the same as when the agency was founded. Although other newspapers now receive the service, they have not bought stock. In accordance with the bylaws of the corporation, no newspaper or person may own more than 10 percent of the stock or of the votes in a stockholders' meeting. The agency's board must include representatives of newspapers from different parts of the country and with different levels of circulation. My father was the first chairman of Noticias Argentinas. After he was assassinated, his place was taken by Ovidio Lagos of the newspaper *La Capital* of Rosario. *La Capital* is one of the most important newspapers in the country, currently selling more than 50,000 copies daily. The next chairman was the director of the newspaper *Rio Negro* in the city of Roca. It has a circulation of 25,000. The vice-chairman is the director of an old, traditional newspaper in a small city, whose daily circulation is about 5,000 copies.

Besides these rules to assure that newspapers from all over the country and of whatever importance participate in running the agency, it is also worth noting that among the stockholders of Noticias Argentinas are newspapers with completely opposing political views. The potential conflict inherent in this situation has demanded a high level of professionalism and objectivity on the agency's part.

With the growing number of news items being transmitted regarding various problems within the country, it has become necessary to carry columnists who analyze and comment upon the news. Often, two or more commentaries reflecting different opinions on the same subject are transmitted. This can be done because journalists with different points of view work for Noticias Argentinas. Such diverse viewpoints are valuable in cities where there is competition and two or more dailies receive our service; each can select its own commentary.

Right now, the difference in rates for various newspapers is fixed according to their importance in a city, with a reduction of 50 percent for afternoon newspapers. The stockholders normally receive a 20 percent discount on rates, as a form of compensation for their efforts in the beginning and for the capital contributions they undoubtedly will continue to make. By Argentine law, no foreigner or corporation with foreign stockholders may be the owner of a news agency. For this reason, the prestigious Buenos Aires *Herald* could not be a stockholder, although it buys the service, just as the Buenos Aires newspapers *La Prensa, La Opinión, Clarín, La Nación, Crónica,* and *La Razón* now do. These important newspapers began to receive our services about two years ago. They have recognized the importance of Noticias Argentinas' coverage in the interior of the country and even in the city of Buenos Aires itself.

With regard to growth, it is hard to imagine that we will increase our clientele. The only remaining possibility is that we sell the service to radio and television, both of which are, in general, state controlled. We cannot hope to improve our quality immediately if this means passing on higher costs to our clients. For the moment we are concentrating on improving the transmission service and increasing the market for our photographic department. Perhaps we could make an effort in the area of specialized services, which some newspapers might want to acquire. As far as overseas sales, all the large news agencies in the world are currently buying our service, and often using it—according to what I have observed in different countries. I have often read with pride in a dispatch the words "according to the private news agency Noticias Argentinas." Basically, we do the journalistic coverage for the large agencies, although they have their own correspondents and normally send their own dispatches and stories as well. However, our journalists are conscious of the responsibility they hold. Their dispatches are generally published in all the newspapers in the interior of Argentina and are the source of many cables from international agencies. This is how we in Argentina have become independent of all government political propaganda. The newspapers themselves found a way to combat the attempt to establish a state news monopoly.

The newspaper of which I am director does not receive Telam's service, only that of Noticias Argentinas. This does not create any problems for us in competing with the large daily newspapers of Buenos Aires, just 40 miles from La Plata. Over the years, we have preferred not to receive Telam's service, considering it an instrument of propaganda. We continue to be proud of our achievement, as much from the technical and professional points of view as from the stand-point of sustaining the basic principles of pluralistic journalism, princi-ples upon which rests the possibility of creating a democratic society in Argentina.

In a world where different and contradictory interests are inter-twined, a knowledge of the truth and a plurality of opinion help to improve the quality of life and facilitate the building of a democracy. All the enemies of democracy, without fail, stand against the idea of a plurality of information. So that it may survive, we must meet the challenge of informing the public, giving them the best of ourselves and of the facts.

10.

THE NONALIGNED NEWS AGENCIES POOL AND THE FREE FLOW OF MEANINGFUL NEWS: An African Viewpoint

BIOLA OLASOPE

The decision of the ministerial conference of nonaligned nations, held in New Delhi, India, from July 8 to 13, 1976, to set up a news agencies pool is as important politically and economically as the decisions made at the first meeting of nonaligned nations at the Bandung Conference of 1955. It is regarded by some as setting in motion the second phase of the liberation of the peoples of Africa, Asia, and Latin America. And it has evoked from the erstwhile imperial powers in the news industry the same kind of reactions that the struggle for political independence evoked during its early days.

Just as the imperialist powers failed to understand why their subjects wanted to be masters in their own houses, so those who dominate and direct the world news industry today appear not to be willing to understand why their clients should want to set up their own businesses. Just as emotionalism, selfishness, and shortsightedness marred the transition from colonialism to independence, so these factors appear to be coming into play in the new situation. And just as independence resulted in a more rational, equitable, and mutually beneficial relationship between former imperialists and former subjects in many cases, so can we expect the new development in the world news industry to lead to a new and more meaningful relationship if it is handled well by both sides.

The situation that has given rise to the present "crisis"—for it seems as if it is regarded as a "crisis" in certain quarters—may be seen in clearer terms if looked at from a geopolitical point of view. From time immemorial, it has been the practice of imperialists to carve out portions of the world exclusively for themselves. The Portuguese and the Spaniards who were the superpowers in the fifteenth and sixteenth centuries drew a line down the middle of what was then regarded as a flat world and each nation claimed half as its exclusive area of influence and operation. At the Berlin Conference of 1884 the European powers carved up Africa in a similar manner. The United States joined them later to carve up the world, outside Europe and North America, as virtually exclusive areas of influence. These decisions have had wide-ranging ramifications, and in spite of the achievement of political independence by the peoples of the former areas of influence, strong vestiges of the old order still remain.

One such vestige is the domination and control of the flow of news in these areas by the news agencies of the former imperialist powers that dominated each other. Reuters dominates the flow of news in the former British colonies. Agence France-Presse (AFP) is stronger than any other news agency in the French-speaking countries, and the two American news agencies, Associated Press (AP) and United Press International (UPI), are in effective control of Latin America. As a result, the flow of news among the countries of Africa, for example, and between them and the rest of the world, is controlled by news agencies based in, owned, and operated by countries outside Africa. This system has been a great impediment to the free flow of news in the world, and this is why the nonaligned nations see a need to change it.

IMPEDIMENTS TO THE FREE FLOW OF NEWS

No one will deny the fact that under the present system dominated by the Western news agencies, the flow of news among African countries is far from satisfactory. One of the reasons for this is that the system was not set up to facilitate such a flow. It was not set up to collect news in Africa for use in Africa by the African media. The prime object of each news agency's operations in Africa has been and still is the collection of news for distribution to its world market. The only other concern these agencies have is to sell the composite news output of their organizations to local news media. The special needs of the African mass media are given no, or at least secondary, consideration as far as African news is concerned. As a result, the scope of the operations of each agency is strictly limited. Reuters and AFP maintain offices only in a few African capitals where their countries have crucial political and economic interests. They also retain a few stringers in a few centers outside the capital. Because of this, their coverage of events in any country is greatly limited. The size of the staff restricts the number of events covered, thus giving attention to just one or two of the many that occur each week in each country.

The decision to report or not report an event is also influenced by its news value to the market the agency serves, a value that is usually a reflection of the political and economic interests of the West. When the reports reach the headquarters of the news agencies, they are passed along with stories from other sources through the processing and filtering machinery that finally determines what is fed to the world. During this process, they lose some details and may have their orientation changed while others of these reports are rejected outright. One may, therefore, discover that by the end of the week only two or three of the 100 or more events reported in the local mass media are mentioned by the international news agencies.

The overall result of this situation is that the Third World countries including the People's Republic of China (PRC), accounting for about two-thirds of the world's population, are alloted less than one-tenth of the news output of the Western-owned news agencies. The principle of equality, either of man or of nations, obviously has no bearing on the agencies' operations. Although no one is suggesting a kind of proportional representation in news output, it is obvious that if the Western news agencies gave all countries or regions similar treatment, the volume and the pattern of world news flow would be very different from what they are today.

Two excuses—one economic, the other political—are usually offered in defense of the present state of world news flow. The economic argument has two aspects, first, that the clients of the so-called international news agencies, that is, the Western mass media, are not interested in ordinary developments in the Third World, and second, that the market in a region like Africa is too small to support any extensive operations. The political argument is that the political center of gravity in the world is not in Africa, Asia, or Latin America, but somewhere in Western Europe and North America.

The conclusions one can draw from the unstated premises of these arguments are obvious. The first is that because the Western-owned news agencies are not public-service, but profit-oriented, organizations, they do not consider it necessary or desirable to ensure a free flow of news at all costs. Second, the agencies believe that the world belongs to the rich and powerful nations and whatever the poor and weak nations do is really not so important unless they do something that may disturb the present political and economic order. These views are two of the key impediments to the free flow of news in a region like Africa.

Another aspect of the problem is the attitude, the preferences, and the prejudices of foreign newsmen. The new states of Africa and the rest of the Third World are today preoccupied with social and economic development. They are building hospitals, schools, roads, skyscrapers. To them, but not to the Western correspondents, this development is what is new and relevant. The voluminous development plans are dismissed in a few paragraphs, if the plans belong to countries that the correspondents fancy; otherwise they are ignored. The development and, indeed, transformation that is going on all around is hardly ever noticed while events or issues that are insignificant or that in no way contribute to the progress of the nation, but rather create a bad image, get interpreted from the Western point of view and are blown up out of all proportion. African countries receive the attention of the Western mass media only when they are involved in coups or rebellions or when those of their leaders who are not considered pro-Western engage in outrageous or embarrassing acts. The developing countries have always complained about this treatment. As the Philippines Foreign Minister Carlos P. Romulo recently said, "The governments of most of these countries feel that, for whatever reason, events there are not being reported fairly, that their policies and actions are being misinterpreted in the Western mass media."

The sense of news value and the editorial judgment of the correspondents of the Western news agencies are therefore a distinct impediment to the free flow of news from the African point of view. The flow is controlled by the whims and caprices of these correspondents. It is only what they choose to report that becomes news and how they write about these choices determines how the rest of the world sees this news. Their deliberate or inadvertent distortions and fabrications are accepted by the innocent reader or listener as facts because they come under the prestigious name of Reuters, AFP, or AP, but in the developing world the well-informed editor and the discerning reader are not deceived.

AFRICA AND THE PRESENT NEWS DISTRIBUTION SYSTEM

African mass media organizations are dependent almost exclusively on the Western-owned news agencies for their supply of news about Africa and the rest of the world. The Nigerian Broadcasting Corporation, for example, subscribes to the services of Reuters and AFP. Nigeria is in the process of setting up its own national news agency, but even the few African countries that already have news agencies of their own still depend heavily on the foreign news agencies for their external news. They do not even have correspondents in other

African countries. Lagos, the capital of Nigeria, is a major power center within the African context, but no African news agency maintains an office there at present. The reasons for this unsatisfactory situation are simple. African countries lack the funds, trained personnel, and facilities needed for setting up and operating an international network for gathering and distributing news.

So the collection and distribution of news about Africa is entirely in the hands of foreign news agencies who owe no loyalty to any African country or institution and who may not fully appreciate the interests and aspirations of the African people. These agencies determine what one African country should know about events in other African countries; they determine what events should be reported and which should not; they determine as well, through careful selection of facts, the emphasis and orientation of each story and, by implication, its impact. As a result, most Africans who read newspapers or listen to radio today see their fellow Africans through the eyes of Western correspondents. Unknowingly, Africans judge issues and interpret events from Western viewpoints. A few newspaper and radio organizations, however, take the trouble to edit and rewrite news agency copy before use, but this can be quite a tedious job for a painstaking editor because the prejudices of the correspondents are so unobtrusively woven into the story that it always takes a bit of effort to identify and eliminate them. The problem is even greater for a broadcasting organization that has to use a news item almost as soon as it comes in.

But through experience one learns to identify some of these distortions and misrepresentations. For example, to us in the Nigerian Broadcasting Corporation, those whom the Western news media describe as "terrorists" in southern Africa are "nationalists" or "freedom fighters." The word "tribesmen" is automatically struck off or replaced with "people," for if there are no U.S. or British tribesmen, there is no reason why the people of Nigeria or Kenya should be referred to in that derogatory and outdated term. Obviously, the editors of the Nigerian Broadcasting Corporation would be spared this time-wasting exercise if they were taking their news from an African news agency.

THE FLOW OF NEWS BETWEEN AFRICA AND THE REST OF THE WORLD

Just as the flow of news within Africa is almost entirely controlled by the Western-owned news agencies, so is the flow between Africa and the rest of the world. And the results are the same. Africa sees the rest of the world through Western eyes. The news agency tapes are flooded with news about the Western world, ranging from Strategic Arms Limitation Talks to American baseball results. On the other hand, there is usually only a trickle of news from the Third World and the socialist countries, and what come from these areas are mainly reports of disaster, dissension, and disruption. There is hardly anything about development or events of a positive, pleasant nature.

In the Nigerian Broadcasting Corporation, we have a program "Window on the World," in which we review major developments around the world each week. This 15-minute program treats four or five events in detail. The writers, who usually go through all the available news agency material, listing the week's major events, invariably find that far more than half the events reported in great detail, by implication expected to be regarded as major, originate in the Western world. On the other hand, it is on very rare occasions that one finds any detailed story about events in the socialist world. Of course, when the Western world latches on to an issue like that of "dissidents" in the Soviet Union, we are fed "ad nauseam" with details on this. As for the nonaligned countries, the few reports of events in these areas are usually short, leaving many questions unanswered, although occasionally events involving a threat to Western economic or political interests, such as the Zairean crisis or a flare-up in the Middle East, are reported in great detail, but with a pro-Western slant.

It is under these circumstances that the material for the program "Window on the World" is compiled. The intention of the producers is to give the listeners an accurate picture of the world in the past week, but by courtesy of Reuters and AFP, the picture of the world is often a thoroughly distorted one, and one which can be traced to the limitations that have been placed on the free flow of news to Africa.

Now, how about the picture of Africa seen by the rest of the world? The situation is a little bit more complex. The rest of the world has to be divided into three parts: the Western world, the rest of the nonaligned states, and the socialist countries. The major news agencies of the West and the socialist countries maintain skeleton operations in Africa. Each bloc receives news about Africa through its own correspondents, who have been trained to recognize what their employers and their clients want to know about Africa. As a result, each group of countries sees the image of Africa that it wants to see and the two images are as different from each other as the ideological orientations and economic interests of the two groups of states. Obviously, neither image is completely accurate because there is no free flow of news in each situation. The stream of news is checked, controlled, broken up, and only a small portion of it is processed for consumption by each group of countries.

But if the news material about Africa that reaches the Western and socialist countries is inadequate and inaccurate, the situation is of their own making. The news agencies that supply the material are subject to the control of the governments or of certain responsible and influential groups in the countries in which they are based. But not so, the nonaligned countries. They are in the same situation as African countries as far as news about Africa is concerned. Because their newspapers and radios subscribe to one or more of the news agencies owned by the advanced countries, the flow of African news to them is also controlled, inadequate, and distorted.

We have, so far, been examining the existing international news gathering and distributing system with particular reference to how it is serving the needs of Africa and the rest of the nonaligned world. It may be pertinent to draw some conclusions at this juncture as to whether or not the system as it is now is ensuring the free flow of news. In fairness to the major news agencies of both the East and the West, there is no evidence that the main objective of establishing them was to ensure an absolutely free flow of news throughout the world, nor are they deliberatelay preventing the free flow of news, but financial, political, cultural, and psychological factors prevent them from being able to ensure a free flow of news throughout the world.

There is no free flow of news between African countries because there is no machinery set up for it. The foreign news agencies that operate in Africa have staff and facilities in just a few centers and the few African news agencies that exist gather news mainly for domestic consumption. As a result, most of the newsworthy events that occur within each African country never get reported to others.

There is no free flow of news from Africa to the outside world. Although some of the major news agencies of the Western and socialist countries operate in Africa, their coverage is limited and their output influenced by the political and economic interests of their countries and clients. As a result, most of the newsworthy events that occur in Africa never get to the notice of the outside world, and what is reported is sometimes distorted.

There is no free flow of news from the rest of the world to Africa. Most of the events that happen in the Third World countries never get reported to Africa because there is no machinery to facilitate unimpeded flow of news within this area. The foreign news agencies determine what Africa should know about the rest of the world.

THE NEED FOR A NEW WORLD ORDER
IN THE NEWS INDUSTRY

The present system of gathering and distributing news is patently unsatisfactory. It does not allow the collection and distribution of a great proportion of the news available in the world. It is lopsided in its operation, concentrating on the developed countries to the detriment of the developing ones, thereby creating a gross and unjustifiable imbalance in the flow of news. The system is also entirely owned and controlled by the advanced countries who use it in different ways to further their own political and economic interests.

Just as there is a need for a new and more equitable world economic order, so there is an obvious and urgent need to replace the present international news gathering and distribution setup with a new arrangement that will facilitate a greater flow of news, a balance in the pattern of flow, and will lead to better understanding, through knowledge, among the nations of the world. Such an arrangement is still a thing of the future. But those who are most aggrieved at the present state of affairs—the nonaligned nations—have taken a decision to make a modest change in the system as it affects them by setting up a news agencies pool.

According to the resolution that was adopted by the New Delhi Ministerial Conference of Nonaligned Countries on the Press Agencies Pool, the objectives of the pool are

> . . . to improve and expand mutual exchange of information and further strengthen cooperation among nonaligned countries.
> . . . to facilitate dissemination of correct and factual information about nonaligned countries as well as the international community in general.
> . . . to fill the gap that exists in this field by providing further information about the nonaligned countries and their policies.

The document also emphasizes the point that "objective information is the basic premise of the Pool, with emphasis on progressive, economic, sociopolitical, and cultural developments as well as mutual cooperation and action."

Looked at dispassionately, these objectives are professionally respectable and politically desirable. The world would be the better for it if they could be realized; the main outcome would be the opening up of the nonaligned countries to one another and to the rest of the world. This would mean a much freer flow of news and a greater volume of news than we have in the world today. There would also be a change in the context and orientation of news from the nonaligned countries. News about the really important events in the nonaligned world—"progressive, economic, sociopolitical, and cultural developments"—would be made available to the world along with the foreign news agencies' usual menu of disaster, dissension, and disruption, and the flow of news would be closer to being balanced. One would therefore expect all lovers of a truly free flow of news in the world to give full and enthusiastic support to this noble project; instead, there have been expressions of misgivings about it in some quarters.

It has been said, for example, that since the news agencies in the nonaligned countries are usually owned by governments, there would be no freedom of the press. This is a non sequitur. AFP is owned by the French government, but no one has accused it of being a mouthpiece of that government; Reuters, through some covert channels, is subsidized and influenced by the British government; and the Central Intelligence Agency (CIA) has confessed that it uses the correspondents of U.S. news agencies abroad as agents. There is no basis for a "holier-than-thou attitude" on the part of the Western news agencies.

The news agencies in the nonaligned countries are being run by professional journalists, some of them with as much experience, expertise, and professional pride as their counterparts in the developed countries. Many of them have gone to jail and detention in defense of press freedom while others are sticking to their convictions in subtler ways. It would be a slur on their integrity to assume that the proposed news agencies pool cannot serve any useful purpose without giving it a chance to prove itself. Nigerian news organizations accept reports of British events by Reuters without doubting the integrity of British journalists; the British must be willing to do likewise with the News Agency of Nigeria. For the British to do otherwise would be to expose themselves to charges of arrogance based on prejudice. After all, it is always better to hear news straight from the horse's mouth. In any event, each editor has the final say over what he decides to publish or broadcast, but prejudice should not prevent him from seeing all that is available before he makes his decision. Just as we in the Nigerian Broadcasting Corporation plow through acres of news agency tapes, sifting the wheat from the chaff, so U.S. or French editors should be willing to do the same, using whatever they finally select in whatever way they choose. This could be a highly educational experience.

It seems that the impression is being given by some critics that the news agencies pool would enjoy a monopoly on news from the nonaligned countries. This is far from the truth. The Western news agencies will definitely lose their monopoly in the area, but the world should be the richer for it. The news agencies pool will make news items available to other news agencies, mass communication media, and other interested organizations.

THE ADVANTAGES OF THE NEWS AGENCIES POOL

The first advantage of the Nonaligned News Agencies Pool is that there would be a more effective coverage of events and distribution of news in the nonaligned countries for the benefit of the world at large. According to the resolution of the New Delhi conference, "each participating Agency will itself prepare and select information on the basis of mutual respect and common interest which will be offered through the Pool" and "all distributing News Agencies will provide in their daily transmission or newscasts a mutually agreed duration of time to be devoted to distribution of news received from other participants." For once, "mutual respect" and "common interest," and not profit or prejudice, will be the guiding factors in the collection and distribution of news. This is a welcome development.

Each news agency in the pool, because of its desire to publicize events in its country and because of its duty to contribute to the pool, can be expected to ensure a regular flow of news from each country. In return, each agency will enjoy a regular flow of news about other countries. All the available material will also be placed at the disposal of the rest of the world. The result would be a sharp increase in the volume of news on the nonaligned countries.

Another advantage is that the economic impediment to the free flow of news would be removed. Since each country will be responsible for the gathering of news within its borders, there should be a relative drop in the cost. The amount AFP or Reuters spends on maintaining one correspondent in Lagos can be used to pay the salaries of 10 local reporters and with better results.

The total outcome is that there will be a freer and more meaningful flow of news within and from the nonaligned countries. The flow of news will be freer because a machinery for facilitating it exists where there was none before. It will be freer because each member of the pool has an interest in contributing to it and because mutual respect and common interest will be the guiding principles. It will be freer because one major impediment to the operations of the Western news agencies in the nonaligned countries—the profit motive—will not come into play and relative cost will be reduced.

The pool will ensure a more meaningful flow of news because it will ensure that the news of the events that are really relevant within the context of the life and aspirations of the nonaligned countries will circulate among them and flow out to the outside world. This would be a more realistic reflection of the totality of newsworthy activities taking place in the area at any given time. The expected increase in the volume of news flowing from the nonaligned countries to the Western countries should go some way in redressing the glaring imbalance that now exists.

The establishment of the Nonaligned News Agencies Pool should therefore be regarded as a necessary and desirable step toward the setting up of a new and more equitable world order in the gathering and dissemination of news.

11.
ATTEMPTS OF THE ARAB WORLD TO PARTICIPATE IN BALANCING THE FLOW OF INFORMATION

MOHAMED ABDEL GAWAD

Since the early 1960s, the Arab countries have been taking part in conferences and seminars aimed at studying the best means to adopt to ensure the free flow of information. They have made progress in deciding what they want and in steering clear of the dangers forecast in foreign speculations that attempt to discredit the authenticity of the reports issuing from these meetings. Such foreign attempts have been much in vogue ever since the Arab countries obtained independence and control over their own affairs.

A fair analyst must bear in mind the circumstances of the Arab states, which inherited problems bequeathed by imperialism, which had plundered their natural resources for hundreds of years, leaving behind nations sapped by poverty and ignorance. Most of the Arab countries had ancient civilizations, which attest to the fact that the people of these nations are not backward by nature but only as a consequence of the circumstances through which these countries have passed. It is strange that the Arab world, the cradle of ancient civilizations and the birthplace of monotheistic religions, should now be entered in the list of backward areas. The Pharaonic, Babylonian, and Assyrian civilizations that flourished in the ancient Arab world knew the importance of communication thousands of years ago. In ancient Egypt, journals were inscribed on stone tablets. The oldest Egyptian journal, a military one inscribed on both sides of stone tablets, was well edited by a certain Ptah. It was a monthly periodical distributed among army commanders and government authorities with a circulation of about 100 copies. Such journalistic activity was not confined to one ruler or one dynasty, but was a system pursued by all the Pharaohs.

In Nineveh, the seat of the Assyrian empire, for another instance, copies of an army journal were found in the form of clay tablets. The historian Flavius Josephus asserts that the Babylonians had writers of annals whose function was to record events like present-day journalists. The Assyrians are credited with the introduction of picture journalism. They used to serialize their victories. Each serial number indicated color pictures of kings and citizens taken captive. These tablets were put on show in the palaces, public halls, and main streets.

The printing press developed and spread at a time when the Arab world lay under the yoke of the Ottoman empire, which disrupted every country it ruled. With the end of the Ottoman rule, the Arab world fell prey to French and British occupation, which tried to eradicate the personality of the area altogether. When the printing press finally came into the Arab world with the French occupation of Egypt in 1798, it could have exercised a major effect if Napoleon had not issued an order severely restricting its use. Article Five of that order stipulated that the Arab printing press should come under the direct control of a Frenchman. No one could print anything without permission from him. Article Six of the order placed the French printing press under the direct control of another Frenchman. The laws of publication continued to be restrictive. Any criticism of government activities or any treatment of matters of government concern were banned. The occupation authorities jailed many Arab journalists and even hanged some of them. Many other Arab journalists were interned, while still others fled to Europe.

Much later, when the Arab nations won their independence, the gratuitous foreign advice was that they should free their mass information media from government tutelage. The Western information media, particularly the news agencies, overlooked the fact that they themselves could not always remain outside the sphere of their governments. Reuters, for instance, played an open role in the service of British propaganda during World War I; Sir Roderick Jones was at the same time manager of the agency and director of propaganda in the British Ministry of Information. No one can assert that the direction of propaganda conformed with the agency's claim of neutrality.

Some of the Western news agencies receive subsidies from their governments whenever such aid is necessary for their survival. Some news agency correspondents have been accused of espionage for their governments in the countries where they are accredited. There are other cases where, apparently, a news agency itself has used the activities of its correspondents to serve political purposes outside the sphere of information. This does not mean that the work of the news agencies necessarily or even frequently conceals suspicious activities or that the correspondents of world news agencies are secret agents of intelligence services, but it does mean that it is remarkable that the Western information media should persist in the claims that the poorly financed news agencies of the Arab countries and other Third World nations should free themselves from depending on government financing or, if they do not, remain permanently suspect.

Imperialism deprived the nations that were under occupation from getting their share of training and experience and left behind poor means of communication. Yet these nations have definitely made tangible progress through experience. They now need solidarity to work out a formula of cooperation in the flow of information.

The big question now is can the world news mechanisms give a helping hand to the Third World groupings in their attempts to achieve this balance? The doors of joint interests and reciprocal benefits are open to anyone who is ready to forgo individual advantage, for this can only produce benefit for one at the expense of the others.

The Arab world has found its way to achieve balance in the flow of information. On the one hand, it welcomes cooperation with the world news agencies, which have their mechanisms and correspondents in every country. The reports of these agencies are printed in the Arab newspapers side by side with the news reports of the national agencies. The national agencies of the Third World see the gloomy pictures about the Third World nations conveyed by the world news agencies. It should be the responsibility of the national agencies to convey to the world the achievements of the Third World countries and to give a true image of the struggle of these countries for more production and development.

The Arab countries are trying to achieve balance in the flow of information through three principle instruments: the Union of Arab News Agencies, the Union of African News Agencies, and the Nonaligned News Agencies Pool. These several instruments are needed because the Arab world comprises many states and extends across large tracts of Asia and Africa. These countries have found it useful to study their case inside a union that embraces all of them, namely the Union of Arab News Agencies. The idea of establishing this union came up at the conference of the directors of Arab news agencies held in Cairo in October 1964.

Since 1963, when the African countries began to prepare for a pan-African news agency, the Arab states situated in Africa have been members of the Union of African News Agencies. The Arab countries located on the African continent constitute an important element for linking the Arab and African unions together in the search for ways of cooperation between the African and Arab countries in the field of information in general and the field of news agencies in particular.

As all the Arab countries are members of the nonaligned group, they participate in supporting the idea of pools. This idea began to bear fruit with the declaration of a number of news agencies of nonaligned countries, such as Tanjug of Yugoslavia and the Middle East News Agency (MENA) of Egypt, that they would work together as a pool.

Dialogue has also started between the Arab and European news agencies. Their first seminar was held in Tunis in 1976 to examine ways of cooperation between the Arab and European news agencies.

These various unions have held many conferences that have worked out important formulas of cooperation. Application of the recommendations that have come out of the conferences can produce tangible results regarding the balance of the flow of information.

THE UNION OF ARAB NEWS AGENCIES AND
THE BALANCING OF INFORMATION

In 1964 the directors of all Arab news agencies then existing held a conference at the Arab League headquarters in Cairo from October 24 to 28. The delegates, who met as a constituent committee, adopted a formal resolution to establish the Union of Arab News Agencies and discussed a proposal to set up a unified Arab news agency.

At that time, many Arab countries still depended entirely on the four world news agencies for coverage of world news, including news of the Arab world. The proposal envisaged a unified Arab news agency that would open bureaus in all the Arab countries and in the main capitals on all continents.

The first conference of the Union of Arab News Agencies was held in Amman on July 24, 1965. The constitution and the statutes of the union were laid down. The Arab League Council ratified them on September 15, 1973. The second conference of the union, in Baghdad in April 1974—10 years after the first planning conference in Cairo—laid down the basic rules for the functioning of the union, amended the constitution and the statutes in keeping with existing conditions, and adopted a set of resolutions and recommendations for the actual start of the union's work. Decisions were taken to establish headquarters for the union and to elect a secretary-general for a three-year term on a full-time basis. A few months after the second conference in Baghdad, the third conference was held in Beirut in November 1974. The union started its work at the beginning of January 1975 in Beirut, after a secretary-general had been elected.

The first article of the union's constitution stipulates: "A union of the national news agencies of the Arab countries is formed within the framework of the Arab League, with a legal personality." The union comprises a general assembly and a general secretariat as its principle mechanism. Membership in the union is divided into active members, associate members, and observers. The active members are all the national news agencies in the Arab world. The associate members are official organizations engaged in the gathering and distribution of news in the Arab countries where no national agencies are operating, as well as branches of agencies existing in Arab countries alongside the national agencies. The observer status is given to world and foreign news agencies, press associations, and international organizations connected with information work, such as the United Nations Educational, Scientific and Cultural Organization (UNESCO).

The General Assembly of the Union of Arab News Agencies consists of representatives of the news agencies that are active members, that is, the board chairmen and the general directors or the editors-in-chief of the Arab national news agencies. Each chief delegate is accompanied by, at most, two advisers. The associate members and observers are invited to attend the meetings of the general assembly, which are held once a year in November, although the general assembly may hold extraordinary meetings at the request of at least three active members. Each member has one vote; resolutions are adopted by ordinary majority.

The general assembly elects the members of the general secretariat of the union, the executive body of the union, from among its active members. The General Assembly of the Union of Arab News Agencies held its fifth conference at the Arab League Secretariat from January 15 to 18, 1977. The conference was attended by representatives from nearly all the national Arab news agencies and by the general director of the Palestinian news agency WAFA (Wakalep Anba El-Falastinieh). I had the honor of being elected president of the union for the current session.

The union encourages the conclusion of agreements for the exchange of news among the Arab news agencies so as to strengthen their cooperation for the subsequent establishment of news pools among neighboring Arab national news agencies in preparation for fulfillment of the union's ultimate aim of creating a central Arab news agency embracing the whole Arab world.

It is noteworthy that the Arab news agencies achieved a large number of news-exchange agreements between 1964 and 1977. Apart from news, these agreements also provided for the exchange of news-reels, features, and photos in addition to the exchange of experience and correspondents. At present MENA distributes the news services of the Saudi Press Agency, Qatar News Agency, and Oman News Agency over its communications network.

A large number of correspondents of Arab, foreign, and world news agencies are operating in Cairo. In this connection, Egypt, with faith in the free flow of information, has lifted the censorship of the work of foreign correspondents that had been in force for many years. It has also decided not to restrict the freedom of any correspondent to report and criticize as he wishes, leaving it to his journalistic conscience. Likewise, Egyptian newspapers and magazines now go to press without any censorship, giving rise to a variety of views and freedom of criticism for all journalists.

MENA has loaned many of its journalists, technicians, and administrative personnel to other Arab news agencies and has for years undertaken the training of large numbers of their personnel.

The establishment of a large Arab news agency would not put an end to the national agencies working in the member states of the union. The large agency would be a kind of pool of the news reports of the local news agencies, which would retransmit these reports to the Arab area and the outside world. The large Arab news agency would definitely introduce some balance in the incoming and outgoing information in the Arab world.

INTER-ARAB COMMUNICATION

Research on a number of Arabic newspapers, conducted by professors and students of the Faculty of Information at Cairo University, showed that until early 1977 Arabic newspapers printed more news of the big powers than of the Arab countries themselves. As a result of this study, some Arabic newspapers began to devote more space to Arab news.

Studies made by the Arab Cable and Wireless Union contributed to the project of establishing a direct communications network that would link the Arab countries together by means of an Arab satellite. The Union of Arab News Agencies has announced that it has completed its economic and technical studies on the utilization of the satellite. The Arab states will start establishing ground stations for the operation of the satellite, which will result in better communications at lower costs.

At present, a large proportion of inter-Arab communications is carried out through networks operating in Europe. Although the Arab states participate in this system with the rest of the Third World countries, the Arab projects also envisage setting up a number of marine cables to facilitate communications on a temporary basis.

Iraq is now linked with the Arab countries through Beirut and Bahrain, Somalia through Britain, Mauritania through France, and the People's Democratic Republic of Yemen through Britain. One marine cable is operating between Cairo and Beirut and another between Cairo and Italy for the communications between Egypt and western Europe. Another marine cable is under construction to link the eastern and western coasts of the Red Sea. Another project under construction is a microwave network between Egypt and Libya to complete the communications between North Africa and Egypt. The network has been completed up to Libya, but the link across Libya and Egypt still remains to be carried out. Another microwave project under construction is to link Egypt with the Sudan.

The basic problem is that these available marine cables incur exorbitant expense. Although the Arab Cable and Wireless Union has recommended lower rates for communications, the objections of some Arab countries have delayed this development.

As far as the Arab news agencies are concerned, the solution would lie in the implementation of the recommendations for lower rates by the public networks operating in the Arab states, and in the conclusion of bilateral agreements with other national news agencies for the transmission of news, since the circuits of the world news agencies are fully loaded. Besides, multilateral agreements between three or more news agencies may lead to the creation of pools that would cut down communications expenses.

Another proposal under discussion is to form a special Arab organization that would set up a communications network in the Arab world. Such an organization would lease various lines of communication, including available public networks, to the Arab news agencies, which would lead to lower expenses.

The technical committees of the Union of Arab News Agencies have issued a set of recommendations. They pointed out that the general assembly has noted that the technical representation of the member agencies is incomplete and that the number of participants is continually declining, which led to the recommendation that the representation of the agencies in the meetings of the engineering committee should be complete.

The technical committees, concerned with ensuring good transmissions among the Arab news agencies, found that interception is due sometimes to the differences in the field of frequencies used by transmitters and have recommended that the switch in frequencies should not exceed 450 HZ/S.

After studying the most practical ways to link the Arab news agencies together, the union's general assembly recommended that each Arab agency having offices in other Arab countries should link these offices with the headquarters of the local national agency at its own expense. In accordance with this recommendation, local lines would be set up in Paris between the office of MENA and the Paris offices of Libya's Arab Revolution News Agency (ARNA), Tunis-Afrique, and the Algerian News Agency. In London, a line was set up between the office of MENA and that of the Arab Revolution News Agency. In Beirut, a line was set up between the office of MENA and the office of the Iraqi News Agency, a second line between the office of ARNA and that of the Iraqi News Agency, a third between the office of ARNA and that of the Syrian News Agency, and a fourth between the office of MENA and that of the Syrian News Agency. Similar lines will be set up in the future to link together the offices of the Arab news agencies in countries in which duplex networks are available.

THE UNION OF AFRICAN NEWS AGENCIES AND THE BALANCING OF INFORMATION

The African Summit Conference of 1963 agreed in principle on the creation of a pan-African news agency. Earlier in the same year, the Union of African News Agencies had been established within the framework of the Organization of African Unity (OAU). The idea of creating a pan-African news agency was taken up by many conferences and technical committee meetings held in various African capitals, but to date nothing concrete has resulted. The idea nearly died, but the OAU ministerial council that met in 1970 asked the secretary-general to revive the idea. Technical studies, however, met with delays that led to postponement of the project.

The Union of African News Agencies includes the Arab countries located in the African continent, namely Egypt, the Sudan, Somalia, Libya, Tunisia, Algeria, Morocco, and Mauritania. The Arabs of Africa thus brought together the members of the Union of African News Agencies and those of the Union of Arab News Agencies, neither of which had been able to create the news agency it aspired to.

Tunis-Afrique held a seminar of the directors of the Arab and African news agencies in Tunis from February 24 to March 2, 1975, for the purpose of studying practical measures to develop the project.

UNESCO and the Arab League took part in sponsoring the seminar, which discussed two subjects, namely, the intensification of the transmission and exchange of news among the national agencies and, second, cooperation between the Arab and African news agencies.

The seminar called attention to the imbalance of relations in the field of news exchange between the African and Arab news agencies, on the one hand, and the world news agencies, on the other. This imbalance, it was agreed, was the result of the vestiges of colonialism and the attempts of neocolonialism and imperialism to deepen that imbalance. The seminar noted the scarcity of the means of communication between the African and Arab countries and their present dependence on the major world news agencies. It concluded that emancipation from this situation would bring forth many benefits, including bilateral and multilateral cooperation through the African and Arab unions.

As regards news exchange, the seminar issued among others the following recommendations:

that the conclusion of bilateral agreements between African and Arab news agencies should be encouraged so that each would act as the correspondent of the other;

that the Arab and African news agencies should depend on the official news bulletins issued by the national news agencies or other official news media in the Arab and African countries in covering the events that take place in each country;

that established news agencies provide technical facilities to the newly created agencies so as to assist them in reception and transmission;

that two offices should be established in the two unions, whose task would be to coordinate the cooperation between the African and Arab news agencies;

that the African and Arab news agencies open offices in African and Arab capitals and appoint correspondents in those capitals, as extensively as possible;

that the correspondents of foreign news agencies operating in African and Arab countries should, whenever possible, be nationals of those countries, and that they should follow the national radio broadcasts and the newspapers of those countries;

that established news agencies receive the reports of the newly founded ones by available means, such as telex, translate them without changes, and relay them to local subscribers under the title of "News of the Afro-Arab World";

that the Arab and African news agencies present to the two unions information on their transmission and reception facilities, their frequencies, their transmission timetables, and the languages used;

that the African and Arab news agencies call on their governments to pay special attention to the development of their wireless networks at home and in the neighboring countries on regional and international scales;

that the agencies of the Arab and African countries, which are nonaligned nations, should be interested in the nonaligned pool and should keep in close contact with it for the benefit of the people of the Third World and their information;

that the Union of African News Agencies should approach the OAU to find out the extent of its preparedness to give material aid for the training of African personnel in the technical and journalistic fields at the existing or established news agencies;

that the member agencies should provide their unions with detailed information on their needs and possibilities in the fields of training and the preparation of personnel, enabling the two unions to coordinate the training courses that existing agencies could provide for the newly created agencies;

that the Executive Committee of the Union of African News Agencies and the General Secretariat of the Union of Arab News Agencies should hold a joint meeting once every two years to examine the progress of work and to propose the best ways of cooperation between the African and Arab news agencies for reference to the general assemblies of the two unions.

Among the recommendations of the technical committee set up at the Tunis seminar were three distinct proposals. The first was an immediate plan to tie up the Arab and African agencies, which led to the following recommendations:

that Arab and African news pools should be established with the participation of all the Arab and African news agencies, particularly those that have technical facilities for news transmission and reception, and that the direct cable lines between Tripoli, Tunis, Algiers, and Rabat, in addition to the line between the Algerian News Agency in Algiers and Dakar and any other similar lines in operation, be exploited;

that joint regional offices should be set up in the African continent, equipped with technical facilities so as to be able to collect the news of the neighboring area of each office and to retransmit it to the rest of the

Arab and African countries. In addition, the facilities of established Arab and African news agencies should be utilized in this respect.

The second proposal was that an approach should be made to UNESCO to provide a comprehensive technical study of the Arab and African countries as regards the present communications facilities possessed by the Arab and African news agencies, the projected facilities, and the facilities under execution. UNESCO should also be requested to draw up a comprehensive chart showing how to connect the Arab and African news agencies by cable and wireless facilities, as well as the existing communications facilities available in the Arab and African countries that could serve Arab and African information.

The third proposal was that, in view of the exorbitant rates of communications between the Arab and African news agencies, the members of the two unions should approach their governments with a view to obtaining special and suitable reductions in this sphere.

A second seminar of the Arab and African news agencies was held in Tripoli from March 26 to 31, 1977, to discuss their cooperation. It reaffirmed the initial resolutions and recommendations and again requested UNESCO assistance.

THE NONALIGNED NEWS AGENCIES POOL AND
THE BALANCING OF INFORMATION

Now we come to the third axis through which the Arab world participates in balancing the flow of information, namely the Nonaligned News Agencies Pool.

The committee for coordinating the work of the news agencies of the nonaligned countries met in Cairo from January 10 to 13, 1977. Since all Arab countries belong to the nonaligned group, they entered into the projected information system.

The coordinating committee noted that 1976 saw increased cooperation among the nonaligned countries in the field of information in general and among their national news agencies in particular. It took cognizance of the reports on the progress of work presented by MENA (Egypt), Tunis-Afrique (Tunisia), and others. It also noted with satisfaction that more than 40 agencies of nonaligned countries in various parts of the world are taking active interest in the exchange of news. The result was increased exchange of the news put out by the agencies of nonaligned countries.

INFORMATION STUDIES IN THE ARAB WORLD

Thus the Arab world connects its news agencies with those of the African countries on the one hand and the nonaligned nations on the other. In this respect, it has spared no effort to develop information studies to turn out generations of well-educated, well-trained journalists.

Information studies were nonexistent in the Arab world until the early 1950s, when the Faculty of Literature, Cairo University, opened an institute of journalism, which enrolled college graduates who worked on Egyptian newspapers and magazines for the M.A. degree after three years of study. Later, the same faculty opened a new division that enrolled secondary school graduates for the B.A. in journalism. Work began in 1954, and the first group was graduated in 1958. These graduates are now working in press establishments in Egypt and the rest of the Arab world. In the early 1970s, Cairo University opened the Faculty of Information for the B.A. degree in information. The faculty consists of three divisions, the first for press and publication, the second for radio and television, and the third for public relations. The faculty also gives the M.A. and the Ph.D. in the three divisions. A number of U.S. and European professors are engaged in the faculty on a full-time basis. The American University in Cairo also graduates large numbers of journalists.

Information and journalism studies are now being offered in a large number of Arab universities, including Baghdad University, King Abdel Aziz University of Jeddah and Riyadh University, and the Call University in the Sudan, as well as the universities of Libya and Tunisia. There are also institutes of journalism in Algeria and in Lebanon, and journalism studies in Syria.

A PICTURE OF ARAB NEWS AGENCIES: MENA

MENA is an Arab news agency affiliated with the Union of African News Agencies; it is also an African news agency affiliated with the Union of African News Agencies; and it is a member of the Nonaligned News Agencies Pool.

The plan to create the MENA dates back to December 15, 1955. The agency began its news work on February 28, 1956, when it put out its first news bulletin, issued by stencil. MENA was the first national news agency in Africa and the Middle East. On March 31, 1956, it began to distribute its news service by ticker to its Egyptian newspaper subscribers. These subscribers jointly owned the shares of the agency, but in January 1962 the ownership went to the state, and MENA became one of the units of the Egyptian General Organization for News and Publication.

In 1956 the agency opened its first offices abroad, in Damascus, Beirut, Amman, and Jerusalem, and it sent correspondents to Khartoum, Kuwait, Rabat, and Ankara. Today it exchanges news with more than 20 agencies in the world. Everyday it puts out 40,000 words in its domestic Arabic service; 30,000 words in its external Arabic service; 25,000 words in its English-language service; and 44,000 words in its English-language economic service. It has 498 subscribers to its various services in Egypt alone and 143 subscribers abroad.

MENA is run by a board of directors consisting of a chairman, five appointed members, two professional members, and five members elected from among the employees. In 1978 the agency will move its headquarters to a newly built 13-floor building equipped with electronic laboratories for film and photo processing, offices for the foreign correspondents and news agencies operating in Egypt, electronic transmitters and receivers, internal elevators, air-pressure pipes and belts for moving the news, central air conditioning, alarm warning devices, a theater, a cinema, a club, and a cafeteria that accommodates 500 employees.

When the agency began its work, it had 40 employees comprising journalists, administrators, and technicians. Now it has 20 times as many. The agency began its Arabic and English transmission abroad in 1962 by Morse telegraph with one-kilowatt shortwave transmitters. In 1962 it began to transmit its Arabic and English news services by teleprinters with five- to ten-kilowatt transmitters beamed on the Arab world and Europe. In 1971 it set up a private transmission station, which has three units, each with 35-kilowatt power, and three others of seven-kilowatt power each, so that its transmission in Arabic can cover the Middle East, the Gulf area, and North Africa, while its transmission in English can cover all Europe and east and southern Africa. In 1973 the agency set up a direct duplex line between Cairo, Paris, and London. The agency also owns a teleprinter reception station operating 20 receivers to intercept the exchange news services and news material of its offices abroad. Most of the agency's offices are supplied with telex equipment, duplex lines, or teleprinters for direct communication with the head office.

The agency transmits a news service in French to west and central Africa and is planning to transmit its English-language news service to the Far East. It is boosting its transmission station with additional aerials. It is also preparing to transmit radio photos in two periods daily. It is expanding its cable circuits, including a Cairo-Beirut-Damascus circuit and a Cairo-Tripoli-Tunis-Algiers-Rabat circuit. The agency is planning to use electronic tickers, and steps are being taken to use the electronic distribution and control system. This has actually begun on the direct circuits between Cairo and Paris, Rome, Tunis, Algiers, and Tripoli.

Some Arab and foreign news agencies disseminate their new services through MENA, namely Qatar News Agency, Deutsche-Presse Agentur (DPA), PARS News Agency of Iran, Universal News Service, the Saudi Press Agency, Oman News Agency, and the Philippine News Agency. MENA intercepts and disseminates Reuters news service and intercepts and disseminates the news service of Agence France-Presse (AFP) in French among the local subscribers and translates it into Arabic and distributes it locally and throughout the Arab world.

MENA has contracts with the television networks of Kuwait, Damascus, Tripoli, Banghazi, Abu Dhabi, Doha, Khartoum, Baghdad, Amman, and Riyadh. It also serves the television networks of Wiesbaden and Hamburg in West Germany; four U.S. networks, namely the National Broadcasting Company (NBC), Columbia Broadcasting System (CBS), American Broadcasting Company (ABC), and UPI TV; and two networks in the United Kingdom, Visnews and International Television News (ITN).

In photos, the agency exchanges services with other agencies in Norway, Hungary, Poland, Spain, Bulgaria, France, Britain, Greece, the Soviet Union, Denmark, East Germany, the People's Republic of China (PRC), Rumania, Holland, Japan, Czechoslovakia, Cuba, Korea, and Yugoslavia.

MENA has offices and correspondents in all Arab capitals as well as Paris, London, Belgrade, and Washington. And at home, MENA covers all the provincial capitals of Egypt with its services and correspondents.

12. DEPTHnews: A Model for a Third World Feature Agency

S. M. ALI

The story of the Press Foundation of Asia (PFA) is, in effect, a capsule story of the press in Asia during the years PFA has existed. If the organization owes its birth in 1967 to the robust idealism that moved the hearts and minds of editors and publishers in Asia in the 1960s, its growth, with all its trials and tribulations, reflects the spirit of a developing society tormented by doubts and fears. For PFA to ignore this crisis—or one might find an even stronger expression to describe the current press situation in Asia—would be to deny its own roots, to discard its own identification, to disown its own parentage. So, paradoxical though it may sound, our weakness lies exactly at our source of strength, the press in Asia. But, then, such is the case with the press in Asia; what is a source of weakness today may turn into a pillar of strength tomorrow, as we have just seen in India. Neither the language of despair nor the sympathy others offer us in our troubles are constructive responses if they diminish our hopes for tomorrow, for we know that joint efforts, if properly channeled, can go a long way in raising the level of mutual relations and, more specifically, in bridging the communication gap between the West and Asia.

THE PFA STORY

PFA was formed in Manila in August 1967 by a group of publishers and editors from Hong Kong, India, Indonesia, Japan, Malaysia, Pakistan, the Philippines, South Korea, Sri Lanka, Taiwan, and Thailand. It was incorporated as a nonprofit trust for consultancy, training, and development in the field of media communications in Asia. Later, publishers and editors of Afghanistan, Australia, Nepal, New Zealand, and Vietnam joined the foundation as members.

The first executives of PFA were Amitabha Chowdhury of India and Tarzie Bittachi of Sri Lanka. The early directors were Esmond Wickremesinghe of Sri Lanka, Jaoquin P. Roces of the Philippines, Koh Jai Wook of South Korea, Sally Aw Sian and Adrian Zecha of Hong Kong, Naoji Yorozu and Susumu Ejiri of Japan, G. Narasimhan of India, Mochtar Lubis of Indonesia, and A. C. Simmons of Singapore.

PFA is run by two bodies: a board of trustees and a board of directors. The board of trustees supports and advises on financial operations; the board of directors represents the press interests of the foundation's members.

The foundation is provided with an endowment fund which was fed in the earlier years by contributions from the member countries' leading publishing concerns. International bodies, such as the Ford and Thomson foundations, the United Nations Fund for Population Activities, the United Nations Educational, Scientific and Cultural Organization (UNESCO), and the International Development Research Centre, have supported PFA programs.

In many aspects of its work, PFA has also cooperated closely with, among others, the United Nations Asian Development Institute, the Economic and Social Commission for Asia and the Pacific, the Asian Development Bank, the East-West Centre, the International Rice Research Institute, and Nihon Shinbun Kyokai (the Association of Editors and Publishers of Japan).

PFA represents and supports national press institutions around the region—the Chinese Language Press Institute in Hong Kong, the Press Institute of India in New Delhi, the Press Foundation of Indonesia in Jakarta, and the Malaysian Press Institute. Aside from its headquarters in Manila, PFA maintains offices in Kuala Lumpur, Bangkok, Tokyo, and Hong Kong to better serve the needs of about 300 newspaper members, from Afghanistan to Indonesia and from South Korea to New Zealand.

As part of its service to Asia's media communication industry, PFA has identified and tackled some of the industry's major problems: newsprint production, printing, product quality, the status of journalists, pricing schemes, promotion, advertising, circulation, newspaper management, and the training of journalists.

In tackling these problems, PFA has, from time to time, come up against a problem that overshadows all other problems of the industry, the problem of press freedom in Asia. The imposition of restrictive practices on the press, in one country after another in Asia, has affected the activities of the PFA. You may wonder why an organization whose president, Mochtar Lubis of Indonesia; founder-trustee, Joaquin Roces of the Philippines; trustee C. G. K. Reddy of India; and former joint chief executive, Johnny Mercado; and countless individual members in different Asian countries have served prison terms for their commitment to press freedom often tends to adopt a low profile on this issue. If the profile is, indeed, a low one, it reflects not an accommodation with the forces hostile to press freedom but a tactical approach that leaves room for quiet diplomacy between editors and publishers in Asia on the one hand and certain governments in the region on the other. This approach, which has worked on a number of occasions, has failed in a few others. But it has helped us to survive and carry out activities that even national governments consider as useful, no matter how much they disregard or distrust PFA's basic commitment to press freedom. Again, while operating under stresses and strains inherent in the present situation, we have also learned to be innovative in conceiving and launching projects, which will later be discussed in detail.

During the first 10 years of operation, the resources of PFA grew in three different, but interrelated, areas: financial, manpower, and projects.

Financial

The foundation, as noted earlier, started with an endowment fund that was fed in the earlier years by contributions from the member countries' leading publishing concerns. Interest generated by the fund as well as by investments made out of this fund, financial support offered by several international bodies, and a continuing grant from the United Nations Fund for Population Activities today constitute the PFA's main financial resource base. Assistance from outside sources has been slowly tapering off, however, but revenue generated by PFA's own projects has helped in reducing the deficit in its operating cost. The financial statement for 1976 shows that at the end of the year, the revenue of the organization in the operating fund was P3,546,623, the equivalent of US$472,883 at the rate of US$1 to 7.5 Philippine pesos, while the endowment fund stood at P2,322,509, the equivalent of US$309,667. Against this, the operating expenses during the year amounted to P4,033,006 or US$537,734, thus showing an operating deficit of US$51,896. Despite this deficit, which is considerably less than in recent years, the endowment fund remains intact. It must also be noted that in addition to the endowment fund, the PFA owns other tangible assets, such as its office premises in downtown Manila; a complete IBM typesetting system; 40 percent equity in Asia Research Systems, Inc., a modern, fully equipped data bank; and several other revenue-generating products.

Manpower

There are now over 80 people on the payroll of PFA, not counting the network of highly trained research assistants and correspondents in the Asia Research Systems, in which PFA is a minority partner. PFA staff is made up mostly of qualified journalists, including many former editors and managing editors of metropolitan dailies, bureau chiefs and correspondents working for the Development, Economics, and Population Themes News (DEPTHnews) network; other staff members are secretaries and the sales team. In terms of nationalities, they come from the Philippines, Thailand, Japan, India, Sri Lanka, Bangladesh, Malaysia, South Korea, Indonesia, Pakistan, Hong Kong, Australia, Canada, Britain, and the United States. It took 10 years for PFA to develop its own reservoir of expertise, by far the most innovative and most professional that one can find in Asia.

Projects

From the time PFA was launched in 1967, one overriding concern of the organization has been to develop an extensive training program involving the various sectors of the profession. In accordance with its charter, PFA has, therefore, concentrated on improving editorial, production, and management techniques through practical seminars and workshops, organized sometimes under PFA's own auspices and sometimes in collaboration with various national institutes or with such associate bodies as the Nihon Shinbun Kyokai and the Thomson Foundation. Through some 50 seminars and workshops held in different parts of Asia in 1967-77 and a once-a-year advanced course in development journalism, PFA and various national institutes have identified and developed new newsbeats, from population and related economic issues to science and technology, from our living heritage in the field of art and culture to interpretative political reporting. What's more, it is primarily through this program that the PFA discovered and deployed new talents in the field of journalism in Asia. Many have returned to their own newspapers with, it is hoped, better skills and wider horizons. Some have stayed on with PFA to help us to launch and develop such other activities as *Data-Asia,* a weekly, 16-page intelligence report of distilled and totally independent research on social, economic, and political development in Asia; the Regional Reference

System, a data bank of vital statistics; *Data-India* and *Data-Fil,* reports modeled after *Data-Asia,* which primarily concentrate on India and the Philippines respectively; *Media,* the monthly journal of Asia's communication industry; and, last but not the least, DEPTHnews, a unique and the only genuinely Asia-based feature service of its kind.

DEPTHnews-THE ONLY ASIA-BASED FEATURE SERVICE

Of the many-sided activities of PFA, DEPTHnews stands out as a lasting contribution to the improvement of the craft and professional competence in Asia. A weekly news and feature service, DEPTHnews introduced and institutionalized the vital beat of development journalism in the region. Since its first weekly packet of articles went out to Asian newspapers in 1969, it has gained a wide reputation for reliability, accuracy, and relevance. The first syllable in DEPTHnews, stands for Development, Economics, and Population Themes, also suggests reporting in depth. Initially, strong UN support gave the unique service a distinct development orientation.

Even before certain governments in Asia raised an outcry about imbalance in news distribution, PFA had realized the need for generating more news and features from within the region for Asian newspapers. What's more, PFA had also realized that what Asian newspapers needed most was a coverage that reflected social relevance and underlined a sense of commitment of Asian journalists to economic development in the broadest sense of the term. It was out of this realization that DEPTHnews was born.

DEPTHnews now comes out every week in ten separate editions: *Depthnews* in English for the region; *Depthnews Philippines* in English, Filipino, Ilocano, Cebuano, and Ilongo; *Depthnews India* in English and Hindi; *Depthnews Indonesia* in Bahasa; *Depthnews Thailand* in Thai. (For Hong Kong, a Chinese edition is being planned.) These multilingual editions are now carried in about 4 million print copies circulated in 12 Asian countries.

Of the six national editions, *Depthnews Philippines* has been the heaviest-used service with an estimated circulation of 1.4 million through English dailies, Tagalog newspapers, vernacular publications, government periodicals, and community newspapers.

In 1972, DEPTHnews branched out into DEPTHnews Asia (DNA); a year later, we launched DEPTHnews Special (DNS). In starting these two services—and on a commercial basis—our basic aim was—and still is—to broaden the scope of the DEPTHnews coverage and, in particular, to report and interpret current political and economic trends in Asia, as seen by Asian journalists. We decided to use DNA mainly for stories dealing with political developments and DNS for reports on economic development and related issues. There is another advantage in having two services, rather than one. In most Asian cities, we have been able to offer the two services to two different newspapers, each getting an exclusive packet of its own choice.

A normal weekly DNA packet contains seven or eight stories, each running 1,000 to 1,200 words. They are mostly analytical pieces on topics of immediate interest. The packet also contains the "Asian Diary," a human-interest column, regarded as good Sunday reading. DNS contains the same number of stories, but generally shorter in length, and a regular commentary.

Newspapers in Asia now subscribing to one or the other services are the *Mainichi Daily News* and *Japan Times* in Tokyo: the *Asian Wall Street Journal* and the *Hong Kong Standard* in Hong Kong; the *Times Journal* and the *Daily Express* in Manila; the *Bangkok Post* and the *Nation* in Bangkok; the *Business Times* and the *Star* in Kuala Lumpur; the *Bangladesh Observer* in Dacca; and the *Kayhan International* in Tehran. We are also about to finalize deals with two Indian papers. DEPTHnews' clients also include one news agency the Jiji Press of Japan, and two prestigious economic journals, *Asian Finance* (a mid-monthly published in Hong Kong) and *Pakistani Economist* (a weekly published in Karachi).

Another dimension to the DEPTHnews operation is a science news feature service, DEPTHnews Science Service (DNSS). This service has the dual objective of improving science news coverage in Asia and following through on the initial impact of science seminars and training courses. At the moment, DNSS stories, averaging three a week, are included in the regular DNA weekly packets.

In our view, the three services, DNA, DNS, and DNSS, merit special attention. We are convinced that put together they provide a ready-made nucleus, a model for a news-cum-feature service with the potential of serving as a bridge across the communication gap between the West and the Third World, between North America and Asia.

This conviction—or, indeed, this claim—is based on several significant achievements. For example, through these three services (for the sake of convenience, just DEPTHnews) we are able to put out some 18 features *a week,* all written and produced by our own correspondents based in different parts of Asia, copy-edited in Manila, and then airmailed to the users of the service in eight major Asian capitals.

Again, since all client newspapers of this service are paying for DEPTHnews features, at rates ranging from US$7,000 per year in case of such major newspapers as the *Asian Wall Street Journal,* the *Busi-*

ness Times of Kuala Lumpur, and the *Bangkok Post* to US$2,500 per year for the *Hong Kong Standard,* the acceptance of the product has passed the professional test. This is further proved by the usage of DEPTHnews features (which varies from 50 to 70 percent). Further, a newspaper such as the *Asian Wall Street Journal* would only apply strictly professional criteria and reject inferior stories.

The success of DEPTHnews is no longer confined to its regular weekly service to its established clients. As proof of its versatility, the service exclusively provides almost one-half the news and feature content of *Asian Finance,* a leading business-cum-investment monthly, at a special fee of US$12,000 per year. From time to time, DEPTHnews correspondents also carry out assignments from client newspapers and help newspapers with special reports and supplements on countries in our region. In 1975 the DEPTHnews bureau in Japan provided editorial material for the *Bangkok Post's* supplement on Japan; and a year later the bureau chief in Tokyo, Eduardo Lachica, now a staff reporter with the *Asian Wall Street Journal,* was assigned to Australia for on-the-spot reportage for the *Financial Times* (London) supplement on Australia.

So the credibility of the service, never in doubt even from the time of its inception, has now been firmly established. It is credibility based on professionalism, objectivity, and total independence from any government or bureaucratic control and influence. This remains the biggest asset of the service as a whole.

Credibility is not enough, however, for a service such as DEPTHnews to survive in this highly competitive field where a number of established news-cum-feature services, mainly from the West, occupy virtually unchallenged positions. To what, then, do we attribute the survival, and indeed the continued growth, of DEPTHnews?

First and foremost, DEPTHnews does not compete either with the wire agencies or with established West-based feature services. It supplements them both qualitatively and quantitatively by concentrating on an area of coverage or a theme that normally either goes by default or calls for a sustained research-oriented approach.

Secondly, our DEPTHnews correspondents are encouraged not only to see economic, social, and political developments in human terms but also to judge these developments in the light of future directions, in the context of hopes and dreams for better life in Asia.

Thirdly, and lastly, the predominantly Asian staff of DEPTHnews has access to such sources in most Asian capitals as are not readily available to visiting Western correspondents. Again, being better aware of national sensitivities than an average foreign journalist, a DEPTHnews correspondent, be he an Indian, a Thai, a Filipino, or even an American who has been trained through the network, knows how far he can go in handling a delicate story without compromising his professional position and without treading on too many tender toes. Maybe, at times, he sacrifices a good story that he would have written if conditions were different. But quite often by sacrificing one story, he manages to write three others. In the end, he still succeeds in maintaining a steady flow of news and information out of this country. This probably explains why a reputable newspaper such as the *Asian Wall Street Journal* makes fair use of DEPTHnews copy from such cities as Jakarta, Manila, and Bangkok, although its own staff reporters blanket these countries.

FUTURE PLANS FOR DEPTHnews

DEPTHnews has reached a stage in its growth when it can be expanded in more ways than one. Our main objective is to find a new market for the service, not simply to generate much needed revenue, but to explore the potential of its role in increasing the flow of information between the West and Asia.

PFA is ready to introduce its service to North America and Europe. We know fully well, however, that we cannot dare do so without the support, cooperation, and assistance of the Western press. While it is for the press in the West to decide how and why it should be involved in such a move, we are more than willing to talk in terms of a joint venture. In our view, it will be a joint venture based not on a profit motive but on our common understanding of the need to increase the flow of information from Asia to the West. It will be based on our awareness that unless we, professional journalists, show the way in bridging the communication gap, a great opportunity will be either lost or foreclosed by some nonprofessional bodies for their own ends.

At the same time, we are prepared to see DEPTHnews serve as a new kind of information channel from the West to Asia. We would like to see a DEPTHnews correspondent, based in Washington, provide the service with features specially written for readers in Asia.

Here is a broad outline of a concerted plan of action, which, if implemented, can turn this concept of working with the Western press into a reality.

1. DEPTHnews will welcome a senior editorial consultant, preferably from the United States, as a member of the DEPTHnews desk in Manila to repackage and produce a minimum of 15 stories a week, specially tailored for the market in the United States and possibly Britain. The raw material input will be the entire DEPTHnews file, carrying original bylines, with background support.

2. A marketing director, preferably with an insight into editorial operations, will be based in New York, responsible for selling the service either
directly to newspapers or chains or through some established news cum
feature services in the United States.
3. A DEPTHnews correspondent will be based in Washington to write on
issues of special interest to Asia.
4. Efforts will be made to raise the productivity of the existing DEPTH-
news network in Asia by increasing its manpower and by introducing
transmission by teleprinter, by arrangement with a wire service, in place
of its present airmail service.
5. Immediate steps will be taken to sell the service to more newspapers
in Asia at subsidized rates related to their ability to pay—for papers such
as *Kabul Times* in Afghanistan and *Bangladesh Times* in Dacca.
6. Possibilities of introducing Asian news and views into the Middle East
and Africa may be explored.

In terms of cost, it will be a sizable undertaking. In the first year
of this proposed expanded operation, DEPTHnews may need an additional US$75,000 in its operating budget. But we sincerely believe that
if an effective marketing strategy is launched, much of this initial
investment can be recovered during the second year, thus allowing us
to scale down the size of further assistance. Finally, the extension of the
service to the Middle East and Africa should well help us to turn the
loss into a modest profit. In the end, DEPTHnews may need no more
than 12 new clients paying the going rates of the *Asian Wall Street
Journal* and the *Business Times* of Kuala Lumpur or the *Bangkok Post.*
What does this additional cost of US$75,000 represent? It probably
represents what a single senior editor of a single publication such as
Time or *Newsweek* earns every year. And it is no more than a fraction
of what several governments in Asia, Africa, and Latin America expect
to spend to filter information through a nonaligned news pool.
Many may be wondering if any serious problems would arise
between this proposed expanded DEPTHnews network and governments in our part of the world. I wish it were possible for me to answer
this question firmly in the negative. But a more honest answer is that
problems may arise but they will not swell into confrontations. Having
operated this service for some years, we have, I think, gained the requisite experience in dealing with Asian governments. Broadly speaking,
whatever be their other reservations, leaders in Asia accept our credibility, recognize our usefulness, concede our instinct for survival.
We doubt if our cooperation with an established professional group
in the United States would make any difference to the scenario. Person-
ally, I feel confident that it may even be welcomed by some in the hope
that a better understanding of Asia's socioeconomic problems in the

West, which DEPTHnews expects to promote through this exercise, would advance their national aspirations. Others may view it as a better alternative to the Third World news pool concept, which is a slow starter in Southeast Asia.

The proposed joint venture may be only a beginning, but a beginning that can give a new dimension to the transit of news round the globe. We believe that the success of this proposed joint venture would, in time, enable PFA to restructure DEPTHnews as a cooperative, based on a partnership between users of the service and equity holders drawn from the profession, regardless of their geographical location. It would be a modest but a rewarding breakthrough in communication between the industrialized West and Asia, a signpost of cooperation that transcends frontiers in our troubled world.

13. NEWS WITH THIRD WORLD PERSPECTIVES:
A Practical Suggestion

NARINDER K. AGGARWALA

Developing countries primarily depend upon the four Western news agencies for news about each other. News about Botswana, more often than not, reaches the people of Zambia through one of the four Western wire services. Worse still, until recently, the Caribbean countries received much of their news about themselves via London through Reuters. The news that the developing countries' media receives from the international wire services is the news written and selected for the Western media. The style, the content, the treatment, and the perspective of practically all the news flowing in and out of the Third World reflects the personality, preferences, and the needs of the Western media.

Even the employment of a substantial number of developing-country reporters by the international wire services will not make any meaningful difference in the kind of news disseminated by these agencies. A case in point is United Press International (UPI), which recently claimed that its Latin American news is written primarily by Latin nationals. Developing-country nationals working for international wire services become conditioned to writing news with a primarily Western audience in mind. It is one of the least stated but most fundamental survival axioms of the journalistic profession that a reporter learns, as quickly as possible, the editorial policies of his or her newspaper or agency and the news preferences and quirks of his or her editor. The adaptation of, and to, the correct slant and treatment follows as a natural corollary.

The views expressed in this chapter are those of the author and not necessarily those of the United Nations or the United Nations Development Programme.

Unquestionably, the world news, as disseminated by the international wire services, has, in the context of North-South relations, a Northern orientation. This is what the developing-country leaders generally refer to when they decry the "one-way" flow of news; they do not mean that the developed countries are not getting any news from the developing countries or vice versa. This is also what Louis Penalaver, Venezuela's Minister of Information, had in mind when he recently asked: "Why should we rely exclusively on foreign news sources, which represent powerful economic interests, to hear about our own neighbors?" The developing countries' demand for measures to correct the existing "imbalance" in world news flows is a call for a change of perspectives on world news, a call to establish a counterflow of news with Third World perspectives—which need not and should not be government-controlled—to supplement that of the Western news media.

The lack of a Third World perspective is obvious in the manner in which Western journalists, rightly or wrongly, discuss the problems, such as employment, food, and population, confronting the developing countries. Their reports, more often than not, either ignore or belittle the efforts of developing countries to alleviate the problems, often against seemingly insurmountable odds. It is not suggested or implied that the media should become subdued or less critical in their exposure of the enormity, as well as the urgency, of problems bedeviling the Third World. But the developing countries do deserve a passing recognition of their development efforts, something strangely missing from Western media reports.

At present, all social, economic, and political developments in the Third World are reported in terms of rightward or leftward shifts in government policies. Land reforms, measures to weaken the stranglehold of a few indigenous business houses over national economies or to encourage the development of national industries to the immediate or potential disadvantage of transnational corporations, and legislation to ensure better monitoring and supervision of national banking and trade institutions are all presented as portents of a country's slide into communist or socialist practice. (No matter that such measures are necessary for a nation's economic survival or well-being of its people. No matter also that many of these measures have been in force in most of the Western countries for decades without any one of them becoming communist or socialist.)

Reporting about similar developments in the Western world is another matter. For example, after the recent local government elections in France, in which the leftist coalition made a near sweep, no international wire service carried a story proclaiming the imminent danger of a socialist/communist takeover of France. True, that would have given a false picture of the political situation in France, but such reporting, ignoring the actual reality in favor of making the news more "sexy," would have been more nearly like the norm in Western dispatches filed from the Third World. This disparity in the treatment of Third World News is even more true of "authoritative reports and commentaries" of roving Western correspondents who claim to become experts on a developing country's complex situation only after a few days' visit.

The intention here is not to challenge the journalistic credentials of the Western media representatives but rather to emphasize that in interpreting developments in the Third World, Western correspondents seem either to lack a proper perspective and/or to give preference, over accuracy, to making news more interesting or salable to its Western users.

When the Third World leaders criticize the Western press for biased and distorted reporting, they are not, generally speaking, questioning the factual accuracy of Western news agencies or the honesty of their correspondents. Distortion, as Juan Somavia, director of the Latin American Institute for Transnational Studies (ILET) in Mexico City, points out, "does not necessarily mean a false presentation of events but rather an arbitrary selection and a slanted evaluation of reality." The alleged objectivity of news presentation, according to him, is belied by an arbitrary use of language, overemphasis on events of no real importance, and the general practice of "making news" by presenting "isolated facts" as a nonexistent whole.

Pressed by the limitation of space (in case of printed media) and of time (in case of radio and television), Western correspondents tend to select only the news that they think is of interest to their readers/subscribers in the industrialized countries either because it is "sensational" or deals with something "strange or exotic." Wars, disasters, famine, riots, and political and military intrigues do make more readable copy than economic development. In this process, the information needs of the Third World are either forgotten or given short shrift.

For example, Tanzania's effort to organize basic rural health services by using paramedics (the Tanzanian version of "barefoot doctors") may not be "sexy" enough for the Western media, but it does present a model to many developing countries. Similarly, the development of inland fisheries in Nepal, the introduction of animal traction for farming in West Africa, and the establishment of the first forest ranger training institute in Honduras may not warrant Western media attention, but they are of great interest to developing countries, showing, as they do, certain progress in meeting the problems of the Third World.

Such news is also important to the developing countries as an agent of change, since an individual's first motivation toward change often comes from "hearing it on the radio," "seeing it on film," or "reading it in the paper." Development news will assume even greater significance for Third World countries as efforts to promote technical cooperation among themselves gain momentum in the coming years.

Tunisia's representative to the United Nations Educational, Scientific and Cultural Organization (UNESCO), Adnan Zmerli, stresses this point: "If Swaziland implements a successful new system for irrigating orange groves, we'd like to hear about it. We also want to know what is happening in Kenya—not just what goes on in Paris, Washington, and Moscow." Zmerli's statement, voicing as it does a sentiment commonly expressed by Third World countries, underscores the failure of the international news agencies to serve Third World information needs.

Admittedly, it is difficult to make development news interesting, but it can be, and is being, done. As long as an action or development has a significant impact on people (all economic and social development activities do), it can make interesting copy. But it needs special skills and training. "High professional skills, higher than ever before, will be needed to make this other [development] news interesting and not dull, and credible to the public," acknowledges Chakravarti Raghavan, former chief editor of the Press Trust of India. There is also urgent need to evolve criteria for assigning appropriate weight to development factors in grading day-to-day news.

Some Western correspondents and commentators have erroneously equated development-oriented news with government-controlled news and information handouts. This is a mistaken view. In covering development news, a journalist can, and should, critically evaluate and report the relevance of a development project to national, and most importantly, local needs; the difference between the planned scheme and its actual implementation; and the differences between its impact on people as claimed by government officials and as it actually is. Thus conceived, a development news story will be markedly different from a government handout and will be similar to features or investigative articles that appear in Western newspapers regularly.

Development journalism, a relatively new genre of reporting in the Third World, is not much different from what usually appears in Western newspapers in community or general news sections. But an international counterpart of community news is missing from Western media files. Also, not all the Third World editors and correspondents, who still operate under the influence of the ultrapolitical orientation acquired during the anticolonial struggle, have taken to development journalism kindly or eagerly. But the market for this kind of journalism is expanding at a relatively rapid pace in the Third World.

Development journalism should not be confused with development support communication programs (DSC), which utilize various media—not just mass but any media—for promoting economic and social development. Development news reporting is only a very minor element of DSC, which in recent years has won many new converts among Third World planners and leaders, primarily due to the efforts of various UN agencies, including the United Nations Development Programme (UNDP), UNESCO, and the United Nations Children's Fund (UNICEF). Paul Fisher, director of the Freedom of Information Center in Columbia, Missouri, is probably referring to the DSC phenomenon when he says: "There is a tendency among leaders of developing countries to favor the views of technicians and specialists who see communication as a tool to achieve certain goals. They are talking about using journalism, using communication, to predetermined ends."

Although Fisher's evaluation is accurate, his inferential criticism and apprehensions are misplaced. There is nothing Machiavellian or alarming in the developing countries' desire to use communication for furthering economic and social development. Communication media have been so used in the Western countries for many decades, particularly in agricultural extension work. The problem arises when the distinction between development communication, primarily a government activity planned and carried out as part of a country's national development program, and the news media, whose effectiveness as a DSC component is inversely related to the degree of government intervention, is blurred. To most Third World leaders, information and communication have unfortunately become synonymous and interchangeable; hence both are seen as subject to government influence and direction.

Some of the more extreme Third World proposals for media control, such as those calling for "the imprisonment of foreign correspondents who insult or misrepresent host countries" or the "licensing of journalists," are merely a reflection of the tremendous frustration that Third World leaders feel about domestic as well as foreign media. It is not too difficult to understand. After all, it was not very long ago that some of the top government leaders in a major Western country, besieged by unrelentingly critical media, were questioning the credentials of nationally known news commentators to analyze and criticize government actions in the name of the general public. They even initiated measures that were openly denounced as "intimidatory" by the media.

This is not to minimize the danger of the growing trend in the Third World toward direct government control of the news media. The danger is accentuated by the need for government subsidies for national news agencies, particularly in the first few years of their operation. But a government-subsidized agency does not necessarily have to be government controlled. The possibility, as well as the level, of official intervention in the operations of a news agency depends very much upon the political philosophy and survival needs of those in power. There is also the fear that a national news agency, in the absence of competition, may willy-nilly become the purveyor of official news. To some extent, it is a justifiable apprehension, but it need not always come true. After all, most developed countries, including Britain and France, have only one national news agency covering the domestic scene, but nobody accuses them of being official mouthpieces.

Contrary to what some critics of the Third World demand for a New Information Order would like us to believe, the flow of news in the world today is not totally "unfettered" or "absolutely" free. Media operations in almost all countries are subject to certain regulations that prohibit the publication of official secrets and news endangering national security. In most industrialized countries, the "management of news," which has been elevated to a fine art, is an everyday phenomenon. Governments can, and do, expel or deny a visa to any foreign correspondent at any time and for almost no reason. Examples of such actions abound, one of the most recent being the expulsion of a U.S. journalist by Britain. Short-notice expulsion is, and will continue to be, an accepted hazard of foreign news reporting. Even now, in many developing countries, foreign news agencies are barred from supplying news directly to a newspaper or a radio station and have to go through a national news agency. Thus, many developing countries already possess the means, if they so desire, to excise or rewrite any news article that they deem unfavorable or slanted.

Few developing countries will agree with the statement attributed to an African diplomat in Nairobi that "we do not want Western journalists in our countries. They should take their news from us." Among those who advocate the institution of a code of social conduct and professional responsibility for news correspondents and call for the establishment of a New Information Order, many are quick to disown any idea of government control over the media. Many others defend the need for such government control "only at the present stage of national development" and "to check the externally funded forces of political and social disequilibrium."

"We are not," says Somavia, who is an ardent critic of the Western media, "advocating government control over the agencies' news flows."

The same view is voiced by Raghavan who contends that national news agencies should be "free of governmental or bureaucratic control, direct or indirect . . . [and should be run] professionally in such a manner that they evoke respect for their professional competence, integrity, and credibility. They should not be vehicles of propaganda."

The Development Dialogue, a Swedish journal advocating Third World causes, had this to say in its Autumn 1976 issue in supporting the call for a New Information Order:

> While it cannot be said that there is no role for governments in information, a role that is as varied as the circumstances, it should be remembered that societies are permanent, and governments—though they may be devoted to the public good—are transient. Societies and the individuals who constitute them are richer in their diversity, needs and aspirations than the states and their bureaucratic machineries—which should only be their servants. A New Information Order and *another* [development] information are not designed to replace the domination of the transnationals by that of national bureaucracies, however well intentioned; they are not a move towards "a more restricted press," but towards a freer one, which would really meet the need to inform and to be informed—one of the fundamental human needs.

THIRD WORLD NEWS AGENCY: STRUCTURE AND OBJECTIVES

What the Third World countries desire primarily is the promotion of a counterflow of world news that will be Southern-oriented, both in content as well as perspective. It will comprise news written and selected with developing country media in mind. The ideal way to achieve this would be for some of the developing countries to expand their national news agencies into international wire services. But this is impracticable, at least at present, since developing countries individually do not possess financial, technical, and human resources needed for operating such global news agencies.

The agreement, among the nonaligned countries, to form a news agencies pool falls far short of the desired objective. In its present form, the agreement, for all practical purposes, provides for no more than a mechanism for exchanging official information or news handouts. Its usefulness, other than as a first-step measure, is questionable since participating governments are unlikely to force their media to publish news, received through the pool, whose credibility they themselves doubt or whose contents colide with their or their allies' policies.

As is the case with industrialized, Western countries, developing nations do not constitute a monolithic ideological bloc. They suffer from mutual rivalries, political as well as economic. Some of them have deep-seated ideological conflicts. They also differ on the interpretation, as well as the implementation, of several important components of the New International Economic Order. In such an environment, a multinational news agencies' pool, not free from government intervention, will founder because of conflicting national pressures. It will not succeed—in terms of its use by developing-country media—because the participating governments will be averse to using or propagating material put out by an agency that is nothing more than a vehicle for distributing official handouts across the border.

What can be done?

Given the limited resources of the Third World, a practical solution would be to set up a truly independent Third World News Agency (TWNA), capable of projecting multiple Third World perspectives in the world news in as much the same way as Associated Press (AP), UPI, Agence France-Presse (AFP), and Reuters project U.S., French and British perspectives in the news they disseminate. Such a news agency would have to reflect the heterogeneous nature of the Third World group. The primary function of the TWNA would be to disseminate news, not to serve causes (any contribution of such a news agency to furthering world peace through better international understanding, for example, would have to be purely incidental). TWNA would also have to be truly multinational in operations—in management as well as in staffing—and free of domination not only by the governments but also by any of the national news agencies. That this would have to be so was clear from the protracted discussions in New Delhi and Colombo in 1976 that preceded the agreement on the Nonaligned News Agencies Pool. "We do not want to exchange British or American domination for domination by Indians or Yugoslavs," an African diplomat is quoted as having remarked in New Delhi, commenting on the intense competition between India and Yugoslavia for leadership of the proposed news agency pool.

TWNA would have a better chance of acceptance by, and support of, Third World countries if it could utilize existing national news gathering machineries, without any diminution of its own credibility. It would also have to steer clear of any involvement in the dissemination of news locally in developing countries (except in response to a direct official request from a country). TWNA's cooperation/adjustment with developing countries would not imply endorsement of any individual country's domestic policies regulating national news media operations. It would simply recognize that the degree of press freedom obtaining in the Third World, as in the Western world, varies from country to country and is designed to meet each country's specific national needs as perceived and determined by the government concerned.

A functional and practicable model of an international news agency, which will have all the above mentioned prerequisites and attributes, requires an organization that, in effect, will be a loose conglomerate of autonomous regional (and where necessary, subregional) news agencies. The proposed TWNA, according to this model, would be several regional news agencies combined into one, with regional agencies drawing upon, as much as possible, existing national news agencies for local news coverage. It will function as any other commercial news agency.

The structural components of the TWNA will include an international office, regional TWNAs, country bureaus, and international bureaus.

International Office

This will be the main executive and administrative unit of the TWNA. It will have no news-gathering or disseminating functions. It will, however, be responsible for administration, financial management, staff training, staff exchanges among various regional TWNAs, and overseeing the smooth functioning of, and cooperation among, the regional units.

One of its most important functions will be staff training. News staff of the TWNA will require training in reporting/writing as well as in cultural, economic, social, and political history of the concerned region. I favor training in the regions themselves, not in Western institutes. I think Third World countries have enough journalists of international repute and standing who can prove extremely valuable in organizing training programs. The TWNA could also attempt to change the ultrapolitical orientation of the senior-level editorial staff of the news media in the Third World, either by involving them in training activities or by arranging special refresher courses and workshops for them.

Regional TWNAs

The regional agency will have the primary responsibility for collecting news and disseminating it to subscriber countries or national

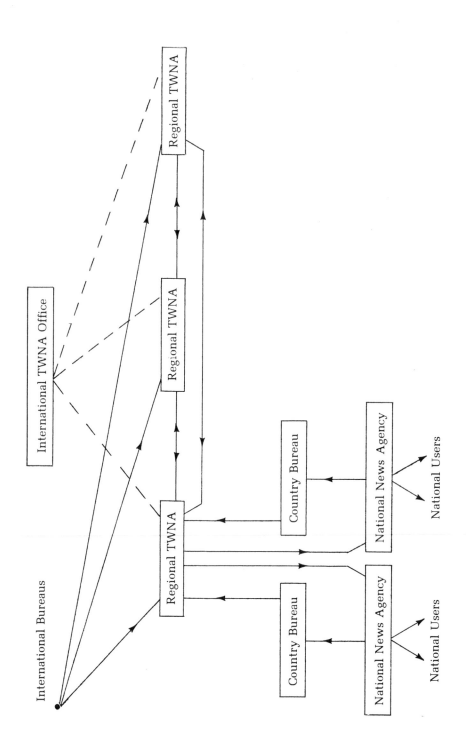

news agencies in the region. It will determine the language (English, French, Arabic, Spanish, and so on) of its news operations. All the news from various country and international bureaus will flow into the regional TWNA office. The regional office will also receive news from, and transmit news to, other regional TWNAs. After editing, collating, synthesizing, and, where necessary, rewriting the news thus received, the regional office will transmit the same directly to subscribing national news agencies that will then distribute the same to their own national users.

Regional TWNA will be responsible for entering into appropriate agreements of cooperation and news exchange with national news agencies. Where such agencies do not exist, regional TWNA may enter into a news exchange agreement with local newspapers or make other arrangements for gathering news. Regional TWNA will also be responsible for implementing any agreement of assistance that the international TWNA office may reach with a developing country for assistance in setting up a national news agency, including training of local staff. It will be responsible for selecting the sites and setting up country or subregional bureaus in the region. It will appoint a senior correspondent to be the chief of each country bureau. The correspondent will not be the national of the country to which he or she is assigned.

Country or Subregional Bureaus

Generally, the bureau will consist of one nonnational correspondent, assisted, if necessary, by local staff. The bureau chief will function as any other foreign correspondent will in the country of his or her attachment. His or her primary function will be to:

1. receive the news gathered by the existing national news agency
2. select news of subregional, regional, or interregional interest
3. rewrite or edit the selected material, as necessary, in the light of his or her own information, making necessary additions and deletions
4. transmit the news to the regional office
5. handle regular coverage in the country of his or her assignment

The bureau chief will be one of the most important functionaries in the TWNA set up, being responsible for building up the credibility of the TWNA as a news disseminator by weaning out unreliable or unverifiable material from national news agency dispatches. He or she will have to have extensive knowledge of the country's, as well as the region's, culture, history, society, economy, and politics.

International Bureaus

The TWNA will need to set up bureaus in major news centers in the Western and the socialist world, such as in New York, London, Paris, Geneva, Moscow, and Peking. These bureaus will serve all the regional TWNAs and will comprise, if necessary, one or more correspondents from each regional TWNA.

Initially, the TWNA will serve only the developing country media. In that sense, it will not change the Third World coverage in the western media. As the TWNA builds up its services, however, and establishes its uniqueness, credibility, and reliability as a news disseminator, it is likely to attract subscribers from the developed countries. The international office, in consultation with regional TWNAs, will at that time determine the form and the means of providing service to the interested developed country media.

The TWNA, through its regional units, will be able to project multiple Third World perspectives on world news. By interposing a country bureau chief, the regional TWNA, although depending on national news agencies, will have the mechanism to select the appropriate news for international dissemination. A major advantage of the TWNA will be the enormous savings in transmission costs that would be incurred if developing countries were to rely on bilateral news exchanges.

To be successful, the TWNA, while relying on the cooperation and support of developing countries, will have to be assured complete freedom from governmental intervention. This should not be difficult since the TWNA will not interfere with the domestic press policies and national news distribution systems of developing countries. Its management will comprise independent professional journalists, not government representatives.

As a first step, it would be necessary to appoint a group of independent, experienced journalists in each region to examine the financial, technical, and staff requirements (including the most important training component) of a regional TWNA. Each group would also make preliminary suggestions as to the location of the regional TWNA's headquarters and country bureaus, as well as the language(s) in which the agency will disseminate news in the region. Such reports could be completed within six months to a year. The next step obviously would be a joint conference of all such regional groups to work out the charter of the TWNA and decide upon the functions and composition of various TWNA units and the location of the international TWNA office. Once the technical feasibility of TWNA was established, the conference could appoint a steering committee to raise the necessary financial and technical resources.

The preceding is a very sketchy model of the proposed TWNA. Many details remain to be investigated, but I think it is a functional model. The TWNA is a practicable, not a utopian, proposition. With its new and unique orientation, the TWNA can become a very valuable, complementary addition to the existing international news gathering and disseminating systems.

14.

UNESCO
and the Press in the
Third World

GUNNAR R. NAESSELUND

It is arguable how legitimate it is to associate the activities of the United Nations Educational, Scientific and Cultural Organization (UNESCO) with the fear expressed that the proliferation of national news agencies—a process encouraged by UNESCO—and their banding together into regional pools—also encouraged by UNESCO—could lead to the exclusion of the established world agencies from these areas and to the consequent shrinkage in the free flow of information in the world.

The development of news agencies and their linking through bilateral, subregional, or regional exchange agreements has been part of UNESCO's program since the early 1950s. We are not aware of any facts that indicate that the risk of government control of media or the exclusion of the Western media can in any country or instance be seen as a consequence of or justified by such assistance.

It is said that UNESCO might have performed a greater service if it had concentrated its efforts on the development of the physical facilities for news agency operations. UNESCO has done so in so far as equipment, training, and operations are concerned, but where telecommunications are concerned UNESCO can only help to identify the user's needs, study discriminatory or exorbitant rates, or point to innovative techniques that might facilitate the operations of news agencies, press, and radio. The telecommunication infrastructure is a matter for the International Telecommunications Union and governments.

UNESCO fully subscribes to the conclusion that what is of more pressing and legitimate concern to outsiders (than internal problems leading to internal press restrictions are) is that internal policies not spill over and restrict the right of any outside agency to collect news from those countries for the rest of the world. By engaging itself and member states in studies of the right to communicate, at the international as well as the national level, UNESCO has embodied this concern in its program.

Also, the Director General of UNESCO in press conferences on November 16, 1976, in Nairobi and on December 14, 1976, in Paris referred to the need for an efficient protection of journalists against arbitrary pressures or reprisals to which they might be subject during the exercise of their profession.

It is the asymmetry of the flow of news based upon the asymmetry in the distribution of world power that is being challenged by the Third World, which argues that:

1. there may be supplementary or corrective news value criteria that have not been identified or tested through the services aimed at the public of primarily industrialized countries;
2. there may be an urgent need now for recognizing the dispersion of power centers that the established institutional routines are slow to identify;
3. there may be a case for trying through public-sector initiatives to identify new demands and to create institutions and outlets that will satisfy those demands.

There is hardly any doubt that the needs of developing countries for "educational," "scientific," or "cultural" information will be constantly growing and that the kind of information needed at their individual stages of development is not identical with the needs of the developed countries being served by the world agencies.

The "nonaligned" movement is in itself a legitimate attempt to create a new "power center" and to tailor a news service to its needs, to the extent that they can be jointly defined. If one such need in the first stage is for government agencies to have "official" accounts available of what is said or done in other nonaligned countries, such a "basic" news service may also be worthwhile. The risk of such a basic official news service being used by a country as a pretext for cutting itself off from the rest of the world's news flow must in all circumstance be negligible.

The argument that the differences within the UN system, when it comes to national attitudes toward news and information, are as irreconcilable as the basic ideologies of the member states and that it is simply impossible, for example, to conceive of a news philosophy or news distribution system that would be acceptable to both Soviet-bloc countries and the Western democracies reveals a basic misconception of UNESCO's role and its means.

The only "news philosophy" within this program is the concept of "the right to communicate" as an extension, within the potentials of modern technologies, of the freedom-of-information concept that was conceived in the age of newspapers and not electronics.

The programs as presented to and approved by the general conference every second year are the concerted actions by member states toward the general goals of UNESCO to work for international understanding and peace. In these activities UNESCO must take account of the existing ideologies or social philosophies to which member states adhere, but it is in no way asked or obliged to present a common philosophy. On the contrary, in its assistance program, to which a part of the regular funds is devoted, UNESCO acts only upon individual member states' requests that are then negotiated and executed on a basis of a bilateral action, into which UNESCO will bring such modalities as are asked for by the member states or assumed by UNESCO to achieve the objectives of the respective projects.

It is of vital importance for the understanding of UNESCO's program of assistance in the development of information media, however, to note that the funds allocated by the general conference for this purpose are limited and would be a fraction of what is needed if they could not be supplemented through other sources. Such sources may be United Nations Development Funds or national funds set aside for multinational activities and provided under funds-in-trust agreements, governed by the general administrative rules, but leading only to the execution of concrete projects agreed upon by a tripartite contract between the recipient country, UNESCO, and the donor country.

For the communication program of UNESCO for the biennium 1977–78, approved in Nairobi, the two divisions over which the program activities are spread (Division of Free Flow of Information and Communication Policies and Division of Development and Application of Communication Systems), the regular budget is respectively $2.3 million and $2.45 million, out of which a total of $0.5 million is available for direct assistance to individual member states upon request. From the United Nations Development Programme (UNDP) about $450,000 is foreseen for communication projects during the two year period and from funds-in-trusts about $350,000.

It is thus only a fraction of the $140 million that the organization reckons to spend during 1977-78 in technical assistance that goes to information and communication. The main reason for this is—as far as UNDP funds are concerned—that aid to news agencies, newspapers, radio stations, and other communication institutions or infrastructures is only in rare cases seen to be conducive to the economic productivity that UNDP funds in general seek to promote. The funds for these activities therefore have to come from elsewhere.

The conclusion of this argument is that UNESCO is—and has always been—well equipped professionally and politically to seek and execute such assistance in the field of communication as its record shows.

COOPERATIVE ASSISTANCE PROGRAMS

The channeling of funds through UNESCO for development of mass media in developing countries would benefit from UNESCO's professional staff in the divisions concerned and the staff's long experience in international assistance. UNESCO would also provide efficient administrative and logistic support services. UNESCO's access to the national authorities concerned and its close contacts with professional organizations in most countries are other advantages as are its extensive reference files on equipment, training, and expertise in communication development. UNESCO would also be able to offer close contact with research, planning and management resources, while knowledge in these fields would be constantly updated through workshops and publication. Last, but not least, UNESCO would allow a neutral, international execution of aid and assistance that would avoid bringing the recipients of the funds into new situations of dependencies.

The Director General of UNESCO may, in accordance with the financial regulations, receive funds from member states and international, regional, or national organizations, both governmental and nongovernmental, for the purpose of paying, at their request, salaries and allowances for personnel, fellowships, grants, equipment, and other related expenses in carrying out certain activities that are consistent with the aims, policies, and activities of the organization, as development of mass media is.

The idea of a joint fund between the International Federation of Editors and Publishers (FIEJ) and UNESCO for graphic media development in the Third World has been unofficially discussed at a recent meeting of representatives of the two organizations and might merit a further study on a wider basis.

It was evident to everybody present during the discussion of the UNESCO communication program and activities at the Nineteenth Session of the General Conference in Nairobi that the amount of financing available for development of mass media and communication systems in the Third World is in glaring contrast with the needs and demands in this field. It was hoped at one point during the discussions in Nairobi that developed countries would demonstrate their appreciation of the urgency of bridging the gap by announcing financial support for these purposes. No firm promises were made, however, but indications of willingness to consider the matter were given by several delegates.

Funds could be earmarked for development purposes in the following general terms. Some might provide assistance in the form of short-term experts' services, fellowships, equipment, and financial aid for the development of media projects, especially those aimed at creating basic media institutions such as news agencies, rural or community newspapers, reading materials for new literates, and extension radio services and at evaluating and upgrading the performance of existing institutions. Other funds could give assistance to, and undertake, preinvestment studies in the field of communication planning, while other monies might be used to undertake advisory missions in the field of formulation and application of communication policies and integrated communication strategies. Providing intellectual and financial assistance for pilot projects aimed at improving the adaptation of technologies and media structures to the specific needs of developing countries is another possible use of earmarked funds, as is the support of and participation in projects aimed at improving the impact of communication in rural development.

If funds were available, UNESCO would initiate the necessary feasibility and preinvestment studies of proposed or suitable projects and establish lists of priorities that would in particular take into consideration the needs of the countries least developed and most disadvantaged in the field of communication. On the following pages is a list of UNESCO programs and publications related to communication as of April 1977.

UNESCO DIVISION OF FREE FLOW OF INFORMATION AND COMMUNICATION POLICIES: Programs and Publication, 1977–78

UNESCO's present program, including research studies and publications, can be grouped into eight general areas. The most multifaceted of these concerns the promotion of a free and balanced flow of information and research on international communication structures. Specifically, this includes "External Broadcasting and International Understanding," a study on the flow of information and its contents, broadcast from other countries to Yugoslavia. The study was published in the Reports and Papers series (E/F/S) in June 1977. In addition the

International Film and Television Council (IFTC) in 1977 completed several papers, published as a document, on the problems of "legal and economic aspects of international communication" as a result of the working group on "Law and Audiovisual Media." Following new approaches to the "free flow of information" another study, undertaken in 1977–78, has analyzed "the concept of a free and balanced flow of information and its political, social and cultural aspects in five different regions of the world." This study will be discussed at an ad hoc working meeting in 1978 and published in the 1978 Reports and Papers series. Another example, a study started in 1974 on the "structure of the international news agencies network," including an analysis of the collection of news and selection criteria for news in some developing countries, was followed in 1977 by two national case studies on the processing of news from international news agency sources in Venezuela and Yugoslavia, giving special attention to the Third World news agency pool arrangement of Tanjug. The study, published as a book in English in 1977, is also being published in French.

Another study, on "the transnational media industries, in particular the marketing patterns of transnational film and television program distribution and the implications for national communication policies and international understanding," which included two country studies in Argentina and Thailand, was finished in 1977 and published in the Reports and Papers series (E/F/S) 1978. It is a follow-up of the study previously published by UNESCO on television traffic around the world, entitled "Television Traffic—a One Way Street." The second study concentrates on the function and role of the transnational corporations in the communication area. Another study, one which was launched in 1974 on the "international typology of radio and television programs," was concluded in 1977–78 and published as a document.

A joint study of cooperating institutions in a number of countries will be undertaken under the coordination of the International Association on Mass Communication Research (IAMCR) on the "image of foreign countries representing different social systems and development states, as portrayed by the mass media."

As a' measure to improve news exchanges a study is being carried out, in cooperation with the International Telecommunications Union and professional organizations, on "rates, facilities, and obstacles to the transmission of press messages within developing countries and between regions." In connection with the measures to improve the news exchanges a document was published in March 1977 on the "circulation of press messages in African States, tariffs for telex and telegrams," followed by a "study on news transmission on a regional level to facilitate cooperative action," published in December 1977. Both documents have limited distribution. Consultations based on this study are being held between representatives of news agencies and media on a regional level to initiate cooperative action, to facilitate news transmissions, and for negotiations with national and/or regional press and telecommunications organizations on measures to counteract high and discrepant rates for the transmission of news from developing countries (including consultant services to governments and regional organizations).

Measures will also be undertaken to strengthen regional and international communication organizations and news agency networks. The measures might be such studies or advisory services as may be requested by the coordinating committee of the Third World news pool.

For the development of news exchanges in Asia, a meeting of experts was organized in 1977 and several background documents, a working paper, and a final report have been and are being prepared for this end. As a follow-up to an earlier meeting, on news agencies in Latin America in Quito in 1975, a feasibility study on regional news exchanges within Latin America, is being carried out. The model of an agreement between news agencies in the region is being prepared for distribution to member states and news agencies for their comments.

The last activity falling in this area results from the recommendations of meetings on news exchange within and among the regions of Africa, the Arab states, and Latin America. Studies based on these recommendations have been undertaken in these regions and in Asia, to identify criteria of news values and principles of crosscultural communication that could promote such exchanges. The conclusions will be published in the series of Reports and Papers on Mass Communication in 1978.

The second area of activity of this UNESCO division concerns the promotion of the international circulation of persons and materials and includes the preparation and publication of the twenty-second issue of *Study Abroad* in 1978 as well as the preparation for publication in 1979 in the Reports and Papers series of a study on "tariff, postal, currency, and freight obstacles to the international circulation of educational, scientific, and cultural materials." In addition, a practical "Guide to the Operation of the Florence Protocol to the Agreement on the Importation of Educational, Scientific and Cultural Materials" was published in August 1977.

Studies on communication and the promotion of communication research represent the third area of activity, including, for example, the international comparative study started in 1975 on "Communication in the Community," which was undertaken in Colombia, Finland, the Federal Republic of Germany, Hungary, Lebanon, Singapore (with a case study in India), and the United Kingdom. This was published in the Reports and Papers series in 1977. Additionally, in collaboration with research institutions, other related studies have been or are being undertaken. One of these concerns the "introduction, use, and consequences of modern communication technology in traditional and modern societies, with particular reference to problems of dependence and the activities of transnational corporations," the results of which will be published in 1979–80. Another study will investigate the historical development of media systems, their functions and institutional structures within given socioeconomic conditions, with an emphasis on the present and future role of communication in society, and will thus constitute a pilot study for a further series of comparative studies to be carried out in selected member states.

The "mass media and the image, role, and social conditions of women," a collection and analysis of communication research work, is another subject of investigation. Comparative studies will also be made on the concept of development and on the role that can be played, now and in the future, by the governments and the media of the developing countries with a view to attaining their political, economic, and cultural sovereignty, as envisaged by the mass media in the developing countries, on the one hand, and by those in the industrialized countries on the other. Meanwhile, research is being organized on methods of communication of the type used to promote "grass roots" participation that will enable all groups of societies to define their own development criteria.

A symposium on "Communication and National Cultures" will be organized in Warsaw, Poland, in 1978 and a report will be prepared by IAMCR. And the concluding example of this third area of activity is the working document and final report prepared in connection with the Latin American Seminar on Communication Research held in August 1977 in Lima, Peru.

The development of documentation centers on communication research is another major area of activity. A report was published in early 1977 on the ad hoc working group of directors and specialists of the International Network of Documentation Centres on Communication Research and Policies, a list of documents and publications in the field of mass communication was published in January 1977, and an inventory of African communication was prepared and produced as a document (for limited distribution) in September 1977. In the late fall of 1977 an ad hoc meeting on the creation of an African Regional Documentation was held in Nairobi and a report on that has been prepared. In addition, in the same year a feasibility study was undertaken regarding the creation of a regional communication documentation center in the Arab states and also in the African region (and was published as a document).

The Intergovernmental Conference on Communication Policies in Asia in June 1978 is the fifth area of activity, which has led to the preparation of several background papers and a working document and will later lead to a final report.

The next area, studies and publications on national communication policies, includes five studies, undertaken in 1976, on national communication policies in Asia, which have been or presently will be published. The countries concerned are India, Sri Lanka, Japan, the Republic of Korea, and Iran. Under preparation are five studies in Africa: in Zaire, Nigeria, and Senegal, and in Zambia or Kenya and Algeria or Egypt. These studies will also be published. Two further European countries, Austria and Belgium, have also offered policy studies.

From three studies (in Colombia, Finland, and Brazil) on various approaches to "National Communication Policy Councils," published in 1977, alternative models that can be applicable to member states will be prepared.

Among the projects that have been finished are two studies undertaken by European research institutes in the United Kingdom and the Federal Republic of Germany to define "indicators for communication development," which were completed in 1977, as well as a survey from the East-West Centre, Hawaii, on "communication planning methodologies and structures" and "a case study on communication structure in Malaysia" as an overview for communication planning.

In addition to studies of particular countries, several contributions for the "handbook on communication planning" will be edited for publication in 1979, dealing with such topics as modeling techniques and simulation; forecasting techniques; techniques of evaluation; economic tools for decision making and for control and implementation of communication plans; and organization theory and institutional communication. And a communication planning workshop, including the development of corresponding instructional materials, designed by Syracuse University and tested in Latin America by the University of Brasilia is being followed up by further studies on the structures and mechanisms for communication planning.

Studies on the right to communicate and studies on mass media councils are the seventh area of activity. Included here is a basic paper prepared in 1976 with a synthesis of the responses received from the member states and professional organizations to a questionnaire. This paper, which also contains the results of a working group held at headquarters, was submitted as a document to the Nineteenth Biennial General Conference. Another example of this category is the working paper for an expert meeting "on the implications of the right to communicate" from different cultural backgrounds that is being prepared and will be published, together with the synthesis of this meeting, as a report to the Twentieth Biennial General Conference. The study on "mass media codes of ethics and mass media councils," published in the fall of 1977, is a third example.

Finally, the preparation of a declaration of fundamental principles governing the use of the mass media has also been a major area of UNESCO activity, and the final report to accompany the revised draft text of the declaration on the fundamental principles governing the use of the mass media was published as a document, together with the revised draft declaration, in December 1977.

15 PRESS CENSORSHIP UNDER INDIRA GANDHI

GEORGE VERGHESE

We have recently been through a remarkable experience in India, a period of emergency lasting 20 months in which censorship was one of the key factors if not the key factor. Information is power, and regimes that want to usurp all authority need to control information. It was not surprising, therefore, that censorship became one of the major instruments of policy.

India has a fairly old tradition of the press, with newspapers going back over 100 years, and a tradition of press freedom, or a struggle for press freedom, that is almost as old. One of the earliest protests of the nationalist movement in the last century was aimed against the Vernacular Press Act of 1878, which sought to suppress the rising generation of Indian-language newspapers that were thought to be preaching sedition. The struggle for press rights and individual liberties has continued from that time on.

In the initial period after independence in 1947, the relations between the Indian press and government were friendly. There was a sense on the part of the press of being deferential to authority, certainly to the personal authority of the then prime minister, Jawaharlal Nehru, one of the great heroes of the independence movement and the nationalist struggle. But as the years went on, the press took on a more critical role, and by the 1960s, the relations were in some degree transformed, the press having taken on an adversary role. This sharpened in the latter 1960s, and particularly from 1969 onward when Indira Gandhi split the Congress party. That was a kind of watershed. A section of the press, larger newspapers called "the monopoly press" because of their

George Verghese was formerly Editor of the *Hindustan Times*.

size and because of their association with big business, was singled out for attack as being antigovernment, antipoor, and in favor of vested interests of various kinds. These papers were accused of not supporting Gandhi's government on acts such as the nationalization of banks and the removal of the privileges of the former Indian princes and of not supporting the Congress party in the elections of 1971.

Pressures also began to mount on the press in the states where control over state advertising was used by some governments to discipline the press. Pressures were applied to remove or to discipline certain "recalcitrant" pressman, newsmen who were critical, who were not amenable to suggestions or advice from the powers that be, and who were exposing things that the government would have preferred to have kept hidden.

During this period, also, the Press Council, a statutory body for the self-regulation of the press, began to get into action by establishing a certain body of case law defining the parameters of press freedom and standards. These regulations—that is, the decrees of the Press Council —were defied by certain state governments. But it is interesting to note that although the central government complained against the attitude of the press and alleged distortions and support of vested interests and so on, it never did bring any case before the Press Council as such. In 1971, in order to deal with this so-called problem of the monopoly press, the central government sought to introduce a bill that would have diffused the ownership of newspapers. This was a means of attacking the so-called monopoly press. That bill was fought and set aside.

Ever since World War II, India has had newsprint control because the bulk of our newsprint is imported from abroad. Because of foreign exchange constraints, the government makes annual newsprint allocations. In 1972 or 1973, acute difficulties concerning the availability of newsprint and the rising costs of imported newsprint led the government to try to introduce a new form of newsprint control by placing a ceiling on the number of pages papers could print. This was struck down by the Supreme Court on an appeal from some of the newspapers; the court held that newsprint control should not be used for purposes of newspaper control.

By 1974, having fought off these attacks on its independence, the press had become increasingly critical of the government for its economic drift, and for the political corruption that had pervaded the whole system. The antigovernment movements in Gujarat and Bihar, led by Jayaprakash Narayan, attracted a great deal of attention in the press and a good deal of sympathy and support. This was the backdrop for the emergency that came in June 1975. Even before the emergency was declared late at night on June 25, the government had imposed a

form of censorship earlier that night by cutting off the electricity supply to the newspapers in Delhi and by raiding newspaper offices in a
number of cities to prevent the country from learning the next day
what had happened later that night in terms of the mass arrests of
political leaders and so on.

With the declaration of emergency on the night of the 25th, formal
censorship was ordered on June 26 under the Defense of India rules.
With that censorship order some guidelines setting out certain dos and
don'ts for the press were issued. These were very extensive as the
following citations indicate.

"The purpose of precensorship," according to the official guidelines,
"is to ensure that no news is published in a manner that contributes to
demoralization about the general situation or the public interest in all
respects as determined by the central government." Nothing should be
published that "will contribute even in a remote way to affect or
worsen the law and order situation," nor about "any action or statement
or event that is likely to cause disaffection between the government and
the people." Nothing should be published that is "likely to convey the
impression of protest or disapproval," "that might bring into hatred or
contempt the government established by law," "that might promote
feelings of enmity and hatred between different classes of citizens in
India," that might result in "the cessation and slowing down of work,"
or that might "encourage people to break prohibitory laws" or "relate
to agitations and violent incidents," or anything "denigrating the institution of the Prime Minister," and so on.

These prohibitions were so broadly stated as to cover anything and
everything. Further, there was a total ban on the publication of the
proceedings of Parliament and the state legislatures, without clearance
by the censor, and also a ban—that is a precensorship ban—on publication of the proceedings of courts and court judgments.

Obviously, the object was to reduce every Indian to an island, to
prevent people from learning what had happened, to muzzle all protest,
all dissent, to ensure conformity, and to prevent any kind of a protest
movement from snowballing and developing into a situation that the
government might not be able to control. There were variations in the
application and operation of censorship in the different states. In some
states all news was, for the whole of the first year, subject to precensorship. In other places, there were censors sitting in newspaper offices.
But in some states, formal precensorship was soon lifted and the guidelines were left to operate on the basis of self-censorship.

Anyone who violated the guidelines was sure to be disciplined in
various ways. A newspaper that violated censorship was placed under
precensorship, which meant that all copy had to be taken to the censor,

page by page, column by column, including the advertisements. This was a form of harrassment. Advertising cutoffs were threatened and advertising was in fact choked off by various means. Presses were sealed. Earlier, certain newspapers belonging to political parties had been closed down. Newspapermen were arrested.

An effort was made to institutionalize the guidelines by legislation. The first enactment was the Prevention of Publication of Objectionable Matters Act, which succeeded in putting the censorship order on the statute book. By placing it in the Ninth Schedule of the Constitution, which is a schedule that encompasses ordinary legislation, the government sought to place it beyond challenge in any court.

Then came the repeal of an act that had been legislated in 1956 that gave newspapers immunity in reporting the proceedings of Parliament. A member of Parliament is entitled to make any observation in the House and be protected. He is not subject to the laws of defamation or libel; no action can be taken against him outside the House. If the newspapers reported him faithfully, they were protected too. This 1956 legislation, introduced by Prime Minister Ghandi's late husband, Feroze Gandhi, was commonly known by his name as the Feroze Gandhi Act. When the Feroze Gandhi Act was repealed, newspapers became liable to action for reporting the proceedings of Parliament or of legislatures in any manner judged to be offensive or prejudicial to the government.

A third move was the abolition of the Press Council. It would obviously be dangerous and unnecessary to have an umpire to oversee fair play if the rules of the game were to be constantly changed to suit the government of the day. So the Press Council disappeared too.

Then followed the takeover of Samachar. There were four independent news agencies in India. The Press Trust of India was the oldest; the United News of India had been established in 1961 to compete with it. These two functioned in the English language. More recently, two Indian-language news agencies had been established: one called Hindustan Samachar, the other Samachar Bharati. The government first thought of taking all four over by an act of nationalization. A draft bill was drawn up and discussed in the cabinet, but was shot down there. The Minister for Information and Broadcasting, however, was authorized to regulate the news agencies. He went about securing what he called the "voluntary" merger of these four news agencies. Every means was used, including pressure on the editorial staff, the management staff, and the proprietors and owners of those newspapers which in turn owned the four news agencies. Thus Samachar came into being early in 1976 as a "voluntary" society, but very much a state-controlled organ.

Samachar was used not merely as an instrument of censorship. There is also positive news management, for which the apparatus of censorship was used. Under the direction of the censor, newspapers would get telephone calls or sometimes messages over the news agency wires, saying that such and such an item should not be published or that it should be published only to the extent of giving the bare news and no comment. But often the directive was that only Samachar should be used, the Samachar copy having been doctored in various ways. So Samachar and censorship became instruments of news management. I know that the journalists in Samachar disapproved of this altogether, but, as in the press generally, there were some who, for various reasons, collaborated, others who were sullen, and a few who left.

There was a proposal to discipline the press further by getting editors to develop a "code of ethics" comprising additional guidelines and prohibitions that the government was anxious should then be given statutory force so that the code too might become an instrument of permanent self-regulation. Interestingly, a committee of editors was appointed by the government to draft this code of ethics, the convener being none other than the chief censor! The object of the exercise was quite clear from the sponsorship, but it did not work. Most of the editors on the committee left in protest and, although some kind of a code was drawn up, it was never endorsed.

Then there was the effort at takeover bids and the exercise of direct pressure on recalcitrant papers. Among the larger newspapers in India is the *Statesman,* which is published in Calcutta and Delhi. There was an attempt to drum up a rather trivial issue that had been inquired into a year or two earlier and dismissed as being completely unfounded about the *Statesman*'s misuse of newsprint. On this trumped-up charge, the *Statesman* got a notice to show cause why the government should not appoint directors to its board. The notice didn't specify how many directors, but the object quite clearly was to name a sufficient number to get a majority and take over the paper.

The *Statesman* took the matter to court, obtained a stay order, and fought the notice. Finally, the government, having no case at all, had to withdraw, but pressure was maintained by cutting off advertisements to the *Statesman.* This was effected by means of a government agency called the Directorate of Audio-Visual Publicity (DAVP), which is an official advertising agency. It controls the placement of all central and municipal government advertising and, after the emergency was declared, all advertising from all public-sector corporations as well. This accounts for a very large chunk, maybe almost half of Indian advertising. Thus if the DAVP put a paper on its blacklist, it could at a stroke deprive it of a very large part of its revenues and force it into financial difficulties. So the *Statesman* was given the DAVP treatment.

This was followed by an attempt to buy out the shares of the *Statesman.* The *Statesman* was a former British-owned company that had passed into Indian hands about 15 years ago. It had been bought by a number of Indian companies, on the basis of no one company's owning more than 13 percent of the shares. The government now tried to get at the shareholders in an effort to secure majority control of the company and thus of the editorial and management staff of the *Statesman,* who were standing firm. This again failed, and the battle continued until almost the end of the emergency period.

Then there was the case of the *Indian Express,* the largest of the Indian newspaper chains in terms of circulation. It publishes multiple editions in English from eight centers, and various Indian-language editions in about four or five different dialects in another four or five centers.

The owner of the *Express* group, Ram Nath Goenka, is a figure who approximates most closely what is called a publisher in the United States. This is a species we don't really have in India; it's an underdeveloped newspaper type, which we must now develop. We have owners, not publishers; we need more publishers.

At the time Goenka was in some difficulties because of bank loans he had received earlier for his newspaper enterprises. Questions were asked about the purposes for which the money had been used, and some cases had been filed against him. The charge was that he had hypothecated or mortgaged, some of his newspaper and newsprint assets and had used the funds for other industrial purposes. This was the lever that he alleges the government used to threaten him and his family with detention unless the *Express* conformed and unless he agreed to certain policy changes and a restructuring of the board.

Goenka was willing to cooperate up to a point, and he negotiated what he thought was a settlement: some change in the stated policy of the paper and a change in the board of directors, which gave the majority vote to the government-named directors. But he retained personnel control under his own charge. Goenka was in the hospital with a heart attack when the new chairman of the board, K. K. Birla, a big industrialist and the chairman and owner of the *Hindustan Times,* another large Indian newspaper group, discharged the editor and tried to take the paper over altogether. This set in motion a chain reaction: Goenka resisted strongly, the earlier agreement broke down, and the heat was turned on the *Express.* In a series of actions, efforts were made to discharge the new replacement editor, who had also proved a very independent man and then, that having failed, the electricity supply was cut off. The *Express* went to court and obtained an order restoring it. The municipal authorities then came and sealed the press on a trumped-up charge of not paying property taxes. That also was successfully contested in court. The banks were then instructed to stop credit to the *Express.* Advertising had been cut earlier by the DAVP and every kind of pressure was employed including precensorship. But the *Express* held out and fought back, a fight that went on right through the emergency.

A number of the larger papers, however, did not resist. This was because their owners and managements feared for their other industrial interests. Unions, being progovernment, sometimes refused to go along with any measures that might result in a confrontation with the government and in possible closure and loss of jobs for their members.

There was nevertheless a number of periodicals and a number of smaller Indian-language papers in the districts around the country that held their ground and fought some very gallant actions. A number of periodicals in English and other languages—*Bhoomiputra, Sadhara, Swalajya, Opinion, Mainstream, Seminar, Himmat,* and many others— stood up to a considerable amount of pressure, fought the issues in court, and obtained favorable stays.

The courts were a major source of support and, throughout the emergency, the judiciary played a notable role in upholding freedom. M. C. Chagle, a former judge of the Bombay High Court, and then Ambassador to the United States, and subsequently Education Minister and External Affairs Minister, made a speech on civil liberties toward the end of 1975. Against the censor's order, a Gujarati paper, the *Bhoomiputra,* published his speech and in consequence was served with a notice for seizure of its press and put under precensorship. The paper took the matter up in the Gujarat High Court. Unlike other cases where specific acts of censorship had been successfully challenged by newspapers, in the Bhoomiputra case the entire censorship order was challenged, together with the guidelines. In the judgment, delivered in the early spring of 1976, the court ruled that "the chief censor's guidelines go very much beyond Rule 48 [of the Defense of India Rules]." The judges said, "The chief censor's guidelines, in our opinion, are thoroughly useless and worthless because the nation which rises like an impregnable citadel above every individual or group of individuals, cannot be apronstringed to the chief censor, nor can its political education and sovereignty be moulded into the cast of the chief censor." This was a very strong judgment, striking down the guidelines and part of the censorship order itself.

The government appealed this judgment to the Supreme Court and asked that the High Court should meanwhile issue a stay on the publication of its judgement. The court heard these arguments and issued another order in which the judges said that it was extraordinary that the government should ask the court to censor its own order striking down censorship! It firmly ruled that this was impossible, saying:

> The censor has no jurisdiction to censor court proceedings, and court proceedings do not and cannot incite people to violence or disturb public order or endanger public safety. The Censorship Order under Rule 51 of the Defense of India Rules was intended to prevent incitement to violence and to safeguard public orders and public safety. Under our Constitution, the court interprets the law and lays it down. The law that we have laid down must hold good at least until the Supreme Court takes a different view. The censor cannot sit in judgment upon our decision and decide which law should be allowed to be made known to the people, and which not.
>
> [The order continued,] ... The censor is not above the court. It is necessary for him to realize that he is subject to the jurisdiction of the court. What is held ultra vires cannot be allowed to operate as intre-vires under the veil of secrecy. We cannot permit the liberty of the people to be under the weight of censorship. We are not inclined to do anything by which deprivation of liberty can be continued even for a moment more.

Despite this specific order, the court's judgement was in fact censored and not allowed to be published. Later on, however, one paper, and then others, did publish the judgment and as a result suffered punitive action. Action was also taken against the judges who delivered this judgment, and a number of other judges who had in other cases given judgments adverse to the government and upholding the liberty of the citizen. They were punished through punitive transfers and other kinds of pressures. Reports on all these actions were also censored.

In short, by means of censorship a climate of fear was created in which even court definitions of what was illegal were not allowed to be reported. More and more, the people had the feeling that, well, this is the law; you must obey the law because there are consequences that follow if you violate it. And many people who might have acted differently, or at least thought differently, had they known that some of these laws were totally illegal and had been struck down in the courts were never permitted to learn the facts.

One had only to look at the censor's orders to see how dishonest the whole operation was. It had nothing to do with the security of the state, with public order, with economic progress. It had everything to do with hiding whatever was embarrassing to the government and in encouraging the propagation of half-truths and untruths through news management. The distinction between party and state was obliterated by the actions of the press information bureau of the Ministry of Information and Broadcasting. The other branches of that ministry—the publications division, the film division, All-India radio and television, which are all government organs—were unashamedly used as propaganda trumpets. And DAVP, the official advertising agency, was used both to punish the recalcitrant and to reward those that collaborated.

The younger journalists and the smaller papers were often more forthright than the big-circulation papers in defending freedom and upholding what they thought was their professional duty. As for the collaborationist press, particularly Samachar and All-India radio and television, their credibility was totally lost.

Efforts were also made by the government to control the foreign press by imposing censorship and guidelines. This was resisted, and ultimately the government found it better to leave the foreign press more or less alone. In the initial period, however, a number of foreign correspondents were expelled.

In February of 1977, Prime Minister Gandhi decided to call an election and announced that censorship would be relaxed, although it would not be removed. The expectation was that fear would linger. On the contrary, the very day after this announcement, a number of newspapers—notably the *Indian Express* and the *Statesman* among the English-language papers, and some among the Indian-language papers and some of the weeklies—began to give voice to everything that had been suppressed during the emergency. Opposition leaders in detention were released. All their statements and activities and their prison diaries were published. The whole mood of the people, which was one of resentment, was captured in the press and began to make very lively reading for everyone. The Delhi edition of the *Indian Express,* which normally had a circulation of about 100,000 copies, registered daily sales of over 300,000 copies within the space of a month. In contrast, the *Hindustan Times,* which continued on a collaborationist path, saw its circulation drop by about 60,000 copies. And this was repeated in other news centers. People were hungry for news; the credibility of the papers that were giving accurate news soared together with their circulation figures.

As the elections drew near, the manifestos of all the opposition parties pledged the removal of censorship and the freeing of the media from governmental shackles. The Congress party was silent on this issue because it thought that censorship had done an excellent job; censorship was something with which the party felt very comfortable.

A number of newspapermen also drafted an election pledge on press freedom that they circulated to all candidates standing for election and asked them to sign, which many did. The election resulted in a victory for the Janata party, which promptly fulfilled its campaign promises by repealing the Prevention of Publication of Objectionable Matters Act and by reenacting the Feroze Gandhi Act, which restored to the press the immunity it had enjoyed in reporting the proceedings of Parliament. The government announced the revival of the Press Council as a self-regulatory mechanism. All the papers that had been on the DAVP blacklist had their advertising restored. Officials who had been in the forefront of news management and information control were reshuffled or dismissed. Radio and television, though still government organs, were permitted full freedom to function as professional media.

The Janata party, in its manifesto and its statements after the election, pledged to give Samachar back its independence, free of any kind of government control. The government also promised full autonomy to radio, television, and the film organizations. Its objective was to ensure for these bodies, whatever their structure, complete independence and autonomy in their day-to-day functioning.

What of the future? Beyond question the emergency proved to have been a great exercise in political education for the whole country, certainly for the press. Previously, the question of press freedom was largely academic. One talked about it, but it was rightly said of the Indian press that it was so busy defending its freedom that it often forgot to exercise it. It was also felt that freedom of the press was something that belonged to editors and newspapers, and that the citizen was not really concerned with it. So when the government talked of disciplining the press by limiting its freedom, people tended to think that the government was disciplining a group of bad guys, monopolists and so on, without realizing that it was their freedom that was at stake. The emergency taught them that freedom of the press is really but a part of the constitutionally guaranteed freedom of speech and expression, which is a fundamental right of the citizen and which, not accidentally, stands first on the list of fundamental freedoms. In the Bill of Rights of the Indian Constitution, freedom of expression comes first, because without that, you cannot articulate any other freedoms. Thus the emergency was a process of political education that has put the whole concept of press freedom and freedom of information—that is, the citizen's right to know and to have access to news—in the forefront of popular political consciousness. And this has filtered right down to the grass roots. Press freedom is no longer an elitist notion. The emergency succeeded in democratizing this basic concept.

As a result of the emergency, there is a new awareness in India within the press and about the press, and I think we are going to have a more demanding readership. There is still some deference to authority and some degree of self-censorship that will have to go. Newspapers that collaborated with the government earlier, have now, in order to compensate, swung all the other way. Maybe it will take a little time for some balance to be restored. Furthermore, with the restored freedom of the press comes another factor: a greater awareness of, or the feeling of a greater need for, social responsibility regarding the role and duty of the press and of the media, generally. Autonomy for radio and television, freedom and independence for the press, yes, but to what end? We talk of the mass media in many countries but to a large extent —and I refer specifically to India—they are really class media. They don't filter down. One of the things that has to be done in order to make press freedom real is to go down to the people so that we no longer communicate only among elites but directly with the people. This suggests some of the tasks that lie ahead for the Indian mass media. With the Janata government advocating a more decentralized society, decentralized communications at the local and community level are going to be very important, particularly important for press freedom, because that is where democracy grows. If the democratic structure takes firm root at the grass roots, then press freedom will be permanently strengthened and will grow from there upward.

16   Press Censorship in South Africa

PERCY QOBOZA

Percy Qoboza was the editor of the World *in Johannesburg, South Africa, when on October 19, 1977, he was arrested and jailed by the Vorster government under the provisions of the Defense Act. The* World *was shut down. On March 10, 1978, when Qoboza was released from prison without ever having had formal charges brought against him, Justice Minister Kruger declared that Qoboza could resume his career as a journalist, but that the* World *could not resume publication. This chapter has been prepared from the transcript of informal remarks Qoboza delivered at the conference on "The Third World and Press Freedom," held in New York City on May 11 to 13, 1977.*

When I consider the Indian experience of press censorship [see the preceding chapter by George Verghese], I have the unmistakable feeling that there were secret meetings between Indira Gandhi and Vorster. Because their strategies seem identical, one is persuaded to think that each had a copy of the censorship policy the other was going to apply to the press and that they had agreed that censorship was the only way they could maintain certain civilized standards and codes and the only way they could preserve the security of the state.

In fact, one of the common fallacies about South Africa, one much encouraged by the South African government's department of information, particularly in the United States, is the notion that South Africa has one of the freest presses one can find around the world. I was horrified in 1976, when I was in Harvard for my Nieman year, to see this fallacy being pronounced again and again in U.S. newspapers; the matter came to a head when then U.S. ambassador to the United Nations Daniel P. Moynihan repeated the fallacy at the United Nations (but it is possible to forgive him for quite a few things).

In the early months of 1977 South Africa moved steadily toward a confrontation with its newspapers. It had long been a traditional sport of the government to present the press in South Africa with all sorts of harrassments and threats—particularly the English-speaking press because the English-speaking press had a very magnificent record of standing up for civil liberties and human rights in the country. This hostility toward the press had been exhibited even more blatantly in June 1976 when the troubles erupted in Soweto and other townships in South Africa.

I'm not quite sure what caused that trouble, but I had known all along it would happen one day. I'm not sure about the beginning of the trouble because I had not been in South Africa for a year. I arrived on June 8, 1976; eight days later the trouble erupted. The claim made by the minister of justice in Parliament—that the whole problem was caused by black power and that black power had been imported into South Africa from the United States—should not be believed, but at the time everybody was looking around the country to see who had just arrived from the United States. So eventually I was caught up in the mess. Any relation between what had happened in South Africa and what I had been doing in the United States was purely coincidental, I can assure you.

Despite the similarities between the Indian and South African situations to which I've alluded, censorship in South Africa is not the blatant type George Verghese has described in India, and this seems to prevent people from seeing that South Africa really does not have a free press in the usual sense of any interpretation of a free press in a free society. There are certain laws and little clauses in the statute book that make editing a newspaper in South Africa, as one wise man observed, like walking through a mine field blindfolded.

My first example of the laws that make life complicated for newspapers in my country may seem unbelievable to outsiders, for there is a law, even in South Africa, that prohibits the promotion of racial hostility. It's an all-embracing law, for one never knows what inflames racial hostility, what causes incitement for one racial group or another. It's a strange law, because everything that has been done in that country and all the laws that have been put on the statute book in that country do, in fact, promote racial hostility. Editors have to be very careful as to just what they put into news stories and they have to be very careful of the editorials they write lest they fall afoul of this law.

The second law that makes life complicated is a law called the Prisons Act. I'm most concerned about this act, because by the nature of the conditions in South Africa three-quarters of its prison population is black, and half of these prisoners are not there because they are criminals in any usual sense, but because they have violated technical laws like the pass laws, which decree where black South Africans can sleep and where they cannot sleep, which decree that at a certain time in the middle of the night, they must take their black faces out of the lily-white areas. Otherwise, if they're caught there, it's a criminal offense. Our jails are crawling with people whose offenses are of that kind.

I'm also concerned because we get some hair-raising stories about what is happening in those prisons and because we, as a newspaper, cannot effectively investigate the conditions under which people are kept in the jails. We may not publish accounts of a released prisoner telling us exactly what was happening behind those walls and, therefore, the whole community, the whole nation, black and white, is left completely in the dark as to what is happening behind those prison walls.

In the early months of 1977 particularly, there were some very sordid stories of people who were arrested, not for any criminal offenses, who were detained under the country's massive security legislation that empowers the police to jail suspects for periods of up to two hours or, in some cases, even up to two years without bringing them before the courts. The police are also entitled to refuse visiting permission to anybody, including wives, parents, and children. At the same time these security laws also prevent any court of law from intervening in cases of such detentions.

With so many people detained under such circumstances, the anxiety of many parents, wives, and children is naturally heightened by the stories filtering out of the prisons, especially when an official account by the police states that a particular prisoner has committed "suicide" in the cell. Yet there has been no way at all through which newspapers could dispute or challenge these official accounts.

Three very close, personal friends of mine, with whom I went to school, died under such circumstances. In the case of one, it's possible that he committed suicide, but the other two, I could swear, had no suicidal tendencies at all, and they had everything going for them. Yet one morning we heard the hair-raising stories that they had taken their lives. In such instances, the government propaganda machinery goes into action; sordid insinuations are made against these dead: that they were members of the Communist party or were what white South Africans term "terrorists" who couldn't bear to face the courts because they would receive lengthy prison sentences.

We just do not believe these stories. We do not believe them because I think we know what's happening in there.

The third law that complicates the work of the press is called the Suppression of Communism Act. The "Communist party" has been with us in South Africa for a long time. First it was used by the government to indoctrinate white South Africans with the fear that the country was facing a real Red threat. This has subsequently become unfashionable because no South African believes it, so today the "Communist Party" label is being used, more and more, to convince the Western world—the United States, France, Britain, and other, less gullible countries—that South Africa is faced with a real Red threat.

In the terms of this law, the government can arbitrarily name an individual a Communist. The person so named is placed under various forms of restriction: a factory worker is not allowed to enter any factory, a teacher is not allowed to enter any teaching institution. Each individual must be in his or her house between 6:00 P.M. and 6:00 A.M. weekdays and on weekends, between Friday 6:00 P.M. and Monday 6:00 A.M. Newspapers must not publish the "Communist's" comments or views on any particular subject, a restriction that was effectively used to gag black opinion in the country. The few white people who have been prosecuted under this law receive very little sympathy from their own people because they're considered "Kaffir lovers." In the United States in the early days of the Old South, they would have been called "nigger lovers."

The fourth in this group of laws is the Defense Act, which seems to be the most draconian of them all. This law was very effectively used in 1976 when South Africa was involved in a war in Angola, yet South Africans did not know that their country was involved in a war because newspapers were not allowed to print the fact. South Africans didn't even know that South African soldiers had penetrated into Angola right up to Luwanda, because newspapers couldn't publish that. Dispatches came through to the newspapers from foreign correspondents, for example, the *Washington Post* reporter Robin Wright, who bravely sent very good dispatches from Angola, reporting exactly how South Africa was involved in that war. There also were dispatches saying South Africa became involved because Henry Kissinger had duped the South African government into it. But South African newspapers were not allowed to publish these dispatches—none of them. It's a measure of the effectiveness of the Defense Act that only nine months later did South Africans know that their country was involved in a war.

In may of 1977 there were five South African prisoners of war in Angola, but under no circumstances were newspapers permitted to publish even a speculative story to ask whether they were in fact still alive or what efforts were being made to get them out. Nor was it permissible, for instance, to report what was happening on the country's borders where the country's troops were involved in a ferocious war with nationalists. No reporters were allowed to go there or even go near because those zones had been declared out of bounds. The South African Defense Force would issue brief statements saying that South African troops had engaged in a confrontation with "terrorists," where two were dead and five arrested, or something of that nature. But no newspaper was allowed to write anything about it.

The Defense Act also contains definitions of and restrictions on what are called "strategic news" and "strategic areas" and so on. An example: the government introduced all kinds of laws to try to preserve energy and fuel. Our gas stations were open only between the hours 6:00 A.M. and 6:00 P.M., Monday through Thursday, and on weekends they had to close from 12:00 midday on Friday until 6:00 A.M. on Monday. Yet our government, in defiance of United Nations' sanctions and in collaboration with certain major petroleum companies, supplied petroleum to Rhodesia, where gas stations were not closed from 6:00 P.M. to 6:00 A.M. Indeed, they were open the whole weekend while ours were closed. This was a very good lead subject, one in which all editors could have had a field day, but we were not permitted to write anything about it.

All these laws in themselves represent the alarming state of mind found in a government that had steadily been going down the drain into the world of authoritarian regimes. The events of the spring of 1977 were an indication of the government's hostility toward the press in South Africa. In my newspaper, four of my reporters and my chief photographer, who had been very efficient indeed in covering the riots and reporting the whole scene as it actually was, were detained under the country's security legislation. Each of them spent four and a half months in jail, without any trial. Two of them were interrogated and assaulted. They were pressured to make incriminating statements against me in particular and the management of the paper in general, both of which they refused to do. After the four and a half months, they were released. In contrast, the other three were not even asked what their names were; the people who detained them simply ignored them until they were released.

I wasn't allowed to see any of these men during this time, nor were their wives and their parents. Our lawyers were told these detentions were no concern of theirs; there was no court of law that could have given these prisoners any form of reprieve. On the day they were released from prison, it became my turn to go to prison, which provoked a massive protest by the media, both in South Africa and abroad, and by agencies like Associated Press (AP), United Press International (UPI), and Reuters, which sent out the story to many countries. As a result, there was a reaction that expedited my release, which otherwise, I believe, would not have taken place.

White reporters posed no threat to the government during this time because they were not allowed into the black townships, and therefore did not get involved in trying to report on what was happening there. Indeed, at one stage, the entire press in South Africa and a lot of overseas media virtually camped out at the premises of the *World* to try to learn from us what was happening. The government couldn't keep us out of Soweto and other black townships for the simple reason that we lived in those areas and were part and parcel of the problem there. For this we paid a very heavy price, and we continue to pay this price. One of my reporters was jailed in January 1977, detained under a law called the Terrorism Act. Four months later neither I nor any of his relatives had seen him. One of the ironies of life is that he was one of those beautiful persons who still believed in the basic goodness of human nature, who still believed that South Africa could be saved without necessarily getting into a confrontation where bloodshed was inevitable. I shuddered to think what will happen the day when he comes back—what his views will be then.

At the end of March 1977 the government went still further, introducing a law in Parliament called the Press Bill, which would have effectively introduced direct censorship in South Africa. There was a unanimous outcry from the press, and for the first time the national papers that normally blindly support the government joined us in decrying this law. I believe that when the South African embassies abroad heard this, in Washington and in London and in Bonn, they were absolutely appalled. I suspect they telexed back to the government to say, "You are putting us in a very invidious position, because the only thing we have at the moment that is going for us is the fact that we have a press that is still reasonably free and vigorous in its criticism of government policy." In any event, the government then called the National Press Union, which is the union that represents newspaper publishers, owners, and representatives of the conference of editors, and said in effect that unless we drew up our own code of ethics, they would proceed with this legislation. Newspaper editors, being as wary as they are, rejected this ultimatum, but the owners and the publishers capitulated. They drew up a code of ethics that was really meaningless, because we editors continued to do what we always did, and we made a definite resolution that if we were called to appear before the Press Council, which was constituted under the chairmanship of a judge whom we didn't trust, we would not answer its summonses if any complaints were lodged against us. Three-quarters of the editors of the National Press Union took a pledge to go to jail rather than subject ourselves to the kind of self-censorship that would necessarily result from that "code of ethics."

The government said that it would wait for a year to see if these restraints were working. We were told quite frankly that we must put our house in order during that year, otherwise the government would proceed with a bill of its own in the following January when Parliament reconvened. A lot of us began looking around in our houses to find out what was in disorder. Finding very little was in disorder, we proceeded as if nothing had happened. In the next few months that followed, with the situation steadily deteriorating in South Africa, with troubles escalating for an economy that was already in dire straits, the role of the press, indeed the very existence of the press, was really very much in question.

Bibliography

Aggarwala, N. "Press Freedom: A Third-World View." *The Interdependent* 4, 1 (January 1977).

Ainslie, R. *The Press in Africa: Communications Past and Present.* London: Victor Gollancz Ltd., 1966.

Alisky, Marvin. "Government-Press Relations in Peru." *Journalism Quarterly* 53, 4 (Winter 1976): 661–665.

Almaney, Adnan. "Governments' Resistance to the Free Flow of International Communication." *Journal of Communication* 22 (March 1972): 77–88.

Amerson, Robert and Herbst, John. *Journalism Training: An Interim Report.* Murrow Reports: Occasional Papers of the Edward R. Murrow Center of Public Diplomacy. Medford: The Fletcher School of Law and Diplomacy, 1978.

Amic. "Information Imbalance Defined at Kandy Conference: Summary Report." *Media Asia* 2, 2 (1975): 69–78.

Bass, Abraham Zisha. "Refining the 'Gatekeeper' Concept: A UN Radio Case Study." *Journalism Quarterly* 46, 1 (Spring 1969): 69–72.

Beltran, S., Luis Ramiro. "TV Etchings in the Minds of Latin Americans: Conservatism, Materialism, and Conformism." *Gazette* 24, 1 (1978): 61–85.

Beltran, Luis Ramiro, and de Cardona, Elizabeth Fox. "Latin American Mass Communication as Influenced by the United States: The Myth of the Free Flow of Information." Paper presented at Fair Communication Policy for International Exchange of Information Conference. East-West Communication Institute, Honolulu, Hawaii, March 28–April 2, 1976.

Berberovic, M. "Non-Alignment and Information." *Review of International Affairs* XXVII, 625 (April 20, 1976): 1–3.

Bergemann, Ralf. "The Monopolistic Organization of News Agencies." *The Democratic Journalist* 9 (1976): 14–17.

Biro, Andras. "An Alternative United Nations Information Model." *Development Dialogue* 1976, 2: 63–75.

Bishop, Robert L. "How Reuters and AFP Coverage of Independent Africa Compares." *Journalism Quarterly* 52, 4 (Winter 1975): 654–662.

Boyd, Douglas. A. *An Analysis of Ten International Radio News Broadcasts in English to Africa.* Murrow Reports: Occasional Papers of the Edward R. Murrow Center of Public Diplomacy. Medford: The Fletcher School of Law and Diplomacy, 1978.

Boyd-Barrett, Oliver. "The World-Wide News Agencies." Paper presented before the International Association for Mass Communication Research. Leipzig, September 12–20, 1974.

Bures, Oldrich, ed. *Developing World and Mass Media.* Prague: International Organization of Journalists, 1975.

Chowdhury, A. "Report to the Annual Assembly of the International Press Institute." *IPI Report* 25, 7 (July 1976): 1–2.

Cole, Richard R. "The Mexican Press System: Aspects of Growth, Control, and Ownership." *Gazette* 21, 2 (1975): 65–81.

Contreras, Eduardo; Larson, James; Mayo, John K.; and Spain, Peter. *The Effects of Cross-Cultural Broadcasting.* Institute for Communication Research of Stanford University. (A study prepared for UNESCO.) Stanford, 1975.

Corradi, Juan E. "Cultural Dependence and the Sociology of Knowledge: The Latin American Case." *International Journal of Contemporary Sociology* 8, 1 (1971): 35–55.

Cowlan, Bert, and Love, Lee M. *A Look at the World's Radio News.* Murrow Reports: Occasional Papers of the Edward R. Murrow Center of Public Diplomacy. Medford: The Fletcher School of Law and Diplomacy, 1978.

The CPU Quarterly (Quarterly of the Commonwealth Press Union), June 1977 [1977 Conference Report, a conference concerning the Third World Press].

"Cultural Imperialism." *New Journalist* (New South Wales), No. 16 (Sept. 1974): 16–22, 29.

Da Costa, Alcino Louis. "A Third World Feature Service." *Development Dialogue* 1976, 2: 51–54.

Dagnino, Evelina. "Cultural and Ideological Dependence: Building a Theoretical Framework." In *Struggles of Dependency,* edited by F. Bonilla and Robert Girling. Stanford, Calif., 1973.

Dajani, Nabil, and Donohue, John. "Foreign News in the Arab Press: A Content Analysis of Six Arab Dailies." *Gazette* 19, (1973) 3: 155–170.

De Cordona, Elizabeth Fox, and Beltran, Luis Ramiro. "Towards the Development of a Methodology to Diagnosis [sic] Public Communications Institutions." Paper presente at the International Broadcast Institute General Meeting, Cologne, September 1–4, 1975.

Fagen, Patricia. "The Media in Allende's Chile." *Journal of Communication* 24, 1 (1974): 59–70.

Fifth Conference of Heads of State or Government of Non-Aligned Countries. "Political Declaration: XXI Press Agencies Pool." NAC/CONF. 5/S.2. Colombo, August 1976.

Fischer, Heinz-Dietrich, and Merrill, John C., eds. *International Communication: Media, Channels, Functions.* New York: Hastings House, 1970.

"Forms of Cultural Dependency: A Symposium." *Journal of Communication* 25, 2 (Spring 1975): 121–193.

Gastil, R. D. "The Comparative Survey of Freedom." *Freedom at Issue* (January–February 1977): 5–15.

Gerbner, George, ed. *Mass Media Policies in Changing Cultures.* New York: John Wiley and Sons, 1977.

Gerbner, George, and Marvanyi, George. "The Many Worlds of the World's Press." *Journal of Communication* 27, 1 (Winter 1977): 52–66.

Gissler, Sig. *World Press Freedom.* Wingspread Symposium, November 1974, Racine, Wisconsin, 1975.

"Governmental Control of Press Advanced by UNESCO Conference." *Freedom at Issue* (September–October 1976): 2–5.

Green, Reginald Herbold. "Mass Communications, the New International Economic Order and Another Development." Paper prepared for the Mexico Seminar on the Role of Information in the New International Order, at Mexico City, May 24–28, 1976.

Gunaratne, Shelton A. "An Asian Contagion." *Index on Censorship* 5 (Summer 1976): 62–63.

Gunaratne, Shelton A. "The Background to the Non-Aligned News Pool: Pros and Cons and Research Findings." *Gazette* 24, 1 (1978): 20–35.

Hanks, William E. "Selected Newspaper Coverage of the 1965 Dominican Revolt." Unpublished paper for the International Communication Association, April 1971.

Harley, W. S. "International Showdown on Press Freedom." U.S. National Commission for UNESCO Background Paper for the Communication Sector, 19th General Conference of UNESCO, October 22–November 22, 1976.

Harms, L. S.; Richstad, Jim; and Kie, Kathleen A., eds. *Right to Communicate: Collected Papers.* Honolulu, Hawaii: Social Sciences & Linguistic Institute, 1976.

Harms, L. S., and Richstad, Jim, eds. *Right to Communicate: Original Essays.* Honolulu, Hawaii, 1976.

Harris, Phil. "An Analysis of the West African Wire Service of an International News Agency." Paper presented to International Association for Mass Communication Research. Leicester, England, 1976.

Hester, Albert M. "An Analysis of News Flow from Developed and Developing Nations." *Gazette* 17, 1/2 (1971): 29–43.

―――. *The Associated Press and News from Latin America: A Gatekeeper and News-Flow Study.* Ph.D. Dissertation, University of Wisconsin, 1972.

―――. "Five Years Foreign News on U.S. Television Evening Newscasts." *Gazette* 24, 1 (1978): 86–95.

―――. "The News from Latin America Via a World News Agency." *Gazette* 20, 2 (1974): 82–91.

―――. "Western News Agencies: Problems and Opportunities in International News." Paper prepared for the Mexico Seminar on the Role of Information in the New International Order, at Mexico City, May 24–28, 1976.

Hicks, Ronald G., and Gordon, Avishag. "Foreign News Content in Israeli and U.S. Newspaper." *Journalism Quarterly* 51, 4 (Winter 1974): 639–644.

Himmelstrand, Ulf. "The Problem of Cultural Translation in the Reporting of African Social Realities." In *Reporting Africa,* edited by Olav Stokke. New York: Africana Publishing Corporation, 1971.

Huq, Edramul. "Present State of Information Flow in Bangladesh." Paper presented at the Regional Conference on Information Imbalance in Asia, at Colombo, Sri Lanka, April 21–25, 1975.

Hurley, Neil P. "Chilean Television: A Case Study of Political Communication." *Journalism Quarterly* 51, 4 (Winter 1974): 683–89.

"In Defence of Press Freedom." *Communicator* [India] (July 1977): 15–31. Various authors.

Ingram, Derek. "The Luxury of Press Freedom: New Nations Cannot Be Judged by Western Standards." *Atlas World Press Review* 23 (November 1976): 45. (Excerpted from the *Ceylon Daily News,* July 14, 1976.)

International Broadcast Institute. *The Global Context for the Formation of Domestic Communication Policy.* London, 1975.

Katz, Elihu and Wedell, George. *Broadcasting in the Third World: Promise and Performance.* Cambridge: Harvard University Press, 1977.

Kaviya, Somkuan. "A Sketch on Thailand's Disadvantages in International Mass Communications." Paper presented at Fair Communication Policy for International Exchange of Information Conference. East-West Communication Institute, Honolulu, Hawaii, March 28–April 2, 1976.

Kawanaka, Yashuhiro. "The Role of Japan in the Flow of News in Asia—Desirability and Feasibility of a World News Agency in Japan." Paper presented at Fair Communication Policy for International Exchange of Information Conference. East-West Communication Institute, Honolulu, Hawaii, March 28–April 2, 1976.

Kekkonen, Urho. "The Free Flow of Information: Towards a Reconsideration of National and International Communication Policies." Address before the Symposium on the International Flow of Television Programmes. University of Tampere, Tampere, Finland, May 21, 1973.

Kim, Kyu Whan. "Information Imbalance in Asia: A Korean Case." Paper presented at the Regional Conference on Information Imbalance in Asia, at Colombo, Sri Lanka, April 21–25, 1975.

Kipp, James E. "Press Coverage of the Havana Conference." *Journalism Quarterly* 44, 3 (Autumn 1967): 542–544.

Kirkpatrick, C. Address to the 19th General Conference, UNESCO, Nairobi, November 1976; memorandum, U.S. National Commission for UNESCO, December 1976.

Knudson, Jerry W. "Whatever Became of 'the Pursuit of Happiness'? The U.S. Press and Social Revolution in Latin America." *Gazette* 20, 4 (1974): 201–214.

Kolosov, Yuri. "East-Bloc View of Global TV." *IPI Report* 22, 4 (April 1973): 1, 4.

Korobelnikov, V. "What is behind the 'freedom of information' concept?" *International Affairs* [Moscow] (February 1976): 105–106; as published in the Congressional Record, S7782 (May 21, 1976).

Lee, John A. R. *Toward Realistic Communication Policies: Recent Trends and Ideas Compiled and Analysed.* Reports and Papers on Mass Communication, no. 76. Paris: Unesco, 1976.

Lent, John A. "Foreign News Content of United States and Asian Print Media. A Literature Review and Problem Analysis." *Gazette* 22, 3 (1976): 169–182.

_____. "Press Freedom in Asia: The Quiet, But Completed, Revolution." *Gazette* 24, 1 (1978): 41–60.

Lindsay, Robert. *Education for Communications Development: The Global View.* Murrow Reports: Occasional Papers of the Edward R. Murrow Center of Public Diplomacy. Medford: The Fletcher School of Law and Diplomacy, 1978.

Liu, Han C., and Gunaratne, Shelton A. "Foreign News in Two Asian Dailies." *Gazette* 18, 1 (1972): 37–41.

McNelly, John T. "Development of News Exchange in Latin America." Working paper for UNESCO meeting of Experts on the Development of News Exchange Arrangements in Latin America, Quito, June 24–30, 1975. COM-76/CONF 63/3, Paris, April 24, 1975.

Maheu, R. Introduction to UNESCO Draft Programs and Budget for 1973–1974, 17 C/S (1974).

Marks, Leonard H. "International Conflict and the Free Flow of Information." *In Control of the Direct Broadcast Satellite: Values in Conflict.* Palo Alto, Calif.: Aspen Institute, Program on Communication and Society, in association with the Office of External Research, U.S. Department of State, 1974.

Martin, L. John. "Analysis of News Agency Coverage of the U.S. Supplied to the Near East and North Africa." USIA Office of Research document R-1-76, January 20, 1976.

Matta, Fernando Reyes. "The Historical Evolution of International News Agencies and Their Growth Towards Domination." Paper prepared for the Mexico Seminar on the Role of Information in the New International Order, at Mexico City, May 24–28, 1976.

———. "The Information Bedazzlement of Latin America." *Development Dialogue* 1976, 2: 29–42.

M'Bow, A. Statement by director-general of UNESCO closing general conference UNESCO/2238 (November 30, 1976); quoted in press release, UN, New York.

Menon, R. Narayan. "Information Imbalance in the Print Media in Asia. Paper presented at the Regional Conference on Information Imbalance in Asia, at Colombo, Sri Lanka, April 21–25, 1975.

Merrill, John C. "Global Patterns of Elite Daily Journalism." *Journalism Quarterly* 45, 1 (Spring 1968): 99–105.

———. *The Elite Press and Great Newspapers of the World.* New York: Pitman, 1968.

———; Bryan, Carter R.; and Alisky, Marvin. *The Foreign Press: A Survey of the World's Journalism.* Baton Rouge: Louisiana State University Press, 1970.

Ministerial Conference of Non-Aligned Countries on Press Agencies Pool. *Constitution of the Pool of Press Agencies of the Non-Aligned Countries* (adopted July 13, 1976).

Ministerial Conference of Non-Aligned Countries on the Press Agencies Pool, New Delhi, July 8–13, 1976. "Resolution on Action Plan for Cooperation in the Field of Information and Mass Media." A/12, July 11, 1976.

Ministerial Conference of Non-Aligned Countries on the Press Agencies Pool, New Delhi, July 8–13, 1976. "The Pool of News Agencies of Non-Aligned Countries." A/P/3/REV II, July 13, 1976.

Mitra, Asok. *Information Imbalance in Asia.* Amic Occasional Papers, no. 5. Singapore, 1975.

Mohamad, Abdullah. "Information Imbalance in Broadcasting in Malaysia." Paper prepared for the Regional Conference on Information Imbalance in Asia, at Colombo, Sri Lanka, April 21–25, 1975.

Mowlana, Hamid. "Trends in Research on International Communication in the United States." *Gazette* 19, 2 (1973): 79–90.

Mujahid, Sharif Al. "Coverage of Pakistan in Three U.S. News Magazines." *Journalism Quarterly* 47, 1 (Spring 1970): 126–130.

Naesseland, Gunnar. "UNESCO Conference on Balanced Communication." (A Report on the November 1974 Conference on Balanced Communication.) *Intermedia* 2, 5 (March 1975): 16–17.

Nafziger, Ralph O. *International News and the Press: An Annotated Bibliography.* New York: Arno Press, 1972.

Nam, Sun Woo. "The Flow of International News into Korea." *Gazette* 16, 1 (1970): 19–24.

Nichols, John Spicer. "LATIN—Latin American Regional News Agency." *Gazette* 21, 3 (1975): 170–181.

Nordenstreng, Kaarle and Schiller, Herbert I. "Helsinki: The New Equation." *Journal of Communication* 26, 1 (Winter 1976): 130–34.

O'Brien, Rita Cruise. "Domination and Dependence in Mass Communications: Implications for the Use of Broadcasting in Developing Countries." *Institute of Development Studies. Bulletin of International Research* 6, 4 (March 1975): 85–99.

Oreh, Onuma O. " 'Developmental Journalism' and Press Freedom. An African View Point." *Gazette* 24, 1 (1978): 36–40.

Ornes, German E. Special Report by the chairman of the Committee on Freedom of the Press and Information, Executive Committee Advisory Council, IAPA. San Jose, Costa Rica, July 12–13, 1976.

Petrusenko, V. *The Monopoly Press or How American Journalism Found Itself in the Vicious Circle of the "Crisis of Credibility".* Prague: International Organization of Journalists.

Pinch, Edward T. *A Brief Study on News Patterns in 16 Third World Countries.*

Murrow Reports: Occasional Papers of the Edward R. Murrow Center of Public Diplomacy. Medford: The Fletcher School of Law and Diplomacy, 1978.

———. "The Third World and the Fourth Estate: A Look at the Non-Aligned News Agencies Pool." Paper prepared for the U.S. Department of State Senior Seminar in Foreign Policy, April 1977.

Pollock, John C., and Cohn, Eileen M. "Political Reporting on Revolution: Cuba in Cross-National Perspective." Paper presented to the International Association for Mass Communication Research. Leicester, England, 1976.

Pool, Ithiel de Sola, and Dizard, Stephen. *International Telecommunications and the Requirements of News Services.* Murrow Reports: Occasional Papers of the Edward R. Murrow Center of Public Diplomacy. Medford: The Fletcher School of Law and Diplomacy, 1978.

Rachty, Gehan. *Foreign News in 9 Arab Countries.* Murrow Reports: Occasional Papers of the Edward R. Murrow Center of Public Diplomacy. Medford: The Fletcher School of Law and Diplomacy, 1978.

Raghavan, Chakravarti. "A New World Communication and Information Structure." *Development Dialogue* 1976, 2: 43–50.

———. "Thoughts of Third World Journalists." *Communicator* [India] 10, 10 (October 1975): 16–20.

Rao, Y. V. Lakshmana. "Information Imbalance: A Closer Look." Paper presented at Fair Communication Policy for International Exchange of Information Conference. East-West Communication Institute, Honolulu, Hawaii, March 28–April 2, 1976.

———. "Information Imbalance in Asia: A Working Paper." Paper prepared for the Regional Conference on Information Imbalance in Asia, in Colombo, Sri Lanka, April 21–25, 1976.

———. "Propaganda Through the Printed Media in the Developing Countries." *The Annals of the American Academy of Political and Social Sciences* 398 (November 1971): 99–103.

"Report of the First Meeting of the Coordination Committee of the Press Agencies Pool of Non-Aligned Countries." Cairo, January 10–12, 1977.

Report of the United States Delegation to the First Intergovernmental [UNESCO] Conference on Communication Policies. San Jose, Costa Rica, July 12–21, 1976.

"Report of the United States Delegation to the Intergovernmental Meeting of Experts to Prepare a Draft Declaration on Fundamental Principles Governing the Use of the Mass Media in Strengthening Peace and International Understanding and in Combating War Propaganda, Racism and Apartheid." Chairman, United States Delegation Ronald F. Stowe (February 2, 1976). Held at UNESCO House, Paris, December 15–22, 1975.

Richstad, Jim, and Bowen, Jackie, eds. *International Communication Policy and Flow: A Working Bibliography.* Honolulu, Hawaii: East-West Communication Institute, November 1976.

Rooy, Maarten. "Developing Media in Developing Countries. A Historical Review of Policies." *Gazette* 24, 1 (1978): 2–10.

Rosengren, Karl Erik and Rikardsson, Gunnel. "Middle East News in Sweden." *Gazette* 20, 2 (1974): 99–116.

Rubin, Barry. "International Censorship: The Pressure for Favorable Coverage is On—and the World's Media are Feeling the Squeeze." *Columbia Journalism Review* (September–October 1975): 55–58.

Schiller, Herbert I. "The Appearance of National-Communications Policies; a New Arena for Social Struggle." *Gazette* 21, 2 (1975): 82–94.

_____. "Authentic National Development Versus the Free Flow of Information and the New Communications Technology." Paper prepared for the International Symposium on Communication: Technology, Impact and Policy. The Annenberg School of Communications, University of Pennsylvania, March 23–25, 1972.

_____. *Communication and Cultural Domination.* White Plains, New York: International Arts and Sciences Press, Inc., 1976.

_____. "Freedom from the 'Free Flow'." *Journal of Communication* 24, 1 (Winter 1974): 110–117.

_____. *The Mind Managers.* Boston: Beacon Press, 1973.

_____. "Transnational Media and National Development." Paper presented at Fair Communication Policy for International Exchange of Information Conference. East-West Communication Institute, Honolulu, Hawaii, March 28–April 2, 1976.

_____, and Smythe, D. "Chile: An End to Cultural Colonialism." *Society* 9, 5 (1972).

Schramm, Wilbur. "Cross-Cultural Communication: Suggestions for the Building of Bridges." Paper presented at Fair Communications Policy for International Exchange of Information Conference. East-West Communication Institute, Honolulu, Hawaii, March 28–April 2, 1976.

──────. *International News Wires and Third World News in Asia.* Murrow Reports: Occasional Papers of the Edward R. Murrow Center of Public Diplomacy. Medford: The Fletcher School of Law and Diplomacy, 1978.

Scotton, James F. "Kenya's Maligned African Press: Time for a Reassessment." *Journalism Quarterly* 52, 1 (Spring 1975): 30–36.

──────. "The Press in Kenya a Decade after Independence: Patterns of Readership and Ownership." *Gazette* 21, 1 (1975): 19–33.

Shukla, V. C. Published address by the president of the Ministerial Conference of Non-Aligned Countries on the Press Agencies Pool, New Delhi, July 8–13, 1976.

Smith, Raymond F. "On the Structure of Foreign News: A Comparison of the *New York Times* and the Indian White Papers." *Journal of Peace Research* 6 (1969): 24–25.

──────. "U.S. News and Sino-Indian Relations: An Extra-Media Study." *Journalism Quarterly* 48, 3 (Fall 1971): 447–458, 501.

Snijders, Max L. "New Information Order Is Incompatible with Democracy." *Gazette* 24, 1 (1978): 11–19.

Somavia, Juan. "The Transnational Power Structure and International Information: Elements of a Third World Policy for Transnational News Agencies." *Development Dialogue* 1976, 2: 15–28.

Sommerlad, E. Lloyd. "Free Flow of Information, Balance and the Right to Communicate." Paper presented at Fair Communication Policy for International Exchange of Information Conference. East-West Institute, Honolulu, Hawaii, March 28–April 2, 1976.

Stokke, Olau. *Reporting Africa! In African and International Mass Media.* Uppsala: Scandinavian Institute of African Studies, 1971.

Sussman, Leonard R. "A Fateful Day for the News Media." *Freedom at Issue* (January–February 1977): 2–4.

──────. "Developmental Journalism: A Backward Idea whose Time Has Come." *Quadrant* 22 (November 1976): 25–31.

_____. "The March Through the World's Mass Media." *Orbis* 20, 4 (Winter 1977): 857–879.

_____. *Mass News Media and the Third World Challenge.* The Washington Papers, vol. 5, no. 46. Beverly Hills and London: Sage Publications, 1977.

_____. "Third World/West Open Media Dialogue, As UNESCO 'Radicalization' Proceeds." *Freedom at Issue* (January–February 1978): 20–28.

Szalai, Alexander, with Croke, Margaret, et al. *The United Nations and the News Media.* New York: Unipub, 1972.

Symposium of the Non-Aligned Countries on Information. Final Report. Tunis, May 26–30, 1976.

Tatarian, Roger. *The Multinational News Pool.* Murrow Reports: Occasional Papers of the Edward R. Murrow Center of Public Diplomacy. Medford: The Fletcher School of Law and Diplomacy, 1978.

Tharoor, Shashi. "Information Imbalances: Communications and the Developing World." *The Fletcher Forum* 1, 2 (Spring 1977): 164–180.

Thirty Years of the International Organization of Journalists in Action. Prague: International Organization of Journalists.

Tiffen, Rod. *Communication and Politics: The Press, the Public and the Third World.* Canberra: Australian Council for Overseas Aid, 1974.

UNESCO. General Conference, Nineteenth Session. "Draft Declaration on Fundamental Principles Governing the Use of the Mass Media in Strengthening Peace and International Understanding and in Combating War Propaganda, Racism and Apartheid. 19 C/91. Nairobi, July 1976.

_____. General Conference, Nineteenth Session. "Draft Resolution submitted by Tunisia: Amendment to the Draft Programme and Budget for 1977–1978." 19 C/DR. 19. Nairobi, September 1976.

_____. Intergovernmental Conference on Communication Policies in Latin America and the Caribbean. Final Report, Com/Md/38. (Held in San Jose, Costa Rica, July 12–21, 1976.) Paris: UNESCO, October 1976.

_____. Intergovernmental Conference on Communication Policies in Latin America and the Caribbean. Provisional Annotated Agenda. (Held in Quito, June 14–23, 1976.)

_____. Meeting of Experts on the Development of News Exchange in Latin America. Final Report, Com/75/Conf 603/4. Quito, June 24–30, 1975.

Proposals for an International Program of Communication Research. Report No: Com/Md/20. Paris, 1971.

_____. Report of the Meeting of Experts on a Draft Declaration Concerning the Role of the Mass Media. Paris, 11–15 March, 1975.

_____. Report of the Meeting of Experts on Communication Policies in Latin America. Com/74/Conf 617/4. (Held in Bogota, July 4–13, 1974.) Paris, October 1974.

_____. Report of the Meeting of Experts on the Development of News Agencies in Africa. Tunis, April 1–0, 1900.

_____. World Communications: A 200 Country Survey of Press, Radio, Television, Film. Paris: The Unesco Press, 1975.

UNESCO Communication Sector, Research and Policies Division. "Report on Ad-Hoc Working Group of Economists on Communication Planning." Paris, April 3–5, 1975.

UNESCO. Conference for the Establishment of UNESCO, London, 1945.

UNESCO. Final Report: Intergovernmental Conference on Communication Policies in Latin America and the Caribbean, Paris, 1976.

UNESCO. From Freedom of Information to the Free Flow of Information, Paris, 1978.

UNESCO. Reports of the General Conferences, 1960, '62, '64, '70, '72, '74, '76.

UNESCO. Report on the Programme of UNESCO—Preparatory Commission, London, 1946.

UNESCO. UNESCO: Twenty Years of Service to Peace, Paris, 1966.

Varis, Tapio. "An East-West Dialogue on the Peaceful Coexistence of Conflicting Ideologies." Journal of Communication 26, 1 (Winter 1976): 120–127.

_____. "The Helsinki Agreements . . . Non-Aligned Country Agreements." Paper presented at Fair Communications Policy for International Exchange of Information Conference. East-West Communication Institute, Honolulu, Hawaii, March 28–April 2, 1976.

Vilanilam, John V. "Foreign News in Two U.S. Newspapers and Indian Newspapers During Selected Periods." *Gazette* 18, 2 (1972): 96–108.

_____. "Ownership versus Developmental News Content: An Analysis of Independent and Conglomerate Newspapers of India." *Gazette* 22, 1 (1976): 1–17.

Weaver, David H. "The Press and Government Restriction: A Cross National Study over Time." *Gazette* 23, 3 (1977): 152–170.

Wilcox, Dennis L. "The Foreign Press in Africa." *International Development Review* 16, 3 (1974).

_____. "What Hope for Free Press in Africa?" *Freedom at Issue* (March–April 1977): 10–13.

Yoshida, Tadashi. "Flow of TV Programmes and News in Asia." *Media Asia* 2, 2 (1975): 82–88.

About the Editor
and Contributors

PHILIP C. HORTON is Director of the Edward R. Murrow Center of Public Diplomacy, the Fletcher School of Law and Diplomacy, Tufts University.

NARINDER K. AGGARWALA is Regional Information Officer for Asia and the Pacific for the United Nations Development Programme (UNDP).

S. M. ALI is Chief Executive of the Press Foundation of Asia (PFA) and Editor-in-Chief of Development, Economics, and Population Themes News (DEPTHnews).

GUIDO FERNANDEZ is Editor-in-Chief and Executive Vice-President of *La Nacion,* San Jose, Costa Rica; Chairman of the Board of Agencia Centroamericana de Noticias (ACAN); and Chairman of the Committee on Freedom of the Press of the Inter-American Press Association (IAPA).

PETER GALLINER is Director of the International Press Institute (IPI).

MOHAMED ABDEL GAWAD is President of the Union of Arab News Agencies and Board Chairman of the Middle East News Agency (MENA).

LEO GROSS is Professor Emeritus of International Law, The Fletcher School of Law and Diplomacy, Tufts University.

PERO IVACIC is General Director of Tanjug, The Yugoslav News Agency.

RAUL KRAISELBURD is Editor of *Diario "El Dia",* La Plata, Argentina; Regional Vice-President (for Argentina, Paraguay, and Uruguay) of the Committee on Freedom of the Press, Inter-American Press Association (IAPA); and Secretary of the Board of Noticias Argentinas.

GUNNAR R. NAESSELUND is Deputy Assistant Director General (Communication) in the Sector of Culture and Communication of the United Nations Educational, Scientific and Cultural Organization (UNESCO).

HILARY NG'WENO is Editor of *The Weekly Review*, Nairobi, Kenya.

BIOLA OLASOPE is Director of News and Current Affairs of the Nigerian Broadcasting Corporation.

PERCY QOBOZA was Editor of *The World*, Johannesburg, South Africa.

MORT ROSENBLUM is a Murrow Fellow of the Council on Foreign Relations.

LEONARD R. SUSSMAN is Executive Director of Freedom House, New York.

ROGER TATARIAN is Professor of Journalism at the California State University at Fresno. Between 1962–72 he was an editor and vice-president of United Press International (UPI).

GEORGE VERGHESE was Editor of the *Hindustan Times.*